INSIGHT ⊙ GUIDES

GREEK

PHRASEBOOK & DICTIONARY

D1413785

Contacting the Editors

Every effort has been made to provide accurate information in this publication, but changes are inevitable. The publisher cannot be responsible for any resulting loss, inconvenience or injury. We would appreciate it if readers would call our attention to any errors or outdated information. We also welcome your suggestions; if you come across a relevant expression not in our phrase book, please contact us at: hello@insightguides.com

All Rights Reserved
© 2016 Apa Digital (CH) AG and Apa Publications (UK) Ltd.

First Edition: 2016
Printed in China

Cover & Interior Design: Pawel Pasternak
Production: AM Services
Production Manager: Vicky Glover
Cover Photo: all Shutterstock

Interior Photos: all Shutterstock

CONTENTS

ACTIVITIES

HEALTH & SAFETY

FOOD & DRINK

GOING OUT

DICTIONARY

PRONUNCIATION

This section is designed to make you familiar with the sounds of Greek using our simplified phonetic transcription. You'll find the pronunciation of the Greek letters explained below, together with their 'imitated' equivalents. This system is used throughout the phrase book; simply read the pronunciation as if it were English, noting any special rules below.

Stress is important in Greek, as often the meaning of the word changes depending upon which syllable is stressed. In written Greek, stress is indicated by a small mark (´) on the syllable to be stressed. In the Greek phonetic transcription, stress is indicated with an underline.

Over the last 25 years, the Greek language has been greatly simplified, with the number of stress and breathing marks reduced; however, one may still encounter words written with the more elaborate stress marks, mainly in older Greek texts.

Please note that the question mark is indicated by the semi-colon (;) in Greek.

CONSONANTS

Letter	Approximate Pronunciation	Symbol	Example	Pronunciation
β	like v in voice	**v**	βάζο	<u>vah</u> • zoh
δ	voiced th, like th in then	**TH**	δεν	THehn
ζ	like z in zoo	**z**	ζω	zoh
θ	unvoiced th, like th in	**th**	θέλω	<u>theh</u> • loh thing
κ	like k in key	**k**	κότα	<u>koh</u> • tah
λ	like l in lemon	**l**	λεμόνι	leh • <u>moh</u> • nee
μ	like m in man	**m**	μαμά	mah • <u>mah</u>
ν	like n in net	**n**	νέο	<u>neh</u> • oh
ξ	like x in fox	**ks**	ξένος	<u>kseh</u> • nohs
π	like p in pen	**p**	πένα	<u>peh</u> • nah

ρ	trilled like a Scottish r	r	ώρα	<u>oh</u> • rah
σ	like s in sit	s	σε	seh
ς*	like s in slim	s	ήλιος	<u>ee</u> • liohs
τ	like t in tea	t	τι	tee
φ	like f in fun	f	φως	fohs
x	like ch in Scottish loch	kh	χαρά	khah • <u>rah</u>
ψ	like ps in tops	ps	ψάρι	<u>psah</u> • ree
γ	like g + h	gh	γάλα	<u>ghah</u> • lah
γγ, γκ	like g in go, but in some cases a more nasal ng as in sing	g	γκαρσόν	gahr • <u>sohn</u>
μπ	like b in bath, but in some cases more like mp as in lamp	b	μπαρ	bahr
ντ	like d in do, but in some cases more like nd as in end	d	ντομάτα	doh • <u>mah</u> • tah
τζ	like j in jazz	j	τζατζίκι	jah • <u>jee</u> • kee
τσ	like ts in lets	ts	τσάντα	<u>tsahn</u> • dah

*This character is used instead of **σ**, when the latter falls at the end of a word.*

VOWELS

Letter	Approximate Pronunciation	Symbol	Example	Pronunciation
α	like a in father	ah	μα	mah
ε	like e in ten	eh	θέλω	<u>theh</u> • loh
η, ι, υ	like ee in keen	ee	πίνω	<u>pee</u> • noh
o, ω	like o in top	oh	πότε	<u>poh</u> • teh
αι	like e in ten	eh	μπαίνω	<u>beh</u> • noh
οι, ει, υι	like ee in keen	ee	πλοίο	<u>plee</u> • oh

VOWEL COMBINATIONS

Letter	Approximate Pronunciation	Symbol	Example	Pronunciation
αυ	1) when followed by θ, κ, ξ, π, σ, τ, φ, χ, ψ, like af in after	**ahf**	αυτός	ahf • <u>tohs</u>
	2) in all other cases, like av in avocado	**ahv**	αύρα	<u>ahv</u> • rah
ευ	1) when followed by θ, κ ξ, π, σ, τ, φ, χ, ψ, like ef in effect	**ehf**	λευκός	lehf • <u>kohs</u>
	2) in all other cases, like ev in ever	**ehv**	νεύρο	<u>nehv</u> • roh
ου	like oo in zoo	**oo**	ούζο	<u>oo</u> • zoh
για, γεια	like yah in yard	**yah**	για	yah
γε, γιε	like ye in yet	**yeh**	γερό	yeh • <u>roh</u>
ειο,γιο	like yo in yogurt	**yoh**	γιος	yohs
γι, γυ, γη	like yea in yeast	**yee**	γύρω	<u>yee</u> • roh
ια, οια	like ia in piano	**iah**	ποια	piah

Greek is a language with a long history. The language has developed over the centuries into the modern Greek spoken today by approximately 11 million people in Greece and Cyprus, as well as Greek-speaking communities within other countries. It is a phonetic language; the sound of each letter does not usually change with its position. The characters may appear confusing at first; don't be put off by this. With a bit of practice most people can read Greek in just a few hours.

HOW TO USE THE APP

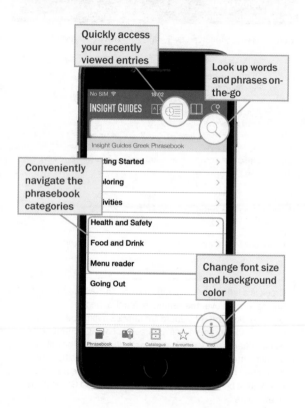

Quickly access your recently viewed entries

Look up words and phrases on-the-go

Conveniently navigate the phrasebook categories

Change font size and background color

Save the most useful everyday words and phrases to your Favorites

Use the Flash Cards Quiz to learn and memorize new words easily

Take all digital advantages of the app: listen to words and phrases pronounced by native speakers

Is there a traditional Greek/an inexpensive restaurant nearby?

Υπάρχει κανένα ελληνικό/φθηνό εστιατόριο εδώ κοντά;

ee·pahr·khee kah·neh·nah
eh·lee·nee·koh/fthee·noh
ehs·tee·ah·toh·ree·oh eh·THoh
kohn·dah

To learn how to activate the app, see the inside back cover of this phrasebook.

GRAMMAR

Greeks generally use **εσείς** (*eh • sees*) the plural form of 'you' with people they do not know well. The familiar, singular form **εσύ** (*eh • see*), is used among friends and with children, but don't worry too much - you will not be considered rude, just friendly!

REGULAR VERBS

Below are three of the main categories of regular verbs in the present tense. Using the endings indicated after the dash, you can use a large number of verbs competently.
Greek verbs are divided in categories that are formed by using certain endings and are conjugated accordingly. Some of the most popular endings are:

– ω *oh*	– έρνω *ehr • noh*
– νω *noh*	– αίνω *eh • noh*
– άζω *ah • zoh*	– ένω *eh • noh*
– άω *ah • oh*	– άσκω *as • koh*
– ήνω *ee • noh*	– όμαι *oh • meh*
– ώνω *oh • noh*	– άμαι *ah • meh*
– έλνω *ehl • noh*	– έμαι *eh • meh*

Είμαι (to be)	Present
I am	**Εγώ είμαι** *eh • goh ee • meh*
You are	**Εσύ είσαι** *eh • see ee • seh*
He is	**Αυτός είναι** *ahf • tohs ee • neh*
She is	**Αυτή είναι** *ahf • tee ee • neh*
We are	**Εμείς είμαστε** *eh • mees eem • ah • steh*
You are	**Εσείς είστε** *eh • sees ee • steh*
They are	**Αυτοί είναι** *ahf • tee ee • neh*

Αφήνω (to let)	Present
I let	**Εγώ αφήνω** *ah • <u>fee</u> • noh*
You let	**Εσύ αφήνεις** *ah • <u>fee</u> • nees*
He lets	**Αυτός αφήνει** *ah • <u>fee</u> • nee*
She lets	**Αυτή αφήνει** *ah • <u>fee</u> • nee*
We let	**Εμείς αφήνουμε** *ah • <u>fee</u> • noo • meh*
You let	**Εσείς αφήνετε** *ah • <u>fee</u> • neh • teh*
They let	**Αυτοί αφήνουν** *ah • <u>fee</u> • noon*

Φέρνω (to bring)	Present
I bring	**Εγώ φέρνω** <u>fehr</u> • noh
You bring	**Εσύ φέρνεις** <u>fehr</u> • nees
He brings	**Αυτός φέρνει** <u>feh</u> • rnee
She brings	**Αυτή φέρνει** <u>fehr</u> • nee
We bring	**Εμείς φέρνουμε** <u>feh</u> • rnoo • meh
You bring	**Εσείς φέρνετε** <u>fehr</u> • neh • teh
They bring	**Αυτοί φέρνουν** <u>fehr</u> • noon

The infinitive/first person of most Greek verbs end in **ω**:
to do   **κάνω** <u>kah</u> • noh

To conjugate this verb, drop the final **ω**, and add the appropriate ending:

Κάνω (to do)	Present
I do	**Εγώ κάνω** *eh • <u>goh</u> <u>kahn</u> • oh*
You do	**Εσύ κάνεις** *eh • <u>see</u> <u>kahn</u> • ees*
(familiar or sing.)	
He does	**Αυτός κάνει** *ahf • <u>tohs</u> <u>kahn</u> • ee*
She does	**Αυτή κάνει** *ahf • <u>tee</u> <u>kahn</u> • ee*
We do	**Εμείς κάνουμε** *eh • <u>mees</u> <u>kahn</u> • oo • meh*
You do *(form., pl.)*	**Εσείς κάνετε** *eh • <u>sees</u> <u>kahn</u> • eh • teh*
They do	**Αυτοί κάνουν** *ahf • <u>tee</u> <u>kahn</u> • oun*

So, by applying this rule you can conjugate another verb ending in **ω**:

Γράφω (to write)	Present
I write	**Εγώ γράφω**
	eh • _goh grahf_ • oh
You write	**Εσύ γράφεις**
	eh • _see grahf_ • ees
He writes	**Αυτός γράφει**
	ahf • _tohs grahf_ • ee
She writes	**Αυτή γράφει**
	ahf • _tee grahf_ • ee
We write	**Εμείς γράφουμε**
	eh • _mees grahf_ • oo • meh
You write	**Εσείς γράφετε**
	eh • _sees grahf_ • eh • teh
They write	**Αυτοί γράφουν**
	ahf • _ee grahf_ • oon

WORD ORDER

Syntax in Greek, especially in everyday spoken language, is very flexible. The standard word order is subject-verb-object, but you can change the order of sentence components to shift emphasis.
Example:
Το τρένο φεύγει τώρα. toh _treh_ • noh _fehv_ • ghee toh • rah
The train leaves now.
You can say the same thing by placing the verb at the beginning of the sentence:
Φεύγει το τρένο τώρα. _fehv_ • ghee toh _treh_ • noh toh • rah
The train leaves now.
Also, use an interrogatory intonation to turn this sentence into a question. The question form can work both with the verb in the beginning and at the end of the sentence.

Τώρα φεύγει το τραίνο; *toh • rah fehv • ghee toh treh • noh*
Is the train leaving now?
Note that, in Greek, the equivalent of a semi-colon (;) is used in place of a question mark.

NEGATION

To form a negative sentence in Greek, add the word **δεν** (*THehn*) before the verb.
Example:

Θέλω *theh • loh*	I want
Δεν θέλω *THehn theh • loh*	I don't want

IMPERATIVES

Imperative sentences are formed by adding the appropriate ending to the stem of the verb. The endings used to form the imperative of a verb are mainly:
α (*ah*), **ε** (*eh*), **ήσου** (*ee • soo*), **άσου** (*ah • soo*).

Examples:		
πηγαίνω	*pee • yeh • noh*	to go
Πήγαινε!	*pee • yeh • neh*	Go!
βιάζομαι	*viah • zoh • meh*	to hurry
Βιάσου!	*viah • soo*	Hurry!

NOUNS & ARTICLES

There are three genders in Greek: masculine, feminine and neuter; all nouns in Greek are assigned a specific gender. The gender of the article changes based on the gender of the noun it modifies.
For example:

She is tall.	**Είναι ψηλή.**	*ee • neh psee • lee*
He is tall.	**Είναι ψηλός.**	*ee • neh psee • lohs*

The article **o** (oh) is used with masculine nouns, **η** (ee) with feminine nouns and **το** (toh) with neuter nouns.

masculine	**ο καφές** oh kah • _fehs_	the coffee
feminine	**η μπίρα** ee _bee_ • rah	the beer
neuter	**το τρένο** toh _treh_ • noh	the train

Greek nouns have four cases: nominative, genitive, accusative and vocative. A simple way to explain their use would be that the nominative indicates the subject, the genitive indicates possession, the accusative indicates the object and the vocative is used to address someone. Don't worry too much about this. In most cases, people will understand what you are saying even if you use a noun with the wrong case. The words in the dictionary are in nominative.

There is no easy way to form the plural. Beginner speakers of Greek should clearly state the number along with the noun to be easily understood.

ADJECTIVES

Adjectives agree with the noun they describe in gender, case and number. The most common ending for a feminine adjective is **–η** _(ee)_, for a masculine adjective it is **–ος** _(ohs)_ and for the neuter **o** _(oh)_.

Example:

Είναι γρήγορος οδηγός. _ee_ • neh _ghree_ • ghoh • rohs
He is a fast driver. oh • THee • _ghohs_

Είναι γρήγορη οδηγός. _ee_ • neh _ghree_ • ghoh • ree
She is a fast driver. oh • THee • _ghohs_

Είναι γρήγορο αυτοκίνητο. _ee_ • neh _ghree_ • ghoh • roh
This is a fast car. ah • ftoh • _kee_ • nee • toh

COMPARATIVES & SUPERLATIVES

The comparative form of adjectives is usually formed by adding the word **πιο** *(pioh)* before the adjective. Also, in certain cases, the comparative may be formed by adding the ending **–ερος** *m (eh•rohs)*, **–ερη** *f (eh•ree)*, **–ερο** *(eh•roh) n* to the stem of an adjective, respectively. To form the superlative of an adjective, add the ending **–ατος** *m (ah•tohs)*, **–ατη** *f (ah•tee)*, **–ατο** *(ah•tee) n* to the stem of the adjective.

POSSESSIVE PRONOUNS

mine	**μου**	moo
yours	**σου**	soo
his/her/its	**του/της/του**	too/tees/too
ours	**μας**	mahs
yours	**σας**	sahs
theirs	**τους**	toos

Example:
Το βιβλίο είναι δικό μου. *toh veev•<u>lee</u>•oh ee•neh thee•<u>koh</u> moo*
This book is mine.

ADVERBS

Adverbs are used to describe the action of verbs. Almost all adverbs are formed by adding the ending **α** *(ah)* to the stem of the adjective.
Example:
Οδηγεί γρήγορα. *oh•THee•<u>yee ghree</u>•ghoh•rah*
He drives quickly.

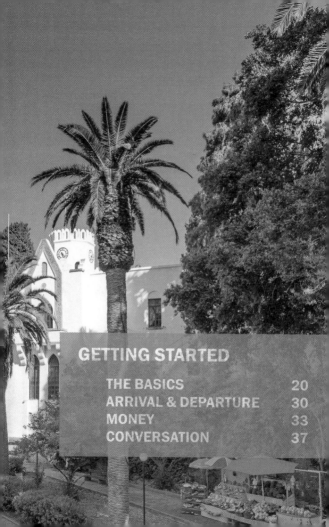

GETTING STARTED

THE BASICS

NUMBERS

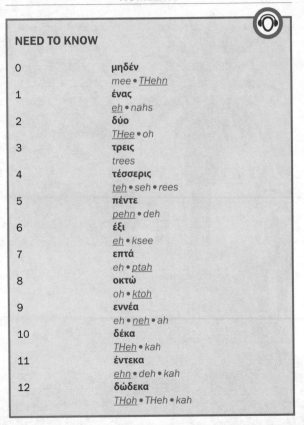

NEED TO KNOW

0	**μηδέν**
	mee • THehn
1	**ένας**
	eh • nahs
2	**δύο**
	THee • oh
3	**τρεις**
	trees
4	**τέσσερις**
	teh • seh • rees
5	**πέντε**
	pehn • deh
6	**έξι**
	eh • ksee
7	**επτά**
	eh • ptah
8	**οκτώ**
	oh • ktoh
9	**εννέα**
	eh • neh • ah
10	**δέκα**
	THeh • kah
11	**έντεκα**
	ehn • deh • kah
12	**δώδεκα**
	THoh • THeh • kah

13	**δεκατρία**
	THeh • kah • <u>tree</u> • ah
14	**δεκατέσσερα**
	THeh • kah • <u>teh</u> • seh • rah
15	**δεκαπέντε**
	THeh • kah • <u>pehn</u> • deh
16	**δεκαέξι**
	THeh • kah • <u>eh</u> • ksee
17	**δεκαεπτά**
	THeh • kah • eh • <u>ptah</u>
18	**δεκαοκτώ**
	THeh • kah • oh • <u>ktoh</u>
19	**δεκαεννέα**
	THeh • kah • eh • <u>neh</u> • ah
20	**είκοσι**
	<u>ee</u> • koh • see
21	**είκοσι ένα**
	<u>ee</u> • koh • see <u>eh</u> • nah
22	**είκοσι δύο**
	<u>ee</u> • koh • see <u>THee</u> • oh
30	**τριάντα**
	tree • <u>ahn</u> • dah
31	**τριάντα ένα**
	tree • <u>ahn</u> • dah eh • nah
40	**σαράντα**
	sah • <u>rahn</u> • dah
50	**πενήντα**
	peh • <u>neen</u> • dah
60	**εξήντα**
	eh • <u>kseen</u> • dah
70	**εβδομήντα**
	ehv • THoh • <u>meen</u> • dah

80	**ογδόντα**
	ohgh • _THohn_ • dah
90	**ενενήντα**
	eh • neh • _neen_ • dah
100	**εκατό**
	eh • kah • _toh_
101	**εκατόν ένα**
	eh • kah • _tohn_ eh • nah
200	**διακόσια**
	THee • ah • _koh_ • siah
500	**πεντακόσια**
	pehn • dah • _koh_ • siah
1,000	**χίλια**
	khee • liah
10,000	**δέκα χιλιάδες**
	THeh • kah khee • _liah_ • THehs
1,000,000	**ένα εκατομμύριο**
	_eh_ • nah eh • kah • toh • _mee_ • ree • oh

ORDINAL NUMBERS

first	**πρώτος** *proh • tohs*
second	**δεύτερος** *THehf • teh • rohs*
third	**τρίτος** *tree • tohs*
fourth	**τέταρτος** *teh • tahr • tohs*
fifth	**πέμπτος** *pehm • ptohs*
once	**μια φορά** *miah foh • rah*
twice	**δύο φορές** *THee • oh foh • rehs*
three times	**τρεις φορές** *trees foh • rehs*

ΕΠΤΑΠΥΡΓΙΟΥ
29

TIME

NEED TO KNOW

What time is it?	**Τι ώρα είναι;** *tee oh • rah ee • neh*
It's noon [midday].	**Είναι μεσημέρι.** *ee • neh meh • see • meh • ree*
At midnight.	**Τα μεσάνυχτα.** *tah meh • sah • neekh • tah*
From nine o'clock. to five o'clock	**Από τις εννέα ως τις πέντε.** *ah • poh tees eh • neh • ah ohs tees* *pehn • deh*
Twenty after [past] four.	**Τέσσερις και είκοσι.** *teh • seh • rees keh ee • koh • see*
A quarter to nine.	**Εννέα παρά τέταρτο.** *eh • neh • ah pah • rah teh • tahr • toh*
5:30 a.m./p.m.	**Πεντέμιση π.μ./μ.μ.** *pehn • deh • mee • see proh* *meh • seem • vree • ahs/meh • tah* *meh • seem • vree • ahs*

DAYS

NEED TO KNOW

Monday	**Δευτέρα**
	THehf • teh • rah
Tuesday	**Τρίτη**
	tree • tee
Wednesday	**Τετάρτη**
	teh • tahr • tee
Thursday	**Πέμπτη**
	pehm • tee
Friday	**Παρασκευή**
	pah • rahs • keh • vee
Saturday	**Σάββατο**
	sah • vah • toh
Sunday	**Κυριακή**
	keer • yah • kee chòo nat

DATES

yesterday	**χτες**
	khtehs
today	**σήμερα**
	see • meh • rah
tomorrow	**αύριο**
	ahv • ree • oh
day	**ημέρα**
	ee • meh • rah
week	**εβδομάδα**
	ehv • THoh • mah • THah
month	**μήνας**
	mee • nahs
year	**χρόνος**
	khroh • nohs

Greece follows a day-month-year format instead of the month-day-year format used in the U.S.
E.g.: July 25, 2008; 25/07/08 = 7/25/2008 in the U.S.

MONTHS

January	**Ιανουάριος** *ee • ah • noo • <u>ah</u> • ree • ohs*
February	**Φεβρουάριος** *fehv • roo • <u>ah</u> • ree • ohs*
March	**Μάρτιος** *<u>mahr</u> • tee • ohs*
April	**Απρίλιος** *ahp • <u>ree</u> • lee • ohs*
May	**Μάιος** *<u>mah</u> • ee • ohs*
June	**Ιούνιος** *ee • <u>oo</u> • nee • ohs*
July	**Ιούλιος** *ee • <u>oo</u> • lee • ohs*
August	**Αύγουστος** *<u>ahv</u> • ghoo • stohs*
September	**Σεπτέμβριος** *sehp • <u>tehm</u> • vree • ohs*
October	**Οκτώβριος** *ohk • <u>toh</u> • vree • ohs*
November	**Νοέμβριος** *noh • <u>ehm</u> • vree • ohs*
December	**Δεκέμβριος** *THeh • <u>kehm</u> • vree • ohs*

SEASONS

spring	**η άνοιξη** *ee <u>ah</u> • nee • ksee*

summer	**το καλοκαίρι**
	toh kah • loh • <u>keh</u> • ree
fall [autumn]	**το φθινόπωρο**
	toh fthee • <u>noh</u> • poh • roh
winter	**ο χειμώνας**
	oh khee • <u>moh</u> • nahs

HOLIDAYS

January 1, New Year's Day	**Πρωτοχρονιά**
	proh • toh • hroh • <u>niah</u>
January 6, Epiphany	**Θεοφάνεια**
	theh • oh • <u>fah</u> • nee • ah
March 25, Annunciation	**Ευαγγελισμός**
	eh • vahn • geh lee • <u>smohs</u>
March 25, National Holiday Proclamation of the Greek War of Independence	**Εθνική εορτή**
	ehth • nee • <u>kee</u> eh • ohr • <u>tee</u>
May 1, May Day	**Πρωτομαγιά**
	proh • toh • mah • <u>yah</u>

August 15, Assumption	**Κοίμηση της Θεοτόκου** _kee_ • mee • see tees theh • oh • _toh_ • koo
October 28, the OXI day	**Εθνική εορτή** ehth • nee • _kee_ eh • ohr • _tee_
December 25, Christmas	**Χριστούγεννα** khrees • _too_ • yeh • nah
Moveable Holidays: Easter	**Πάσχα** _pahs_ • khah
Shrove Monday (Greek Orthodox)	**Καθαρή Δευτέρα** kah • thah • _ree_ THeh • _fteh_ • rah
Pentecost	**Αγίου Πνεύματος** ah • _yee_ • oo _pnehv_ • mah • tohs

Each city and town has a patron saint. The saint's
holy day, also known as a name day, is a local public holiday.

(i)

The most important holidays in Greece are religious celebrations such as Easter and Christmas, with Easter being the most sacred holiday. The traditional celebrations usually start on Good Friday with a procession of the Epitaph (Bier) symbolizing the tomb of Christ. On Holy Saturday evening, the resurrection mass takes place when everyone goes to church at around 11:00 p.m. with unlit candles. At midnight the bells are rung and the priest comes out of the church to pass the Holy Light to the congregation. This is the largest religious gathering.

In most places, the crowds fill the streets outside the church, traffic is blocked and there are usually fireworks right after midnight. After this, it is customary to eat a soup called **μαγειρίτσα** (mah • ghee • ree • tsah), made from the lamb's internal organs.

On Sunday the celebration is usually taken outdoors. Whole families come together to roast a lamb on the spit, a big feast lasting the whole day. If you are in the countryside you will see large parties of people roasting the lamb and you may even be invited to join them. Even in the big cities, don't be surprised if you see people doing the same on their rooftops!

Another major holiday is March 25th, which is a day of remembrance of the start of the Greek War of Independence. On this day there is a military parade in every major city.

ARRIVAL & DEPARTURE

NEED TO KNOW

I'm here on vacation [holiday]/business.	**Είμαι εδώ για διακοπές/δουλειά.** _ee • meh_ eh • _THoh_ yah THiah • koh • _pehs_/THoo • _liah_
I'm going to…	**Θα…** _thah…_
I'm staying at the…Hotel.	**Μένω στο…ξενοδοχείο.** _meh • noh stoh…_ kseh • noh • THoh • _khee_ • oh

BORDER CONTROL

I'm just passing through.	**Απλώς περνώ από εδώ.** ahp • _lohs_ pehr • _noh_ ah • _poh_ eh • _THoh_
I would like to declare…	**Θα ήθελα να δηλώσω…** thah _ee_ • theh • lah nah THee • _loh_ • soh…
I have nothing to declare.	**Δεν έχω να δηλώσω τίποτα.** THehn _eh_ • khoh nah THee • _loh_ • soh _tee_ • poh • tah

Ελεγχος Εισιτηρίων
Check-in 30-157

Προς Εξόδους
All Gates A, B

YOU MAY HEAR...

Το εισιτήριο/διαβατήριό σας, παρακαλώ.
toh ee • see • tee • ree • oh/
THee • ah • vah • tee • ree • oh
sahs pah • rah • kah • loh

Your ticket/ passport, please.

Ποιος είναι ο σκοπός του ταξιδιού σας;
piohs ee • neh oh skoh • pohs too
tah • ksee • THee • oo sahs

What's the purpose of your visit?

Πού μένετε;
poo meh • neh • teh

Where are you staying?

Πόσο καιρό θα μείνετε;
poh • soh keh • roh thah mee • neh • teh

How long are you staying?

Με ποιον είστε εδώ;
meh piohn ee • steh eh • THoh

Who are you with?

Έχετε τίποτα να δηλώσετε;
eh • kheh • the tee • poh • tah nah
THee • loh • seh • teh

Do you have anything to declare?

Πρέπει να πληρώσετε φόρο για αυτό.
preh • pee nah plee • roh • seh • teh
foh • roh yah ahf • toh

You must pay duty on this.

Παρακαλώ ανοίξτε αυτή την τσάντα.
pah • rah • kah • loh ah • nee • ksteh
ahf • tee teen tsah • ndah

Please open this bag.

YOU MAY SEE...

ΤΕΛΩΝΕΙΟ — customs
teh • loh • <u>nee</u> • oh

ΑΦΟΡΟΛΟΓΗΤΑ ΕΙΔΗ — duty-free goods
ah • foh • roh • <u>loh</u> • yee • tah <u>ee</u> • THee

ΕΙΔΗ ΓΙΑ ΔΗΛΩΣΗ — goods to declare
<u>ee</u> • THee yah <u>THee</u> • loh • see

ΤΙΠΟΤΑ ΓΙΑ ΔΗΛΩΣΗ — nothing to
<u>tee</u> • poh • tah yah <u>THee</u> • loh • see declare

ΕΛΕΓΧΟΣ ΔΙΑΒΑΤΗΡΙΩΝ — passport control
<u>eh</u> • leh • ghohs THee • ah • vah •
tee • <u>ree</u> • ohn

ΑΣΤΥΝΟΜΙΑ — police
ah • stee • noh • <u>mee</u> • ah

MONEY

NEED TO KNOW

Where is...?	**Πού είναι...;** *poo ee • neh...*
the ATM	**το αυτόματο μηχάνημα ανάληψης** *toh ahf • toh • mee • khah • nee • mah ah • nah • lee • psees*
the bank	**η τράπεζα** *ee trah • peh • zah*
the currency exchange office	**γραφείο ανταλλαγής συναλλάγματος** *ghrah • fee • oh ahn • dah • lah • ghees see • nah • lahgh • mah • tohs*
What time does the bank open/close?	**Τι ώρα ανοίγει/κλείνει η τράπεζα;** *tee oh • rah ah • nee • ghee/klee • nee ee trah • peh • zah*
I'd like to change dollars/pounds into euros.	**Θα ήθελα να αλλάξω μερικά δολάρια/ λίρες σε ευρώ.** *thah ee • theh • lah nah ah • lah • ksoh meh • ree • kah THoh • lah • ree • ah/ meh • ree • kehs lee • rehs seh ehv • roh*
I want to cash some traveler's checks [cheques].	**Θα ήθελα να εξαργυρώσω μερικές ταξιδιωτικές επιταγές.** *thah ee • theh • lah nah eh • ksahr • yee • roh • soh meh • ree • kehs tah • ksee THee • oh • tee • kehs eh • pee • tah • yehs*

AT THE BANK

Can I exchange foreign currency/ get a cash advance here?	**Μπορώ να αλλάξω συνάλλαγμα εδώ;/να πάρω μετρητά προκαταβολικά εδώ;** *boh • roh nah ah • lah • ksoh see • nah • lahgh • mah eh • THoh/nah pah • roh meh • tree • tah proh • kah • tah • voh lee • kah eh • THoh*
What's the exchange rate?	**Ποια είναι η τιμή συναλλάγματος;** *piah ee • neh ee tee • mee see • nah • lahgh • mah • tohs*
How much is the fee?	**Πόση προμήθεια χρεώνετε;** *poh • see proh • mee • thee • ah khreh • oh • neh • teh*
I think there's a mistake.	**Νομίζω έγινε λάθος.** *noh • mee • zoh eh • ghee • neh lah • thohs*
I've lost my traveler's checks.	**Έχασα τις ταξιδιωτικές επιταγές μου.** *eh • khah • sah tees tah • ksee • THee • oh • tee • kehs eh • pee • tah • yehs moo*
My card was lost.	**Χάθηκε η κάρτα μου.** *khah • thee • keh ee kahr • tah moo*
My credit cards have been stolen.	**Μου έκλεψαν τις πιστωτικές μου κάρτες.** *moo ehk • leh • psahn tees pees • toh • tee • kehs moo kahr • tehs*

YOU MAY SEE...

In 2002, the Greek drachma was replaced with the European Union currency, euro, € (**ευρώ** *ehv • roh*), which is divided into 100 cents (**λεπτό** *lehp • toh*).
Coins: 1, 2, 5, 10, 20, 50 cents; €1, 2
Notes: €5, 10, 20, 50, 100, 200, 500

My card doesn't
work.
Η κάρτα μου δεν λειτουργεί.
ee kahr • tah moo THehn lee • toor • ghee

The ATM ate my card.
Το ATM κράτησε την κάρτα μου.
toh ATM krah • tee • seh teen kahr • tah moo

For Numbers, see page 20.

YOU MAY SEE…

ΕΙΣΑΓΕΤΕ ΤΗΝ ΚΑΡΤΑ	insert card
ee • sah • yeh • teh teen kahr • tah	
ΑΚΥΡΩΣΗ	cancel
ah • kee • roh • see	
ΔΙΑΓΡΑΦΗ	clear
THee • ahgh • rah • fee	
ΕΙΣΑΓΕΤΕ	enter
ee • sah • yeh • teh	
PIN	PIN
peen	
ΑΝΑΛΗΨΗ	withdraw
ah • nah • lee • psee	
ΑΠΟ ΛΟΓΑΡΙΑΣΜΟ ΟΨΕΩΣ	from checking
ah • poh loh • ghahr • yahz • moh	[current]
oh • pseh • ohs	account
ΑΠΟ ΛΟΓΑΡΙΑΣΜΟ ΤΑΜΙΕΥΤΗΡΙΟΥ	from savings
ah • poh loh • ghahr • yahz • moh	account
tah • mee • ehf • tee • ree • oo	
ΑΠΟΔΕΙΞΗ	receipt
ah • poh • THee • ksee	

All major foreign currencies, traveler's checks and Eurocheques are widely accepted at banks and currency exchange offices throughout Greece. In addition, ATMs can be found outside most main banks; these accept VISA, MasterCard, American Express, Eurocard and a variety of other international bank and credit cards.

Banks are generally open Monday through Friday from 7:30 a.m. or 8:00 a.m. to 2:30 p.m. (1:30 p.m. on Friday). Centrally located banks are also open on Saturday. Currency exchange offices usually stay open until late evening.

CONVERSATION

NEED TO KNOW

Hello.	**Χαίρετε.**
	kheh • reh • teh
How are you?	**Πώς είστε;**
	pohs _ee_ • steh
Fine, thanks.	**Καλά, ευχαριστώ. Εσείς;**
And you?	kah • _lah_ ehf • khah • ree • _stoh_
	eh • _sees_
Excuse me!	**Συγγνώμη!**
	seegh • _noh_ • mee
Do you speak	**Μιλάτε Αγγλικά;**
English?	mee • _lah_ • the ahng • lee • _kah_
What's your name?	**Πώς λέγεστε;**
	pohs _leh_ • yeh • steh
My name is…	**Λέγομαι…**
	leh • ghoh • meh…
Nice to meet you.	**Χαίρω πολύ.**
	kheh • roh poh • _lee_
Where are you from?	**Από πού είστε;**
	ah • _poh_ poo ee • steh
I'm from the U.S./U.K.	**Είμαι από τις Ηνωμένες Πολιτείες/το**
	Ηνωμένο Βασίλειο.
	ee • _meh_ ah • _poh_ tees ee • noh • _meh_ • nehs
	poh • lee • _tee_ • ehs/toh
	ee • noh • _meh_ • noh vah • _see_ • lee • oh
What do you do?	**Τι δουλειά κάνετε;**
	tee THoo • _liah_ _kah_ • neh • teh
I work for…	**Δουλεύω για…**
	THoo • _leh_ • voh yah…

I'm a student.	**Είμαι φοιτητής** m/**φοιτήτρια** f. _ee_ • meh fee • tee • _tees_/ fee • _tee_ • tree • ah
I'm retired.	**Είμαι συνταξιούχος.** _ee_ • meh seen • dah • ksee • _oo_ • khohs
Do you like...?	**Σου αρέσει...;** soo ah • _reh_ • see...
Goodbye.	**Γεια σας.** yah sahs
See you later.	**Τα λέμε αργότερα.** tah _leh_ • meh ahr • _ghoh_ • teh • rah

---

In Greek, Mrs. is **κυρία** (kee • _ree_ • ah), Mr. is **κύριος**
(kee • _ree_ • ohs) and Miss is **δεσποινίς** (THehs • pee • _nees_).
Greek has a formal and an informal form of 'you': **γεια σας**
(yah sahs) and **γεια σου** (yah soo), respectively. The informal
is used between friends or when addressing children. Use
the formal **γεια σας** unless prompted to do otherwise.

LANGUAGE DIFFICULTIES

Do you speak English?	**Μιλάτε Αγγλικά;** mee • _lah_ • teh ahng • lee • _kah_
Does anyone here speak English?	**Μιλάει κανείς εδώ Αγγλικά;** mee • _lah_ • ee kah • _nees_ eh • _THoh_ ahng • lee • _kah_
I don't speak Greek.	**Δεν μιλώ Ελληνικά.** THehn mee • _loh_ eh • lee • nee • _kah_

Could you speak more slowly?	**Μπορείτε να μιλάτε πιο αργά;**
	boh • ree • the nah mee • lah • teh pioh ahr • ghah
Could you repeat that?	**Μπορείτε να το επαναλάβετε;**
	boh • ree • the nah toh eh • pah • nah • lah • veh • teh
Excuse me!	**Συγγνώμη!**
	seegh • noh • mee
What was that?	**Τι είπατε;**
	tee ee • pah • teh
Can you spell it?	**Μπορείς να το συλλαβίσεις;**
	boh • rees nah toh see • lah • vee • sees
Can you write it down, please?	**Μου το γράφετε παρακαλώ;**
	moo toh ghrah • feh • teh pah • rah • kah • loh
Can you translate this for me?	**Μπορείτε να μου μεταφράσετε αυτό;**
	boh • ree • teh nah moo meh • tahf • rah • seh • teh ahf • toh
What does this/ that mean?	**Τι σημαίνει αυτό/εκείνο;**
	tee see • meh • nee ahf • toh/eh • kee • noh
I (don't) understand.	**(Δεν) Καταλαβαίνω.**
	(THehn) kah • tah • lah • veh • noh
Do you understand?	**Καταλαβαίνετε;**
	kah • tah • lah • veh • neh • teh

YOU MAY HEAR...

Μιλώ (μόνο) λίγα Αγγλικά.
mee • loh (moh • noh) lee • ghah ahng • lee • kah

I speak (only) a little English.

Δεν μιλώ Αγγλικά.
THehn mee • loh ahng • lee • kah

I don't speak English.

MAKING FRIENDS

Hello.	**Χαίρετε.**
	kheh • reh • teh
Good morning.	**Καλημέρα.**
	kah • lee • _meh_ • rah
Good afternoon/	**Καλησπέρα.**
evening.	kah • lee • _speh_ • rah
Good night.	**Καληνύχτα.**
	kah • lee • _neekh_ • tah
My name is…	**Λέγομαι…**
	leh • ghoh • meh…
What's your name?	**Πώς λέγεστε;**
	pohs _leh_ • yehs • teh
I'd like to introduce	**Θα ήθελα να σας συστήσω τον** m /**την** f …
you to…	thah _ee_ • theh • lah nah sahs
	sees • _tee_ • soh tohn/teen…
Pleased to meet you.	**Χαίρω πολύ.**
	kheh • roh poh • _lee_
How are you?	**Πώς είστε;**
	pohs _ees_ • teh
Fine, thanks.	**Καλά, ευχαριστώ.**
	kah • _lah_ ehf • khah • rees • _toh_
And you?	**Εσείς;**
	eh • _sees_

Greeks shake hands when they meet for the first time
and on subsequent meetings. With close friends,
it is customary to exchange kisses on both cheeks when
meeting and parting. It is polite to address people you meet
for the first time by their surname until prompted to use their
first name.

TRAVEL TALK

I'm here...	**Είμαι εδώ...**
	ee • meh eh • THoh...
on business	**για δουλειά**
	yah THoo • lee • ah
vacation [holiday]	**για διακοπές**
	yah THiah • koh • pehs
studying	**για σπουδές**
	yah spoo • THehs
I'm staying here for...	**Μένω εδώ για...**
	meh • noh eh • THoh yah...
I've been here...	**Είμαι εδώ...**
	ee • meh eh • THoh...
a day	**μια ημέρα**
	miah meh • rah
a week	**μια εβδομάδα**
	miah ehv • THoh • mah • THah
a month	**ένα μήνα**
	eh • nah mee • nah
Where are you from?	**Από πού είστε;**
	ah • poh poo ee • steh
I'm from...	**Είμαι από...**
	ee • meh ah • poh...

For Numbers, see page 20.

PERSONAL

Who are you with?	**Με ποιον/ποιαν είστε;**
	meh piohn/piahn <u>ee</u> • steh
I'm on my own.	**Είμαι μόνος** *m* **/μόνη** *f* **μου.**
	<u>ee</u> • meh <u>moh</u> • nohs/<u>moh</u> • nee moo
I'm with…	**Είμαι με…**
	<u>ee</u> • meh meh…
my husband/wife	**τον σύζυγο/την σύζυγό μου**
	tohn <u>see</u> • zee • ghoh/teen
	<u>see</u> • zee • <u>ghoh</u> moo
my boyfriend/ girlfriend	**τον φίλο/την κοπέλα μου**
	tohn <u>fee</u> • loh/teen koh • <u>peh</u> • lah moo
a friend	**ένα φίλο** *m* **/μια φίλη** *f*
	<u>eh</u> • nah <u>fee</u> • loh/miah <u>fee</u> • lee
a colleague	**έναν συνάδελφο**
	<u>eh</u> • nahn see • <u>nah</u> • THehl • foh
When's your birthday?	**Πότε είναι τα γενέθλιά σου;**
	<u>poh</u> • teh <u>ee</u> • neh tah
	gheh • <u>nehth</u> • lee • <u>ah</u> soo
How old are you?	**Πόσο χρονών είσαι;**
	<u>poh</u> • soh khroh • <u>nohn</u> <u>ee</u> • seh
I'm…	**Είμαι…**
	<u>ee</u> • meh…

Are you married?	**Είστε παντρεμένος;**
	ee • steh pah • dreh • <u>meh</u> • nohs
I'm...	**Είμαι...**
	ee • meh...
single	**ελεύθερος** m **/ελεύθερη** f
	eh • <u>lehf</u> • theh • rohs/eh • <u>lehf</u> • theh • ree
in a relationship	**δεσμευμένος** m **/δεσμευμένη** f
	THehs • mehv • <u>meh</u> • nohs/
	THehs • mehv • <u>meh</u> • nee
engaged	**αρραβωνιασμένος**
	ah • rah • voh • niah • <u>zmeh</u> • nohs
married	**παντρεμένος** m **/παντρεμένη** f
	pahn • dreh • <u>meh</u> • nohs/
	pahn • dreh • <u>meh</u> • nee
divorced	**διαζευγμένος** m **/διαζευγμένη** f
	THee • ah • zehv • <u>ghmeh</u> • nohs/
	THee • ah • zehv • <u>ghmeh</u> • ee
separated	**σε διάσταση**
	seh THee • <u>ah</u> • stah • see
I'm widowed.	**Είμαι χήρος** m **/χήρα** f.
	ee • meh <u>khee</u> • rohs/khee • rah
Do you have children/ grandchildren?	**Έχετε παιδιά/εγγόνια;**
	eh • kheh • the peh • <u>THyah</u>/
	eh • <u>goh</u> • niah

WORK & SCHOOL

What do you do?	**Τι δουλειά κάνετε;**
	tee THoo • <u>liah</u> kah • neh • teh
What are you studying?	**Τι σπουδάζετε;**
	tee spoo • <u>THah</u> • zeh • teh
I'm studying...	**Σπουδάζω...**
	spoo • <u>THah</u> • zoh...
I...	**Εγώ...**
	Eh • ghoh

work full-/part-time	δουλεύω με πλήρη/μερική απασχόληση
	THoo • _lehv_ • oh meh _plee_ • ree/
	meh • ree • _kee_ ah • pah • _skhoh_ • lee • see
am unemployed	**δεν δουλεύω**
	THehn THoo • _lehv_ • oh
work at home	**δουλεύω στο σπίτι**
	THoo • _lehv_ • oh stoh _spee_ • tee
Who do you work for...?	**Για ποιον δουλεύετε...;**
	yah piohn THoo • _leh_ • veh • teh...
I work for...	**Δουλεύω για...**
	THoo • _leh_ • voh yah...
Here's my business card.	**Ορίστε η κάρτα μου.**
	oh • _ree_ • steh ee _kahr_ • tah moo

WEATHER

What's the weather forecast for tomorrow?	**Τι λέει η πρόβλεψη του καιρού για αύριο;**
	tee _leh_ • ee ee _proh_ • vleh • psee too
	keh • _roo_ yah _ah_ • vree • oh
What beautiful/ terrible weather!	**Τι ωραίος/απαίσιος καιρός!**
	tee oh • _reh_ • ohs/
	ah • _peh_ • see • ohs keh • _rohs_
It's cool/warm.	**Έχει δροσιά/ζέστη.**
	_eh_ • khee roh • _siah/zeh_ • stee

It's cold/hot.	**Κάνει κρύο/ζέστη.**
	kah • nee <u>kree</u> • oh/<u>zeh</u> • stee
It's rainy/sunny.	**Ο καιρός είναι βροχερός/ηλιόλουστος.**
	oh keh • <u>rohs</u> <u>ee</u> • neh vroh • kheh • <u>rohs</u>/
	ee • <u>lioh</u> • loo • stohs
It's snowy/icy.	**Έχει παγωνιά.**
	<u>eh</u> • khee pah • ghoh • <u>niah</u>
Do I need a jacket/	**Να πάρω ζακέτα/ομπρέλα;**
an umbrella?	*nah <u>pah</u> • roh zah • <u>keh</u> • tah/*
	ohm • <u>breh</u> • lah

For Seasons, see page 26.

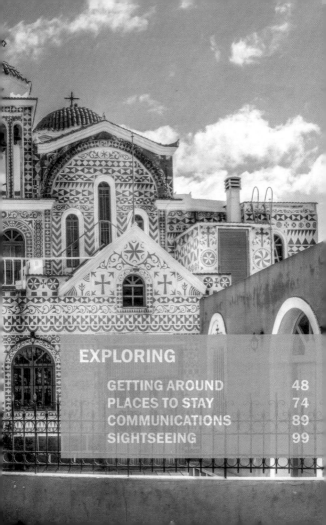

EXPLORING

GETTING AROUND

<table>
<tr><td colspan="2">NEED TO KNOW 🎧</td></tr>
<tr><td>How do I get to town?</td><td>Πώς μπορώ να πάω στην πόλη;
pohs boh • <u>roh</u> nah <u>pah</u> • oh steen <u>poh</u> • lee</td></tr>
<tr><td>Where's...?</td><td>Πού είναι...;
poo <u>ee</u> • neh...</td></tr>
<tr><td>the airport</td><td>το αεροδρόμιο
toh ah • eh • roh • <u>THroh</u> • mee • oh</td></tr>
<tr><td>the train [railway] station</td><td>ο σταθμός των τρένων
oh stahth • <u>mohs</u> ton treh • nohn</td></tr>
<tr><td>the bus station</td><td>ο σταθμός των λεωφορείων
oh stahth • <u>mohs</u>
tohn leh • oh • foh • <u>ree</u> • ohn</td></tr>
<tr><td>the metro station</td><td>ο σταθμός του μετρό
oh stahth • <u>mohs</u> too meh • <u>troh</u></td></tr>
<tr><td>How far is it?</td><td>Πόσο απέχει;
<u>poh</u> • soh ah • <u>peh</u> • khee</td></tr>
<tr><td>Where can I buy tickets?</td><td>Από πού μπορώ να αγοράσω εισιτήρια;
ah • <u>poh</u> poo boh • <u>roh</u> nah
ah • ghoh • <u>rah</u> • soh ee • see • <u>tee</u> • ree • ah</td></tr>
</table>

A one-way/ return-trip ticket.	**Ένα απλό εισιτήριο/εισιτήριο με επιστροφή;**
	eh • nah ahp • loh ee • see • tee • ree • oh/ ee • see • tee • ree • oh meh eh • pees • troh • fee
How much?	**Πόσο;**
	poh • soh
Is there a discount?	**Υπάρχει μειωμένο εισιτήριο;**
	ee • pahr • khee mee • oh • meh • noh ee • see • tee • ree • oh
Which…?	**Ποια…;**
	piah…
gate	**είσοδος**
	ee • soh • THohs
line	**γραμμή**
	ghrah • mee
platform	**πλατφόρμα**
	plaht • fohr • mah
Where can I get a taxi?	**Πού μπορώ να βρω ταξί;**
	poo boh • roh nah vroh tah • ksee
Please take me to this address.	**Παρακαλώ πηγαίνετέ με σε αυτή τη διεύθυνση.**
	pah • rah • kah • loh pee • yeh • neh • the meh seh ahf • tee tee THee • ehf • theen • see
Where can I rent a car?	**Πού μπορώ να νοικιάσω ένα αυτοκίνητο;**
	poo boh • roh nah nee • kee • ah • soh eh • nah ahf • toh • kee • nee • toh
Can I have a map?	**Μπορώ να έχω ένα χάρτη;**
	boh • roh nah eh • khoh eh • nah khahr • tee

TICKETS

When's...to Athens?	**Πότε αναχωρεί...για Αθήνα;** _poh_ • the ah • nah • khoh • _ree_...yah ah • _thee_ • nah
the (first) bus	**το (πρώτο) λεωφορείο** toh (proh • toh) leh • oh • foh • _ree_ • oh
the (next) flight	**η (επόμενη) πτήση** ee (eh • _poh_ • meh • nee) ptee • see
the (last) train	**το (τελευταίο) τρένο** toh (teh • lehf • _teh_ • oh) treh • noh
Where can I buy tickets?	**Από πού μπορώ να αγοράσω εισιτήρια;** ah • _poh_ poo boh • _roh_ nah ah • ghoh • _rah_ • soh ee • see • _tee_ • ree • ah
One ticket./Two tickets.	**Ένα εισιτήριο./Δύο εισιτήρια.** _eh_ • nah ee • see • _tee_ • ree • oh/THee • oh ee • see • _tee_ • ree • ah
For today/tomorrow.	**Για σήμερα/αύριο.** yah _see_ • meh • rah/_ahv_ • ree • oh
A first/economy class ticket.	**Ένα πρώτης/οικονομικής θέσης εισιτήριο.** _eh_ • nah proh • tees/ ee • koh • noh • mee • _kees theh_ • sees ee • see • _tee_ • ree • oh
A...ticket.	**Ένα εισιτήριο....** _eh_ • nah ee • see • _tee_ • ree • oh
one-way	**χωρίς επιστροφή** khoh • _rees_ eh • pee • stroh • _fee_
return trip	**με επιστροφή** meh eh • pee • stroh • _fee_
business class	**για θέση business** yah _theh_ • see business
How much?	**Πόσο;** _poh_ • soh

Is there a discount for…?	**Υπάρχει μειωμένο εισιτήριο για…;**
	ee • pahr • khee mee • oh • meh • noh
	ee • see • tee • ree • oh yah…
children	**παιδιά**
	peh • THyah
students	**φοιτητές**
	fee • tee • tehs
senior citizens	**ηλικιωμένοι**
	ee • lee • kee • oh • meh • nee
tourists	**τουρίστες**
	too • ree • stehs
The express bus/ express train, please.	**Το λεωφορείο express/ τρένο express, παρακαλώ.**
	toh leh • oh • foh • ree • oh express/ treh • noh express, pah • rah • kah • loh
The local bus/train, please.	**Το τοπικό λεωφορείο/τρένο, παρακαλώ.**
	toh toh • pee • koh leh • oh • foh • ree • oh/ treh • noh, pah • rah • kah • loh
I have an e-ticket.	**Έχω e-ticket.**
	eh • khoh ee tee • keht
Can I buy a ticket on the bus/train?	**Μπορώ να αγοράσω εισιτήριο στο λεωφορείο/ τρένο;**
	boh • roh nah ah • ghoh • rah • soh ee • see • tee • ree • oh stoh leh • oh • foh • ree • oh/treh • noh
Do I have to stamp the ticket before boarding?	**Πρέπει να σφραγίσω το εισιτήριο πριν ανέβω;**
	preh • pee nah sfrah • yee • soh toh ee • see • tee • ree • oh preen ah • neh • voh
Can I return on the same ticket?	**Μπορώ να επιστρέψω με το ίδιο εισιτήριο;**
	boh • roh nah eh • pee • streh • pso meh toh ee • THioh ee • see • tee • ree • oh
I'd like to…my reservation	**Θα ήθελα να…την κράτησή μου.**
	Thah ee • theh • lah nah…teen krah • tee • see moo

cancel	ακυρώσω
	ah • kee • roh • soh
change	αλλάξω
	ah • lah • ksoh
confirm	επιβεβαιώσω
	eh • pee • veh • veh • oh • soh

For Days, see page 25.

AIRPORT TRANSFER

How much is a taxi to the airport?	Πόσο κοστίζει το ταξί ως το αεροδρόμιο;
	poh • soh kohs • tee • zee toh tah • ksee ohs toh ah • eh • roh • THroh • mee • oh
To…Airport, please.	Στο…αεροδρόμιο, παρακαλώ.
	stoh…ah • eh • roh • THroh • mee • oh pah • rah • kah • loh
My airline is…	Πετάω με την εταιρία…
	peh • tah • oh meh teen eh • teh • ree • ah…
My flight leaves at…	Η πτήση μου φεύγει στις…
	ee ptee • see moo fehv • ghee stees…
I'm in a rush.	Βιάζομαι.
	vee • ah • zoh • meh
Can you take an alternate route?	Μπορείτε να πάτε από άλλο δρόμο;
	boh • ree • teh nah pah • teh ah • poh ah • loh THroh • moh
Can you drive faster/slower?	Μπορείτε να πάτε πιο γρήγορα/αργά;
	boh • ree • teh nah pah • teh pioh ghree • ghoh • rah/ahr • ghah

For Time, see page 24.

YOU MAY SEE...

ΑΦΙΞΕΙΣ *ah • fee • ksees*	arrivals
ΑΝΑΧΩΡΗΣΕΙΣ *ah • nah • khoh • ree • sees*	departures
ΠΑΡΑΛΑΒΗ ΑΠΟΣΚΕΥΩΝ *pah • rah • lah • vee ah • pohs • keh • vohn*	baggage claim
ΑΣΦΑΛΕΙΑ *ah • sfah • lee • ah*	security
ΠΤΗΣΕΙΣ ΕΣΩΤΕΡΙΚΟΥ *ptee • sees eh • soh • teh • ree • koo*	domestic flights
ΠΤΗΣΕΙΣ ΕΞΩΤΕΡΙΚΟΥ *ptee • sees eh • ksoh • teh • ree • koo*	international flights
ΕΛΕΓΧΟΣ ΑΠΟΣΚΕΥΩΝ *eh • legh ah • pos • keh • vohn*	check-in
E-TICKET CHECK-IN *ee • tee • keht tsehk • een*	e-ticket check-in
ΠΥΛΕΣ ΕΠΙΒΙΒΑΣΗΣ *pee • lehs eh • pee • vee • vah • sees*	boarding gates

YOU MAY HEAR...

Με ποια εταιρία πετάτε; *meh piah eh • teh • ree • ah peh • tah • teh*	What airline are you flying?
Τοπική ή Διεθνή; *toh • pee • kee ee THee • ehth • nee*	Domestic or International?
Σε ποιον τερματικό σταθμό; *seh piohn tehr • mah • tee • koh stahth • moh*	What terminal?

CHECKING IN

Where is the check-in desk for flight...?	**Πού είναι το γραφείο παράδοσης αποσκευών για την πτήση...;** *poo ee • neh toh ghrah • fee • oh ah • rah • THoh • sees ah • poh • skeh • vohn yah teen tee • see...*
My name is...	**Λέγομαι...** *leh • ghoh • meh...*
I'm going to...	**Πηγαίνω...** *pee • gheh • noh...*
I have...	**Έχω...** *eh • khoh*
one suitcase	**μία βαλίτσα** *mee • ah vah • lee • tsah*
two suitcases	**δύο βαλίτσες** *THee • oh vah • lee • tsehs*
one piece of hand luggage	**μία χειραποσκευή** *mee • ah khee • rah • poh • skehv • ee*
How much luggage is allowed?	**Πόσο είναι το επιτρεπόμενο βάρος;** *poh • soh ee • neh toh eh • pee • treh • poh • meh • noh vah • rohs*
Is that pounds or kilos?	**Είναι σε λίβρες ή σε κιλά;** *ee • neh seh lee • vrehs ee seh kee • lah*
Which terminal?	**Σε ποιο τέρμιναλ;** *seh pi • oh teh • rmee • nahl*
Which gate does flight...leave from?	**Από ποια έξοδο φεύγει η πτήση...;** *ah • poh piah eh • ksoh • THoh fehv • yee ee ptee • see...*
I'd like a window/ an aisle seat.	**Θα ήθελα μια θέση στο παράθυρο/ διάδρομο.** *thah ee • theh • lah mee • ah theh • see toh pah • rah • thee • roh/THe • ah • THroh • moh*
When do we leave/ arrive?	**Πότε φεύγουμε/φθάνουμε;** *poh • the fehv • ghoo • meh/fthah • noo • meh*

YOU MAY HEAR...

Ο επόμενος!
oh eh • poh • meh • nohs
Next!

Το εισιτήριο/διαβατήριο σας, παρακαλώ.
toh ee • see • tee • ree • oh/
THee • ah • vah • tee • ree • oh
sahs pah • rah • kah • loh
Your ticket/
passport, please.

Πόσες αποσκευές έχετε;
poh • sehs ah • poh • skeh • vehs
eh • kheh • teh
How much
luggage
do you have?

Έχετε υπέρβαρο.
eh • kheh • teh ee • pehr • vah • roh
You have excess
baggage.

Αυτό είναι πολύ βαρύ/μεγάλο για αποσκευή χειρός.
ahf • toh ee • neh poh • lee
vah • ree/meh • gha • loh yah
ah • pohs • keh • vee khee • rohs
That's too heavy/
large for
a carry-on
[to carry on
board].

Φτιάξατε τις βαλίτσες σας μόνος σας *m /***μόνη σας** *f*;
ftee • ah • ksah • teh tees vah • lee • tses
sahs moh • nohs sahs/moh • nee sahs
Did you pack
these bags
yourself?

Σας έδωσε κανείς να μεταφέρετε κάτι;
sahs eh • THoh • seh kah • nees nah
meh • tah • feh • reh • the kah • tee
Did anyone give
you anything
to carry?

Αδειάστε τις τσέπες σας.
ah • THiah • steh tees tseh • pehs sahs
Empty your
pockets.

Βγάλτε τα παπούτσια σας.
vghahl • teh tah pah • poo • tsiah sahs
Take off your
shoes.

Τώρα αρχίζει η επιβίβαση για την πτήση...
toh • rah ahr • khee • zee ee
eh • pee • vee • vah • see yah teen ptee • see...
Now boarding
flight...

Is flight...delayed?	**Υπάρχει καθυστέρηση στην πτήση...;**
	e • _pahr_ • khee kah • thee • <u>steh</u> • ree • see
	steen <u>tee</u> • see...
How late will it be?	**Πόσο θα αργήσει;**
	<u>poh</u> • soh thah ahr • <u>ghee</u> • see

LUGGAGE

Where is/are...?	**Πού είναι...;**
	poo <u>ee</u> • neh...
the luggage carts [trolleys]	**τα καροτσάκια αποσκευών**
	tah kah • roh • <u>tsah</u> • kee • ah ah • pohs • keh • <u>vohn</u>
the luggage lockers	**οι θυρίδες**
	ee thee • <u>ree</u> • THehs
the luggage claim	**η φύλαξη αποσκευών**
	ee <u>fee</u> • lah • ksee h • poh • skeh • <u>vohn</u>
I've lost my luggage.	**Έχασα τις αποσκευές μου.**
	<u>eh</u> • khah • sah tees ah • pohs • keh • <u>vehs</u> moo
My luggage has been stolen.	**Μου έκλεψαν τις αποσκευές.**
	moo <u>ehk</u> • leh • psahn tees ah • pohs • keh • <u>vehs</u>
My suitcase was damaged.	**Η βαλίτσα μου χάλασε στη μεταφορά.**
	ee vah • <u>lee</u> • tsah moo <u>khah</u> • lah • seh stee eh • tah • foh • <u>rah</u>

FINDING YOUR WAY

Where is/are...?	**Πού είναι...;**
	poo <u>ee</u> • neh...
the currency exchange office	**το γραφείο ανταλλαγής συναλλάγματος**
	toh ghrah • <u>fee</u> • oh ahn • dah • lah • <u>ghees</u> ee • nah • <u>lahgh</u> • mah • tohs

the car hire	**το γραφείο ενοικιάσεως αυτοκινήτων**
	toh ghrah • fee • oh
	eh • nee • kee • ah • seh • ohs
	ahf • toh • kee • nee • tohn
the exit	**η έξοδος**
	ee eh • ksoh • THohs
the taxis	**τα ταξί**
	tah tah • ksee
Is there...into town?	**Υπάρχει...για την πόλη;**
	ee • pahr • khee...yah teen poh • lee
a bus	**λεωφορείο**
	leh • oh • foh • ree • oh
a train	**τρένο**
	treh • noh
a metro	**μετρό**
	meh • troh

For Asking Directions, see page 69.

For Asking Directions, see page 69.

TRAIN

How do I get to the (main) train station?	**Πώς πάνε στον (κεντρικό) σιδηροδρομικό σταθμό;**
	pohs pah • neh stohn (kehn • dree • koh) see • THee • roh • THroh • mee • koh stahth • moh
How far is it?	**Πόσο απέχει;**
	poh • soh ah • peh • khee
Where is/are...?	**Πού είναι...;**
	poo ee • neh...
the ticket office	**το γραφείο εισιτηρίων**
	toh ghrah • fee • oh ee • see • tee • ree • ohn
the information desk	**το γραφείο πληροφοριών**
	toh ghrah • fee • oh plee • roh • foh • ree • ohn

the luggage lockers	**οι θυρίδες** *ee thee • <u>ree</u> • THehs*
the platform	**η αποβάθρα** *ee ah • poh • <u>vahth</u> • rah*
Could I have a schedule [timetable]?	**Μπορώ να έχω ένα πρόγραμμα δρομολογίων;** *boh • <u>roh</u> nah eh • khoh eh • nah <u>proh</u> • ghrah • mah THroh • moh • loh • <u>yee</u> • ohn*
How long is the trip?	**Πόση ώρα διαρκεί το ταξίδι;** *<u>poh</u> • see <u>oh</u> • rah THee • ahr • <u>kee</u> toh tah • <u>ksee</u> • THee*
Is it a direct train?	**Είναι απευθείας τρένο;** *ee • neh ah • pehf • <u>thee</u> • ahs treh • noh*
Do I have to change trains?	**Χρειάζεται να αλλάξω τρένο;** *khree • <u>ah</u> • zeh • the nah ah • <u>lah</u> • ksoh <u>treh</u> • noh*
Is the train on time?	**Το τρένο είναι στην ώρα του;** *toh <u>treh</u> • noh ee • neh steen <u>oh</u> • rah too*

For Tickets, see page 50.

YOU MAY SEE...

ΠΡΟΣ ΑΠΟΒΑΘΡΕΣ *prohs ah • poh • <u>vahth</u> • rehs*	to the platforms
ΠΛΗΡΟΦΟΡΙΕΣ *plee • roh • foh • <u>ree</u> • ehs*	information
ΚΡΑΤΗΣΕΙΣ *krah • <u>tee</u> • sees*	reservations
ΑΙΘΟΥΣΑ ΑΝΑΜΟΝΗΣ *<u>eh</u> • thoo • sah ah • nah • moh • <u>nees</u>*	waiting room
ΑΦΙΞΕΙΣ *ah • <u>fee</u> • ksees*	arrivals
ΑΝΑΧΩΡΗΣΕΙΣ *ah • nah • khoh • <u>ree</u> • sees*	departures

DEPARTURES

When is the train to...?	**Πότε φεύγει το τρένο για...;** *<u>poh</u> • teh <u>fehv</u> • ghee toh <u>treh</u> • noh yah...*
Is this the right platform for...?	**Είναι αυτή η σωστή αποβάθρα για το τρένο για...;** *ee • neh ahf • <u>tee</u> ee sohs • <u>tee</u> ah • poh • <u>vahth</u> • rah yah yah toh <u>treh</u> • noh yah...*
Where is platform...?	**Πού είναι η αποβάθρα...;** *poo <u>ee</u> • neh ee ah • poh • <u>vahth</u> • rah...*
Where do I change for...?	**Πού αλλάζω για...;** *poo ah • <u>lah</u> • zoh yah...*

ON BOARD

Can I sit here/open the window?	**Μπορώ να καθίσω εδώ/ ανοίξω το παράθυρο;** *boh • <u>roh</u> nah kah • <u>thee</u> • soh eh • <u>THoh</u>/ ah • <u>nee</u> • ksoh toh pah • <u>rah</u> • thee • roh*

That's my seat.	**Νομίζω αυτή είναι η θέση μου.**
	noh • mee • zoh ahf • tee ee • neh
	ee theh • see moo
Here's my reservation.	**Να η κράτησή μου.**
	nah ee krah • tee • see moo

> (i)
>
> The Greek train system is operated by OSE (**ΟΣΕ, Οργανισμός Σιδηροδρόμων Ελλάδος** _oh • seh, ohr • ghah • neez • mohs_ see • THee • roh • THroh • mohn _eh • lah • THohs_). The network is quite limited and, though the journey is scenic, is usually quite slow.
> The I/C, Intercity (**Υπερταχεία** _ee • pehr • tah • khee • ah_), makes few stops, but is more expensive. Make sure you reserve a seat in advance. All trains have bars and a sleeping car for longer journeys.

BUS

Where's the bus station?	**Πού είναι ο σταθμός λεωφορείων;**
	poo ee • neh oh stahth • mohs leh • oh • foh • ree • ohn
How far is it?	**Πόσο απέχει;**
	poh • soh ah • peh • khee
How do I get to…?	**Πώς πάνε σε…;**
	pohs pah • neh seh…
Is this the bus to…?	**Είναι αυτό το λεωφορείο για…;**
	ee • neh ahf • toh toh leh • oh • foh • ree • oh yah…
Could you tell me when to get off?	**Μπορείτε να μου πείτε πού να κατέβω;**
	boh • ree • teh nah moo pee • teh poo nah kah • teh • voh

Do I have to change buses?	**Χρειάζεται να αλλάξω λεωφορείο;**
	khree • ah • zeh • teh nah ah • lah • ksoh leh • oh • foh • ree • oh
Stop here, please!	**Σταματείστε εδώ, παρακαλώ!**
	stah • mah • tees • teh eh • THoh pah • rah • kah • loh

For Tickets, see page 50.

YOU MAY SEE... 👁

ΣΤΑΣΗ ΛΕΩΦΟΡΕΙΩΝ	bus stop
stah • see leh • oh • foh • ree • ohn	
ΕΙΣΟΔΟΣ/ΕΞΟΔΟΣ	enter/exit
ee • soh • THohs/eh • ksoh • THohs	
ΑΚΥΡΩΣΤΕ ΤΟ ΕΙΣΙΤΗΡΙΟ ΣΑΣ	validate your
ah • kee • roh • steh toh	ticket
ee • see • tee • ree • oh sahs	

YOU MAY HEAR...

Επιβιβαστείτε!	All aboard!
eh • pee • vee • vahs • tee • teh	
Τα εισιτήριά σας, παρακαλώ.	Tickets, please.
tah ee • see • tee • ree • ah sahs	
pah • rah • kah • loh	
Πρέπει να αλλάξετε σε...	You have to
preh • pee nah ah • lah • kseh • teh seh...	change at...
Επόμενη στάση...	Next stop...
eh • poh • meh • nee stah • see...	

METRO

Where's the nearest metro station?	**Πού είναι ο κοντινότερος σταθμός του μετρό;**
	poo ee • neh oh koh • ndee • noh • teh • rohs stahth • mohs too meh • troh
Could I have a map of the metro?	**Μπορώ να έχω ένα χάρτη του μετρό;**
	boh • roh nah eh • khoh eh • nah khahr • tee too meh • troh
Which line should I take for…?	**Ποια γραμμή πρέπει να πάρω για…;**
	piah ghrah • mee preh • pee nah pah • roh yah…
Which direction?	**Προς ποια κατεύθυνση;**
	prohs piah kah • tehf • theen • see
Where do I change for…?	**Πού αλλάζω για…;**
	poo ah • lah • zoh yah…
Is this the right train for…?	**Είναι αυτό το σωστό τρένο για…;**
	ee • neh ahf • toh toh sohs • toh treh • noh yah…
How many stops to…?	**Πόσες στάσεις μέχρι…;**
	poh • sehs stah • sees meh • khree
Where are we?	**Πού είμαστε;**
	poo ee • mahs • the

For Finding your Way, see page 56.

(i)

Athens is the only Greek city currently served by a **μετρό** *(meh • troh)*, subway. Before boarding public transportation you need to buy a ticket at the special kiosks or automatic ticketing machines marked **ΕΙΣΙΤΗΡΙΑ** *(ee • see • tee • ree • ah)*. Validate your ticket in the machine, found by the platform, before you get on. In Athens, tickets are valid for 90 minutes and can be used for buses, metro, trolleybuses, trams and part of the suburban railway. Daily, weekly or monthly tickets and reduced fares are available.

BOAT & FERRY

When is the ferry to...?	**Πότε φεύγει το φέρρυ-μπωτ για...;** _poh • the fehv • ghee toh feh • ree boht yah..._
Can I take my car onboard?	**Μπορώ να επιβιβάσω το αυτοκίνητό μου;** _boh • roh nah eh • pee • vee • vah • soh toh ahf • toh kee • nee • toh moo_
What time is the next sailing?	**Πότε είναι ο επόμενος απόπλους;** _poh • teh ee • nehoh eh • poh • meh • nohs ah • poh • ploos_
Can I book a seat/cabin?	**Μπορώ να κλείσω θέση/καμπίνα;** _boh • roh nah klee • soh theh • see/ kah • bee • nah_
How long is the crossing?	**Πόσο διαρκεί το πέρασμα;** _poh • soh THee • ahr • kee toh peh • rah • smah_
Where are the life jackets?	**Πού είναι τα σωσίβια;** _poo ee • neh tah soh • see • vee • ah_

For Weather, see page 44.

YOU MAY SEE...

ΝΑΥΑΓΟΣΩΣΤΙΚΗ ΛΕΜΒΟΣ _nah • vah • ghoh • sohs • tee • kee lehm • vohs_	life boats
ΣΩΣΙΒΙΑ _soh • see • vee • ah_	life jackets

It is likely that after your arrival in Athens, you will be heading straight for the port of Piraeus to catch a ferry. The harbor front is lined with ticket agents; ferry prices are fixed. Each agent tends to sell tickets for one company serving a particular route. A window display (usually in Greek and English) will tell you exactly what islands that ferry goes to. Sleeping on the deck is allowed, but make sure to take a sleeping bag and wear warm clothes, even in July! Once on an island, you may decide to go on an island tour. Several converted fishing boats run daily trips. Note that throwing anything into the sea off a boat deck is an offense in Greece, and you will be fined if caught.

TAXI

Where can I get a taxi?	**Πού μπορώ να βρω ταξί;** *poo boh • roh nah vroh tah • ksee*
Can you send a taxi?	**Μπορείτε να στείλετε ταξί;** *boh • ree • teh nah stee • leh • te tah • ksee*
Do you have the number for a taxi?	**Έχετε το τηλέφωνο για ταξί;** *eh • kheh • teh toh tee • leh • foh • noh yah tah • ksee*
I'd like a taxi now/ for tomorrow at…	**Θα ήθελα ένα ταξί τώρα/για αύριο στις…** *thah ee • theh • lah eh • nah tah • ksee toh • rah/yah ahv • ree • oh stees…*
Pick me up at (place/time)…	**Ελάτε να με πάρετε από/στις…** *eh • lah • the nah meh pah • reh • teh ah • poh/stees…*
I'm going to…	**Πηγαίνω…** *pee • gheh • noh…*
this address	**σε αυτή τη διεύθυνση** *seh ahf • tee tee THee • ehf • theen • see*

the airport	**στο αεροδρόμιο**
	stoh ah • eh • roh • THroh • mee • oh
the train [railway] station	**στον σιδηροδρομικό σταθμό**
	stohn see • THee • roh • THroh • mee • koh stahth • moh
I'm late.	**Έχω αργήσει.**
	eh • hoh ahr • ghee • see
Can you drive faster/slower?	**Μπορείτε να πάτε πιο γρήγορα/αργά;**
	boh • ree • teh nah pah • teh pioh gree • ghoh • rah/ahr • ghah
Stop/Wait here.	**Σταματήστε/Περιμένετε εδώ.**
	stah • mah • tee • steh/ peh • ree • meh • neh teh eh • THoh
How much?	**Πόσο;**
	poh • soh
You said it would cost…euros.	**Είπατε ότι θα κόστιζε…ευρώ.**
	ee • pah • the oh • tee thah kohs • tee • zeh…ehv • roh
Keep the change.	**Κρατείστε τα ρέστα.**
	krah • tees • teh tah rehs • tah
A receipt, please.	**Μια απόδειξη, παρακαλώ.**
	miah ah • poh • THee • ksee pah • rah • kah • loh

ⓘ

In Athens, licensed taxis are yellow with a blue stripe.
In all major cities, fares are fixed. For longer distances
you should agree to a fare before the trip. Tipping is not
compulsory, but it is common to round up the amount due.

YOU MAY HEAR...

Πού μπορώ να;
poo boh • roh nah

Where to?

Πού είναι η διεύθυνση;
poo ee • neh ee THee • ehf • theen • see

What's the
address?

BICYCLE & MOTORBIKE

I'd like to hire...	**θα ήθελα να νοικιάσω...**
	thah ee • theh • lah nah nee • kiah • soh...
a bicycle	**ένα ποδήλατο**
	eh • nah poh • THee • lah • toh
a moped	**ένα μοτοποδήλατο**
	eh • nah moh • toh • poh • THee • lah • toh
a motorbike	**μία μοτοσικλέτα**
	mee • ah moh • toh • see • kleh • tah
How much per day/week?	**Πόσο κοστίζει την ημέρα/την εβδομάδα;**
	poh • soh koh • stee • zee teen ee • meh • rah/tee ehv • THoh • mah • THah
Can I have a helmet/lock?	**Μπορώ να έχω ένα κράνος/μία κλειδαριά;**
	boh • roh nah eh • khoh eh • nah krah • nohs/mee • ah klee • THah • riah

CAR HIRE

Where can I hire a car?	**Πού μπορώ να νοικιάσω ένα αυτοκίνητο;** poo boh • roh nah nee • <u>kiah</u> • soh eh • nah ahf • toh • <u>kee</u> • nee • toh
I'd like to hire…	**Θα ήθελα να νοικιάσω ένα…** thah <u>ee</u> • theh • lah nah nee • <u>kiah</u> • soh <u>eh</u> • nah…
a cheap/small car	**ένα φτηνό/μικρό αυτοκίνητο** <u>eh</u> • nah ftee • <u>noh</u>/mee • <u>kroh</u> ahf • toh • <u>kee</u> • nee • toh
a 2-/4-door car	**δίπορτο/τετράπορτο αυτοκίνητο** <u>ee</u> • poh • rtoh/teh • <u>trah</u> • poh • rtoh ahf • toh • <u>kee</u> • nee • toh
an automatic/ manual car	**αυτόματο αυτοκίνητο/ αυτοκίνητο με συμπλέκτη** ahf • <u>toh</u> • mah • toh ahf • toh • <u>kee</u> • nee • toh/ ahf • toh • <u>kee</u> • nee • toh meh see • <u>bleh</u> • ktee
a car with air- conditioning	**αυτοκίνητο με κλιματισμό** ahf • toh • <u>kee</u> • nee • toh meh klee • mah • tee • <u>smoh</u>
a car seat	**παιδικό κάθισμα αυτοκινήτου** peh • THee • <u>koh kah</u> • thee • smah ahf • toh • kee • <u>nee</u> • too
How much…?	**Πόσο κάνει…;** <u>poh</u> • soh <u>kah</u> • nee…
per day/week	**την ημέρα/εβδομάδα** teen ee • <u>meh</u> • rah/ehv • THoh • <u>mah</u> • THah
per kilometer	**το χιλιόμετρο** toh khee • lee • <u>oh</u> • meht • roh
for unlimited mileage	**για απεριόριστη απόσταση** yah ah • peh • ree • <u>oh</u> • rees • tee ah • <u>poh</u> • stah • see

with insurance	**με ασφάλεια** *meh ah • sfah • lee • ah*
Are there any discounts?	**Υπάρχει έκπτωση;** *ee • pahr • khee ehk • ptoh • see*

YOU MAY HEAR...

Έχετε διεθνή άδεια οδήγησης;
eh • kheh • the THee • ehth • nee
ah • THee • ah oh • THee • ghee • sees

Do you have an international driver's license?

Μπορώ να δω το διαβατήριό σας, παρακαλώ;
boh • roh nah THoh toh
THee • ah • vah • tee • ree • oh sahs
pah • rah • kah • loh

May I see your passport, please?

Θέλετε ασφάλεια;
theh • leh • teh ah • sfah • lee • ah

Do you want insurance?

Υπάρχει μία προκαταβολή των...
ee • pahr • khee miah
proh • kah • tah • voh • lee tohn...

There is a deposit of...

Παρακαλώ υπογράψτε εδώ.
pah • rah • kah • loh
ee • poh • ghrah • psteh eh • THoh

Please sign here.

FUEL STATION

Where's the next fuel station, please?	**Πού είναι το επόμενο βενζινάδικο,** **παρακαλώ;** *poo ee • neh toh eh • poh • meh • noh* *vehn • zee • nah • THee • koh* *pah • rah • kah • loh*
Fill it up, please.	**Γεμίστε το, παρακαλώ.** *yeh • mee • steh toh pah • rah • kah • loh*

...liters, please.	**...λίτρα βενζίνη, παρακαλώ.** *...lee • trah vehn • zee • nee* *pah • rah • kah • loh*
I'll pay in cash/by credit card.	**Θα πληρώσω τοις μετρητοίς/με πιστωτική** **κάρτα.** *thah plee • roh • soh tees meh • tree • tees/* *meh pee • stoh • tee • kee kah • rtah*

For Numbers, see page 20.

YOU MAY SEE...

ΑΠΛΗ *ah • plee*	regular
ΣΟΥΠΕΡ *soo • pehr*	premium [super]
ΝΤΗΖΕΛ *dee • zehl*	diesel

ASKING DIRECTIONS

Is this the right road to...?	**Είναι αυτός ο σωστός δρόμος για...;** *ee • neh ahf • tohs oh sohs • tohs* *THroh • mohs yah...*
How far is it to...?	**Πόσο μακριά είναι για...;** *poh • soh mahk • ree • ah ee • neh yah...*
Where's...?	**Πού είναι...;** *poo ee • neh...*
...Street	**η οδός...** *ee oh • THohs...*
this address	**αυτή η διεύθυνση** *ahf • tee ee THee • ehf • theen • see*
the highway [motorway]	**η εθνική οδός** *ee ehth • nee • kee oh • THohs*

Can you show me on the map?	**Μπορείτε να μου δείξετε στο χάρτη;** *boh • ree • the nah moo THee • kseh • teh stoh khahr • tee*
I'm lost.	**Έχω χαθεί.** *eh • hoh khah • thee*

PARKING

Can I park here?	**Μπορώ να παρκάρω εδώ;** *boh • roh nah pahr • kah • roh eh • THoh*
Is there a parking lot [car park] nearby?	**Υπάρχει χώρος στάθμευσης εδώ κοντά;** *ee • pahr • khee khoh • rohs stath • mehf • sees eh • THoh kohn • dah*
Where's…?	**Πού είναι…;** *poo ee • neh*
the parking garage	**το πάρκινγκ** *toh pah • rkee • ng*
the parking meter	**το παρκόμετρο** *toh pah • rkoh • meh • troh*
How much…?	**Πόσο κοστίζει…;** *poh • soh koh • stee • zee…*
per hour	**την ώρα** *teen oh • rah*
per day	**την ημέρα** *teen ee • meh • rah*
overnight	**τη νύχτα** *tee neeh • khtah*

Parking in large cities, particularly Athens, can be a problem as spaces are limited. It is likely that you will need to park in an indoor or outdoor parking lot. Prices vary greatly, depending on your location.

YOU MAY HEAR...

ευθεία/ίσια *ehf • thee • ah/ee • see • ah*	straight ahead
στα αριστερά *stah ah • rees • teh • rah*	on the left
στα δεξιά *stah THeh • ksee • ah*	on the right
στη/μετά τη γωνία *stee/meh • tah tee ghoh • nee • ah*	on/around the corner
απέναντι *ah • peh • nahn • dee*	opposite
πίσω *pee • soh*	behind
δίπλα *THee • plah*	next to
μετά *meh • tah*	after
βόρεια/νότεια *voh • ree • ah/noh • tee • ah*	north/south
ανατολικά/δυτικά *ah • nah • toh • lee • kah/THee • tee • kah*	east/west
στο φανάρι *stoh fah • nah • ree*	at the traffic light
στη διασταύρωση *stee THee • ah • stahv • roh • see*	at the intersection

YOU MAY SEE...

ΑΠΑΓΟΡΕΥΕΤΑΙ Η ΕΠΙ ΤΟΠΟΥ ΣΤΡΟΦΗ   no u-turn
ah • pah • ghoh • <u>reh</u> • veh • teh ee eh
<u>pee</u> <u>toh</u> • poo stroh • <u>fee</u>

ΥΠΟΧΡΕΩΤΙΚΗ ΠΑΡΑΧΩΡΗΣΗ   yeld
ΠΡΟΤΕΡΑΙΟΤΗΤΑΣ
ee • pohkh • reh • oh • tee • <u>kee</u>
pah • rah • <u>khoh</u> • ree • see
proh • teh • reh • <u>oh</u> • tee • tahs

ΥΠΟΧΡΕΩΤΙΚΗ ΔΙΑΚΟΠΗ ΠΟΡΕΙΑΣ   stop
ee • pohkh • reh • oh • tee • <u>kee</u>
THee • ah • koh • <u>pee</u> poh • <u>ree</u> • ahs

ΠΕΡΙΟΧΗ ΑΠΑΓΟΡΕΥΣΗΣ   no parking
ΣΤΑΘΜΕΥΣΗΣ
peh • ree • oh • <u>khee</u>
ah • pah • <u>ghoh</u> • rehf • sees
<u>stahth</u> • mehf • sees

ΑΠΑΓΟΡΕΥΕΤΑΙ Η ΣΤΑΣΗ ΚΑΙ Η   no stopping
ΣΤΑΘΜΕΥΣΗ
ah • pah • ghoh • <u>reh</u> • veh • teh ee
<u>stah</u> • see keh ee <u>stahth</u> • mehf • see

ΜΟΝΟΔΡΟΜΟΣ   one way
moh • <u>noh</u> • THroh • mohs

BREAKDOWN & REPAIR

My car broke down/won't start.	**Το αυτοκίνητό μου χάλασε/δεν παίρνει μπρος.** toh ahf • toh • <u>kee</u> • nee • <u>toh</u> moo <u>khah</u> • lah • seh/THehn <u>pehr</u> • nee brohs
Can you fix it today?	**Μπορείτε να το επισκευάσετε σήμερα;** boh • <u>ree</u> • teh nah toh eh • pees • keh • <u>vah</u> • seh • the <u>see</u> • meh • rah
When will it be ready?	**Πότε θα είναι έτοιμο;** poh • teh thah <u>ee</u> • neh <u>eh</u> • tee • moh
How much?	**Πόσο;** poh • soh
I have a puncture/ flat tyre (tire).	**Έχω σκασμένο λάστιχο.** eh • khoh skah • <u>zmeh</u> • noh <u>lah</u> • stee • khoh

For Time, see page 24.

ACCIDENTS

There's been an accident.	**Έγινε ένα ατύχημα.** <u>eh</u> • yee • neh <u>eh</u> • nah ah • <u>tee</u> • khee • mah
Call an ambulance/ the police.	**Καλέστε ένα ασθενοφόρο/την αστυνομία.** kah • <u>lehs</u> • teh <u>eh</u> • nah ahs • theh • noh • <u>foh</u> • roh/teen ahs • tee • noh • <u>mee</u> • ah

For Police, see page 148.

PLACES TO STAY

NEED TO KNOW

Can you recommend a hotel?	**Μπορείτε να μου συστήσετε ένα ξενοδοχείο;** boh • _ree_ • teh nah moo sees • _tee_ • seh • teh _eh_ • nah kseh • noh • THoh • _khee_ • oh
I have a reservation.	**Έχω κλείσει δωμάτιο.** _eh_ • khoh klee • see THoh • _mah_ • tee • oh
My name is...	**Λέγομαι...** _leh_ • ghoh • meh...
Do you have a room...?	**Έχετε ελεύθερο δωμάτιο...;** _eh_ • kheh • the eh • _lehf_ • theh • roh THoh • _mah_ • tee • oh...
for one/two	**μονόκλινο/δίκλινο** moh • _noh_ • klee • noh/_THee_ • klee • noh
with a bathroom	**με μπάνιο** meh _bah_ • nioh
with air--conditioning	**με κλιματισμό** meh klee • mah • teez • _moh_
For tonight.	**Γι' απόψε.** yah • _poh_ • pseh
For two nights.	**Για δύο βράδια.** yah _THee_ • oh _vrah_ • THee • ah
For one week.	**Για μια εβδομάδα.** yah _mee_ • ah ev • THoh • _mah_ • THah
How much?	**Πόσο;** _poh_ • soh

Do you have anything cheaper?	**Έχετε τίποτα φθηνότερο;** *eh • kheh • the tee • poh • tah fthee • noh • teh • roh*
When's check-out?	**Τι ώρα πρέπει να αδειάσουμε το δωμάτιο;** *tee oh • rah preh • pee nah ah • THee • ah • soo • meh toh THoh • mah • tee • oh*
Can I leave this in the safe?	**Μπορώ να αφήσω αυτό στη θυρίδα;** *boh • roh nah ah • fee • soh ahf • toh stee thee • ree • THah*
Could we leave our baggage here until...?	**Μπορούμε να αφήσουμε τα πράγματά μας εδώ ως τις...;** *boh • roo • meh nah ah • fee • soo • meh tah prahgh • mah • tah mahs eh • THoh ohs tees...*
Could I have the bill/a receipt?	**Μπορώ να έχω τον λογαριασμό/μιααπόδειξη;** *boh • roh nah eh • hoh tohn loh • ghahr • yahs • moh/miah ah • poh • THee • ksee*
I'll pay in cash/by credit card.	**Θα πληρώσω τοις μετρητοίς/με πιστωτική κάρτα.** *thah plee • roh • soh tees meht • ree • tees/meh pees • toh • tee • kee kahr • tah*

SOMEWHERE TO STAY

Can you recommend a hotel?	**Μπορείτε να μου συστήσετε ένα ξενοδοχείο...;** *boh • ree • teh nah moo sees • tee • seh • teh eh • nah kseh • noh • THoh • khee • oh...*

Can you recommend...?	**Μπορείτε να προτείνετε...;**
	boh • ree • teh nah proh • tee • neh • teh
a hostel	**ένα ξενώνα**
	eh • nah kseh • noh • nah
a campsite	**ένα μέρος για κάμπινγκ;**
	eh • nah meh • rohs yah kahm • peeng
a bed and breakfast	**ένα δωμάτιο με πρωινό**
	eh • nah THoh • mah • tee • oh meh proh • ee • noh
What is it near?	**Πού κοντά είναι;**
	poo kohn • dah ee • neh
How do I get there?	**Πώς πάω εκεί;**
	pohs pah • oh eh • kee

AT THE HOTEL

I have a reservation.	**Έχω κλείσει δωμάτιο.**
	eh • hoh klee • see THoh • mah • tee • oh
My name is...	**Λέγομαι...**
	leh • ghoh • meh...
Do you have a room...?	**Έχετε δωμάτιο...;**
	eh • kheh • the THoh • mah • tee • oh...
with a bathroom [toilet]/shower	**με μπάνιο/ντους**
	meh bah • nioh/doo
with air- -conditioning	**με κλιματισμό**
	meh klee • mah • teez • moh
that's smoking/ non-smoking	**για καπνιστές/μη καπνιστές**
	yah kahp • nees • tehs/mee kahp • nees • tehs
For tonight.	**Γι' απόψε.**
	yah • poh • pseh
For two nights.	**Για δύο βράδια.**
	yah THee • oh vrah • THiah

For one week.	**Για μία εβδομάδα.**
	yah mee • ah ev • THoh • mah • THah
Does the hotel have...?	**Έχει το ξενοδοχείο...;**
	eh • khee toh kseh • noh • THoh • khee • oh...
a computer	**υπολογιστή**
	ee • poh • loh • ghees • tee
an elevator [lift]	**ασανσέρ**
	ah • sahn • sehr
(wireless) internet service	**υπηρεσία (ασύρματου) internet**
	ee • pee • reh • see • ah (ah • seer • mah • too)
	een • tehr • neht
room service	**υπηρεσία δωματίου**
	ee • pee • reh • see • ah THoh • mah • tee • oo
a pool	**πισίνα**
	pee • see • nah
a gym	**γυμναστήριο**
	gheem • nahs • tee • ree • oh
I need...	**χρειάζομαι...**
	khree • ah • zoh • meh...
an extra bed	**άλλο ένα κρεβάτι**
	ah • loh eh • nah kreh • vah • tee
a cot	**ένα ράντζο**
	eh • nah rahn • joh
a crib	**ένα παιδικό κρεβάτι**
	eh • nah peh • THee • koh kreh • vah • tee

ⓘ

If you didn't reserve a place to stay before your trip,
visit the local tourist information office for a list of places to
stay. Booking ahead is recommended in the high season,
from July to the end of August.

Greece offers a large variety of accommodation options: **Ξενοδοχεία** (ksehn • oh • THoh • <u>khee</u> • ah), hotels; **Διαμερίσματα** (THee • ah • meh • <u>reez</u> • mah • tah), furnished apartments; **Δωμάτια** (THoh • <u>mah</u> • tee • ah) furnished rooms, with or without a private bath; **Παραδοσιακά δωμάτια** (pah • rah • THoh • see • ah • <u>kah</u> THoh • <u>mah</u> • tee • ah), apartments in traditional but renovated homes; **Ξενώνας νεότητας** (kseh • <u>noh</u> • nahs neh • <u>oh</u> • tee • tahs), youth hostels; **Κάμπινγκ** (<u>kahm</u> • peeng) campsites and more.

PRICE

How much per night/week?	**Πόσο κάνει τη βραδιά/την εβδομάδα;** <u>poh</u> • soh <u>kah</u> • nee tee vrah • <u>iah</u>/teen ehv • o • <u>mah</u> • ah
Does the price include breakfast/ sales tax [VAT]?	**Η τιμή συμπεριλαμβάνει πρωινό/ΦΠΑ;** ee tee • <u>mee</u> seem • beh • ree • lahm • <u>vah</u> • nee proh • ee • <u>noh</u>/fee • pee • <u>ah</u>
Are there any discounts?	**Έχει έκπτωση;** <u>eh</u> • khee <u>ehk</u> • ptoh • see

PREFERENCES

Can I see the room?	**Μπορώ να δω το δωμάτιο;** boh • <u>roh</u> nah doh toh THoh • <u>mah</u> • tee • oh
I'd like a...room.	**Θα ήθελα...δωμάτιο.** tha <u>ee</u> • theh • lah...THoh • <u>mah</u> • tee • oh
better	**καλύτερο** kah • <u>lee</u> • teh • roh
bigger	**μεγαλύτερο** meh • ghah • <u>lee</u> • teh • roh

cheaper	**πιο φθηνό** pioh fthee • <u>noh</u>
quieter	**πιο ήσυχο** pioh <u>ee</u> • see • khoh
I'll take it.	**Θα το πάρω.** thah toh <u>pah</u> • roh
No, I won't take it.	**Όχι, δεν θα το πάρω.** <u>oh</u> • khee, THen thah toh <u>pah</u> • roh

QUESTIONS

Where's…?	**Πού είναι…;** poo <u>ee</u> • neh…
the bar	**το μπαρ** toh bahr
the bathroom	**το μπάνιο** toh <u>bah</u> • nioh
the elevator [lift]	**το ασανσέρ** toh ah • sahn • <u>sehr</u>
Can I have…?	**Μπορώ να έχω…;** boh • <u>roh</u> nah <u>eh</u> • khoh…
a blanket	**μια κουβέρτα** miah koo • <u>vehr</u> • tah
an iron	**ένα σίδερο** <u>eh</u> • nah <u>see</u> • THeh • roh
the room key/ key card	**το κλειδί δωματίου/την κάρτα** toh klee • <u>THee</u> THoh • mah • <u>tee</u> • oo/ teen <u>kahr</u> • tah
a pillow	**ένα μαξιλάρι** <u>eh</u> • nah mah • ksee • <u>lah</u> • ree
soap	**σαπούνι** sah • <u>poo</u> • nee
toilet paper	**χαρτί υγείας** khahr • <u>tee</u> ee • <u>ghee</u> • ahs

a towel	**μια πετσέτα μπάνιου** *miah peh • tseh • tah bah • nee • oo*
Can I use this adapter here?	**Μπορώ να χρησιμοποιήσω αυτόν τον προσαρμοστή εδώ;** *boh • roh nah khree • see • moh • pee • ee • soh ahf • tohn tohn proh • sahr • mohs • tee eh • THoh*
How do I turn on the lights?	**Πώς ανάβουν τα φώτα;** *pohs ah • nah • voon tah foh • tah*
Could you wake me at…?	**Μπορείτε να με ξυπνήσετε στις…;** *boh • ree • teh nah meh kseep • nee • seh • teh stees…*
Could I have my things from the safe?	**Μπορώ να έχω τα πράγματά μου από τη θυρίδα;** *boh • roh nah eh • khoh tah prahgh • mah • tah moo ah • poh tee thee • ree • THah*
Is there mail/ a message for me?	**Υπάρχει αλληλογραφία/κάποιο μήνυμα για μένα;** *ee • pahr • khee ah • lee • lohgh • rah • fee • ah/ kah • pioh mee • nee • mah yah meh • nah*
Do you have a laundry service?	**Έχετε υπηρεσία πλυντηρίων;** *eh • kheh • teh ee • pee • reh • see • ah plee • dee • ree • ohn*

YOU MAY HEAR...

Το διαβατήριό σας/την πιστωτική σας κάρτα, παρακαλώ.
toh ee • ah • vah • tee • ree • oh sahs/teen pees • toh • tee • kee sahs kahr • tah pah • rah • kah • loh

Your passport/ credit card, please.

Παρακαλώ συμπληρώστε αυτό το έντυπο.
pah • rah • kah • loh seem • blee • rohs • teh ahf • toh toh ehn • dee • poh

Please fill out this form.

Υπογράψτε εδώ.
ee • pohgh • rahp • steh eh • THoh

Sign here.

PROBLEMS

There's a problem.	**Υπάρχει ένα πρόβλημα.**
	ee • _pahr_ • hee eh • nah _prohv_ • lee • mah
I've lost my key/key card.	**Έχασα το κλειδί/την κάρτα μου.**
	_eh_ • hah • sah toh klee • _THee_/teen _kahr_ • tah moo
I've locked myself out of my room.	**Κλειδώθηκα έξω από το δωμάτιό μου.**
	klee • _THoh_ • thee • kah eh • ksoh ah • _poh_ toh THoh • _mah_ • tee • _oh_ moo
There's no hot water/toilet paper.	**Δεν υπάρχει ζεστό νερό/χαρτί υγείας.**
	Then ee • _pahr_ • khee zeh • _stoh_ neh • _roh_/khahr • _tee_ ee • _yee_ • ahs
The room is dirty.	**Το δωμάτιο είναι βρώμικο.**
	Toh THoh • _mah_ • tee • oh _ee_ • neh _vroh_ • mee • koh
There are bugs in our room.	**Υπάρχουν έντομα στο δωμάτιο μας.**
	ee • _pahr_ • hoon _ehn_ • doh • mah stoh THoh • _mah_ • tee • _oh_ mahs
...is broken.	**...είναι σπασμένος** m /**σπασμένη** f / **σπασμένο** n.
	...ee • neh spahs • _mehn_ • ohs/spahs • _mehn_ ee/spahs • _mehn_ • oh
Can you fix...?	**Μπορείτε να φτιάξετε...;**
	boh • _ree_ • teh nah _ftiah_ • kseh • teh...
the air conditioning	**τον κλιματισμό**
	tohn klee • mah • teez _moh_
the fan	**τον ανεμιστήρα**
	tohn ah • neh • mee • _stee_ • rah
the heating	**τη θέρμανση**
	tee _thehr_ • mahn • see
the light	**το φως**
	toh fohs
the TV	**την τηλεόραση**
	teen tee • leh • _oh_ • rah • see

the toilet	**την τουαλέτα** *teen too • ah • leh • tah*
I'd like to move to another room.	**Θα ήθελα να μεταφερθώ σε άλλο δωμάτιο.** *thah ee • theh • lah nah meh • tah • fehr • thoh she ah • loh THoh • mah • tee • oh*

YOU MAY SEE...

ΩΘΗΣΑΤΕ/ΕΛΞΑΤΕ *oh • thee • sah • teh/ehl • ksah • teh*	push/pull
ΜΠΑΝΙΟ/ΤΟΥΑΛΕΤΑ *bah • nioh/too • ah • leh • tah*	bathroom/ restroom [toilet]
ΝΤΟΥΣ *dooz*	shower
ΑΣΑΝΣΕΡ *ah • sahn • sehr*	elevator [lift]
ΣΚΑΛΑ *skah • lah*	stairs
ΠΛΥΝΤΗΡΙΟ *pleen • dee • ree • oh*	laundry
ΜΗΝ ΕΝΟΧΛΕΙΤΕ *meen eh • nohkh • lee • teh*	do not disturb
ΠΥΡΟΣΤΕΓΗΣ ΘΥΡΑ *pee • rohs • teh • ghees thee • rah*	fire door
ΕΞΟΔΟΣ ΚΙΝΔΥΝΟΥ *eh • ksoh • THohs keen • THee • noo*	emergency exit
ΥΠΗΡΕΣΙΑ ΑΦΥΠΝΙΣΗΣ *ee • pee • reh • see • ah ah • feep • nee • sees*	wake-up call

---

Tipping depends largely on your class of hotel; the higher the class, the more generous the tip. As a guideline, a euro or two per service rendered is recommended in standard hotels.

CHECKING OUT

When's check-out?	**Τι ώρα πρέπει να αδειάσουμε το δωμάτιο;** *tee oh • rah preh • pee nah ah • THee • ah • soo • meh toh THoh • mah • tee • oh*
Could we leave our baggage here until…?	**Μπορούμε να αφήσουμε τα πράγματά μας εδώ ως τις…;** *boh • roo • meh nah ah • fee • soomeh tah prahgh • mah • tah mahs eh • THoh ohs tees…*
Can I have an itemized bill/a receipt?	**Μπορώ να έχω έναν αναλυτικό λογαριασμό/μια απόδειξη;** *boh • roh nah eh • khoh eh • nah nah • nah • lee • tee • koh loh • ghahr • yahz • moh/miah ah • poh • ee • ksee*
I think there's a mistake in this bill.	**Νομίζω ότι έγινε ένα λάθος στο λογαριασμό.** *noh • mee • zoh oh • tee eh • yee • neh eh • nah lah • thohs stoh loh • ghahr • yahz • moh*
I'll pay in cash/by credit card.	**Θα πληρώσω τοις μετρητοίς/με πιστωτική κάρτα.** *thah plee • roh • soh tees meht • ree • tees/ meh pees • toh • tee • kee kahr • tah*

RENTING

I've reserved an apartment/a room.	**Έχω κλείσει ένα διαμέρισμα/δωμάτιο.** *eh • hoh klee • see eh • nah ee • ah • meh • rees • mah/ oh • mah • tee • oh*
My name is…	**Λέγομαι…** *leh • ghoh • meh…*

Can I have the key/key card?	**Μπορώ να έχω το κλειδί/την κάρτα;**	
	boh • roh nah eh • hoh toh klee • THee/teen kahr • tah	
Are there…?	**Υπάρχουν…;**	
	ee • pahr • khoon…	
dishes	**πιάτα**	
	piah • tah	
pillows	**μαξιλάρια**	
	mah • ksee • lah • ree • ah	
sheets	**σεντόνια**	
	sehn • doh • niah	
towels	**πετσέτες**	
	peh • tseh • tehs	
kitchen utensils	**οικιακά σκεύη**	
	ee • kee • ah • kah skeh • vee	
When do I put out the bins/recycling?	**Πότε να βγάλω έξω τα σκουπίδια/ την ανακύκλωση;**	
	poh • teh nah vghah • loh eh • ksoh tah skoo • pee • THiah/teen ah • nah • kee • kloh • see	
…has broken down.	**…χάλασε.**	
	…khah • lah • seh	
How does…work?	**Πώς λειτουργεί…;**	
	pohs lee • toor • ghee…	
the air-conditioner	**το κλιματιστικό**	
	toh klee • mah • tees • tee • koh	
the dishwasher	**το πλυντήριο πιάτων**	
	toh plee • ndee • ree • oh piah • tohn	
the freezer	**ο καταψύκτης**	
	oh kah • tah • psee • ktees	
the heater	**ο θερμοσίφωνας**	
	oh thehr • moh • see • foh • nahs	
the microwave	**ο φούρνος μικροκυμάτων**	
	oh foor • nohs meek • roh • kee • mah • tohn	

the refrigerator	**το ψυγείο**
	toh psee • ghee • oh
the stove	**η κουζίνα**
	ee koo • zee • nah
the washing machine	**το πλυντήριο**
	toh pleen • dee • ree • oh

In Greece the electricity supply is 220 V, with standard continental 2-pin or 3-pin plugs. A multi-adapter is recommended.

DOMESTIC ITEMS

I need…	**Χρειάζομαι…**
	khree • ah • zoh • meh…
an adapter	**έναν προσαρμοστή**
	eh • nahn proh • sahr • mohs • tee
aluminum foil	**λίγο αλουμινόχαρτο**
	lee • ghoh ah • loo • mee • noh • khahr • toh
a bottle opener	**ένα τιρμπουσόν**
	eh • nah teer • boo • sohn
a broom	**μια σκούπα**
	miah skoo • pah
a can opener	**ένα ανοιχτήρι**
	eh • nah ah • neeh • tee • ree
cleaning supplies	**μερικά καθαριστικά**
	meh • ree • kah kah • thah • rees • tee • kah
a corkscrew	**ένα τιρμπουσόν**
	eh • nah teer • boo • sohn
detergent	**λίγο απορρυπαντικό**
	lee • ghoh ah • poh • ree • pahn • dee • koh
dishwashing liquid	**λίγο υγρό πιάτων**
	lee • ghoh ee • ghroh piah • tohn

bin bags	**μερικές σακκούλες σκουπιδιών**
	meh • ree • <u>kehs</u> sah • <u>koo</u> • lehs skoo • pee • THee • <u>ohn</u>
a light bulb	**μια λάμπα**
	miah <u>lah</u> • mbah
matches	**μερικά σπίρτα**
	meh • ree • <u>kah</u> <u>speer</u> • tah
a mop	**μια σφουγγαρίστρα**
	miah sfoo • ghahr • <u>ees</u> • trah
napkins	**χαρτοπετσέτες**
	khah • rtoh • peh • <u>tseh</u> • tehs
paper towels	**χαρτοπετσέτες**
	khah • rtoh • peh • <u>tseh</u> • tehs
plastic wrap [cling film]	**διαφανή μεμβράνη**
	THee • ah • fah • <u>nee</u> mehm • <u>vrah</u> • nee
a plunger	**μια βεντούζα**
	miah vehn • <u>doo</u> • zah
scissors	**ένα ψαλίδι**
	<u>eh</u> • nah psah • <u>lee</u> • THee
a vacuum cleaner	**μια ηλεκτρική σκούπα**
	miah ee • lehk • tree • <u>kee</u> <u>skoo</u> • pah

For In the Kitchen, see page 198.

AT THE HOSTEL

Do you have any places left for tonight?	**Έχετε θέση για απόψε;**
	<u>eh</u> • kheh • teh theh • see yah ah • <u>poh</u> • pseh
Can I have...?	**Μπορώ να έχω...;**
	boh • <u>roh</u> nah <u>eh</u> • khoh...
a single/ double room	**μονό/διπλό δωμάτιο**
	moh • <u>noh</u>/THee • <u>ploh</u> THoh • <u>mah</u> • tee • oh

a blanket	**μια κουβέρτα**
	miah koo • vehr • tah
a pillow	**ένα μαξιλάρι**
	eh • nah mah • ksee • lah • ree
sheets	**σεντόνια**
	sehn • doh • niah
a towel	**μια πετσέτα μπάνιου**
	miah peh • tseh • tah bah • nioo
Do you have lockers?	**Έχετε ντουλάπια;**
	eh • kheh • teh doo • lah • piah
What time are the doors locked?	**Τί ώρα κλειδώνετε;**
	tee oh • rah klee • THoh • neh • the
Do I need a membership card?	**Χρειάζομαι κάρτα μέλους;**
	khree • ah • zoh • meh kahr • tah meh • loos
Here's my international student card.	**Αυτή είναι η διεθνής φοιτητική μου κάρτα.**
	ahf • tee ee • neh ee THee • eh • thnees fee • tee • tee • kee moo kahr • ta

GOING CAMPING

Can I camp here?	**Μπορώ να κάνω κάμπινγκ εδώ;**
	boh • roh nah kah • noh kahm • peeng • THoh
Is there a campsite near here?	**Υπάρχει χώρος κάμπινγκ εδώ κοντά;**
	ee • pahr • khee khoh • rohs kahm • peeng eh • THoh kohn • dah
What is the charge per day/week?	**Ποιό είναι το κόστος για την ημέρα/την εβδομάδα;**
	pioh ee • neh toh kohs • tohs yah teen ee • meh • rah/ehv • THoh • mah • THah
Are there...?	**Υπάρχουν...;**
	ee • pahr • hoon...
cooking facilities	**ηλεκτρική κουζίνα**
	ee • lehk • tree • kee koo • zee • nah

electrical outlets	**πρίζες**
	pree • zehs
laundry facilities	**πλυντήρια**
	pleen • _dee_ • ree • ah
showers	**ντους**
	dooz
tents for hire	**σκηνές για ενοικίαση**
	skee • nehs yah eh • nee • _kee_ • ah • see
Where can I empty the chemical toilet?	**Πού μπορώ να αδειάσω τη χημική τουαλέτα;**
	poo bohroh nah ah • THee • _ah_ • soh tee khee • meekee too ah • _leh_ • tah

For In the Kitchen, see page 198.

YOU MAY SEE...   👁

ΠΟΣΙΜΟ ΝΕΡΟ	drinking water
poh • see • moh neh • _roh_	
ΑΠΑΓΟΡΕΥΕΤΑΙ Η ΚΑΤΑΣΚΗΝΩΣΗ	no camping
ahpah • ghoh • _reh_ • vehteh ee kah • tahs • _kee_ • nohsee	
ΜΗΝ ΑΝΑΒΕΤΕ ΦΩΤΙΑ	no fires/
meen ah • _nah_ • veh • teh foh • tee • _ah_	barbecues

COMMUNICATIONS

NEED TO KNOW

Where's an internet cafe?	**Πού υπάρχει internet cafe;**
	poo ee • _pahr_ • khee
	een • tehr • neht kah • _feh_
Can I access the internet/check e-mail here?	**Μπορώ να μπω στο internet/να ελέγξω τα e-mail μου εδώ;**
	boh • _roh_ nah boh stoh
	een • tehr • _neht_/nah
	eh • _lehng_ • ksoh tah ee • meh • eel
	moo eh • _THoh_
How much per hour/half hour?	**Πόσο χρεώνεται η ώρα/μισή ώρα;**
	poh • soh hreh • _oh_ • neh • teh ee
	_oh_ • rah/mee • _see oh_ • rah
How do I connect/log on?	**Πώς μπορώ να συνδεθώ/μπω;**
	pohs boh • _roh_ nah
	seehn • THeh • _thoh/boh_
I'd like a phone card.	**Θα ήθελα μια τηλεκάρτα.**
	thah _ee_ • theh • lah miah
	tee • leh • _kahr_ • tah
Can I have your phone number?	**Μπορώ να έχω τον αριθμό τηλεφώνου σας;**
	boh • _roh_ nah eh • hoh tohn
	ah • reeth • _moh_ tee • leh • _foh_ • noo sahs
Here's my number/ e-mail address.	**Ορίστε το τηλέφωνό μου/e-mail μου.**
	oh • _rees_ • teh toh tee • _leh_ • foh • _noh_
	moo/ee • _meh_ • eel moo
Call me.	**Πάρτε με τηλέφωνο.**
	pahr • teh meh tee • _leh_ • foh • noh

E-mail me.	**Στείλτε μου e-mail.**
	<u>steel</u> • teh moo ee • <u>meh</u> • eel
Hello. This is…	**Εμπρός. Είμαι…**
	ehm • <u>brohs</u> ee • <u>meh</u>…
I'd like to speak to…	**Θα ήθελα να μιλήσω με…**
	thah <u>ee</u> • theh • lah nah mee • <u>lee</u> • soh meh…
Repeat that, please.	**Επαναλάβετέ το, παρακαλώ.**
	eh • pah • nah • <u>lah</u> • veh • <u>teh</u> toh pah • rah • kah • <u>loh</u>
I'll be in touch.	**Θα επικοινωνήσω μαζί σας.**
	thah eh • pee • kee • noh • <u>nee</u> • soh mah • <u>zee</u> sahs
Bye.	**Αντίο.**
	ah • <u>dee</u> • oh
Where is the nearest/main post office?	**Πού είναι το κοντινότερο/κεντρικό ταχυδρομείο;**
	poo ee • neh toh koh • ndee • <u>noh</u> • teh • roh/ kehn • dree • <u>koh</u> tah • khee • THroh • <u>mee</u> • oh
I'd like to send this to…	**Θα ήθελα να στείλω αυτό σε…**
	thah <u>ee</u> • theh • lah nah <u>stee</u> • loh ahf • <u>toh</u> seh…

ONLINE

Where's an internet cafe?	**Πού υπάρχει ένα internet cafe;**
	poo ee • <u>pahr</u> • khee eh • nah een • tehr • <u>neht</u> kah • <u>feh</u>
Does it have wireless internet?	**Έχει ασύρματο internet;**
	<u>eh</u> • khee ah • <u>seer</u> • mah • toh een • tehr • <u>neht</u>

What is the WiFi password?	**Ποιος είναι ο κωδικός πρόσβασης για το WiFi;**
	piohs ee • neh oh koh • THee • kohs proh • svah • sees yah toh WiFi
Is the WiFi free?	**Το WiFi είναι δωρεάν;**
	toh WiFi ee • neh THo • reh • ahn
Do you have bluetooth?	**Έχετε bluetooth;**
	eh • kheh • teh bluetooth
How do I turn the computer on/off?	**Πώς ανοίγει/κλείνει ο υπολογιστής;**
	pohs ah • nee • ghee/klee • nee oh ee • poh • loh • ghees • tees
Can I...?	**Μπορώ...;**
	boh • roh...
access the internet here	**να έχω πρόσβαση στο internet από εδώ**
	nah eh • hoh prohs • vah • see stoh een • tehr • neht ah • poh eh • THoh
check e-mail	**να ελέγξω τα e-mail μου**
	nah eh • leng • ksoh tah ee • meh • eel moo
print	**εκτυπώσω**
	ehk • tee • poh • soh
plug in/charge my laptop iPhone/iPad	**να συνδέσω/φορτίσω το laptop/iPhone/iPad**
	nah seen • THeh • soh toh laptop/iPhone/iPad
access Skype	**να μπω στο Skype**
	nah boh stoh Skype
How much per hour/half hour?	**Πόσο χρεώνεται η ώρα/μισή ώρα;**
	poh • soh hreh • oh • neh • teh ee oh • rah/mee • see oh • rah
How do I...?	**Πώς μπορώ να...;**
	pohs boh • roh nah
connect/disconnect	**συνδεθώ/αποσυνδεθώ**
	seen • theh • THoh/ah • poh • seen • theh • THoh

log on/off	**συνδεθώ/αποσυνδεθώ**
	seen • theh • THoh/
	ah • poh • seen • theh • THoh
type this symbol	**πληκτρολογήσω αυτό το σύμβολο**
	pleek • troh • loh • ghee • soh ahf • toh toh
	seem • voh • loh
What's your e-mail?	**Ποιο είναι το e-mail σας;**
	pioh ee • neh toh ee • meh • eel sahs
My e-mail is...	**Το e-mail μου είναι...**
	toh ee • meh • eel moo ee • neh...
Do you have a scanner?	**Έχετε σαρωτή;**
	eh • kheh • teh sah • roh • tee

YOU MAY SEE...

ΚΛΕΙΣΙΜΟ	close
klee • see • moh	
ΔΙΑΓΡΑΦΗ	delete
THee • ahgh • rah • fee	
EMAIL	e-mail
ee • meh • eel	
ΕΞΟΔΟΣ	exit
eh • ksoh • THohs	
ΒΟΗΘΕΙΑ	help
voh • ee • thee • ah	
ΕΦΑΡΜΟΓΗ ΑΜΕΣΟΥ	instant
ΜΗΝΥΜΑΤΟΣ	messenger
eh • fahr • moh • yee ah • meh • soo	
mee • nee • mah • tohs	
INTERNET	internet
een • tehr • neht	

YOU MAY SEE...

ΣΥΝΔΕΣΗ	login
seen • theh • see	
ΝΕΟ (ΜΗΝΥΜΑ)	new (message)
neh • oh mee • nee • mah	
ON/OFF	on/off
ohn/ohf	
ΑΝΟΙΧΤΟ	open
ah • neekh • toh	
ΕΚΤΥΠΩΣΗ	print
ehk • tee • poh • see	
ΑΠΟΘΗΚΕΥΣΗ	save
ah • poh • thee • kehf • see	
ΑΠΟΣΤΟΛΗ	send
ah • pohs • toh • lee	
ΟΝΟΜΑ ΧΡΗΣΤΗ	username
oh • noh • mah khrees • tee	
ΚΩΔΙΚΟΣ ΠΡΟΣΒΑΣΗΣ	password
koh • THee • kohs prohs • vah • sees	
ΑΣΥΡΜΑΤΟ INTERNET	wireless internet
ah • seer • mah • toh een • tehr • neht	

SOCIAL MEDIA

Are you on Facebook/ Twitter?	**Είστε στο Facebook/Twitter;**
	ee • steh stoh Facebook/Twitter
What's your username?	**Ποιο είναι το όνομα χρήστη;**
	pioh ee • neh toh oh • noh • mah khree • stee
I'll add you as a friend.	**Θα σε προσθέσω ως φίλο.**
	thah seh proh • stheh • soh ohs fee • loh

I'll follow you on Twitter.	**Θα σε ακολουθώ στο Twitter.**
	thah seh ah • koh • loo • <u>thoh</u> stoh Twitter
Are you following...?	**Ακολουθείς...;**
	ah • koh • loo • <u>thees</u>
I'll put the pictures on Facebook/Twitter.	**Θα βάλω τις φωτογραφίες στο Facebook/ Twitter.**
	thah <u>vah</u> • loh tees foh • toh • ghrah • <u>fee</u> • ehs sto Facebook/Twitter
I'll tag you in the pictures.	**Θα σε σημειώσω στις φωτογραφίες.**
	thah seh see • mee • <u>oh</u> • soh stees foh • toh • ghrah • <u>fee</u> • ehs

---

YOU MAY HEAR...

Ποιος είστε;	Who's calling?
piohs <u>ee</u> • steh	
Περιμένετε, παρακαλώ.	Hold on, please.
peh • ree • <u>meh</u> • neh • the pah • rah • kah • <u>loh</u>	
Θα σας συνδέσω.	I'll put you
thah sahs seen • THeh • soh	through.
Θέλετε να αφήσετε μήνυμα;	Would you like to
<u>theh</u> • leh • teh nah ah • <u>fee</u> • seh • teh <u>mee</u> • nee • mah	leave a message?
Ξανακαλέστε αργότερα/σε δέκα λεπτά.	Call back later/
ksah • nah • kah • <u>lehs</u> • teh ahr • <u>ghoh</u> • teh • rah/she eh • kah lehp • <u>tah</u>	in ten minutes.
Να σας πάρει εκείνος/εκείνη;	Can he/she call
nah sahs <u>pah</u> • ree eh • <u>kee</u> • nohs/ eh • <u>kee</u> • nee	you back?
Ποιος είναι ο αριθμός σας;	What's your
piohs <u>ee</u> • neh oh ah • reeth • <u>mohs</u> sahs	number?

PHONE

> ⓘ Throughout Greece, even in remote areas, there are plenty of public phones; these are mainly card operated. Phone cards can be purchased from **περίπτερα** (peh • ree • pteh • rah), kiosks. You can also purchase a **κάρτα για κινητό** (kah • rtah yiah kee • nee • toh) prepaid card for your wireless phone from any of the conveniently located wireless phone stores.

A phone card/ prepaid phone, please.	**Μια τηλεκάρτα/χρονοκάρτα.** *miah tee • leh • kahr • tah/ khroh • noh • kahr • tah*
How much?	**Πόσο;** *poh • soh*
Where's the pay phone?	**Πού είναι ένα καρτοτηλέφωνο;** *poo ee • neh toh kahr • toh • tee • leh • foh • noh*
What's the area/ country code for...?	**Ποιος είναι ο κωδικός περιοχής/χώρας για...;** *piohs ee • neh oh koh • THee • kohs peh • ree • oh • khees/khoh • rahs yah...*
What's the number for Information?	**Ποιος είναι ο αριθμός για Πληροφορίες;** *piohs ee • neh oh ah • reeth • mohs yah plee • roh • foh • ree • ehs*
I'd like the number for...	**Θα ήθελα έναν αριθμό για...** *thah ee • theh • lah eh • nahn ah • reeth • moh yah...*
I'd like to call collect [reverse the charges].	**Θέλω να τηλεφωνήσω με αναστροφή χρέωσης.** *theh • loh nah tee • leh • foh • nee • soh meh ah • nah • stroh • fee khreh • oh • sees*
My phone doesn't work here.	**Το τηλέφωνό μου δεν λειτουργεί εδώ.** *toh tee • leh • foh • noh moo THehn lee • toor • ghee eh • THoh*
What network are you on?	**Σε ποιο δίκτυο είσαι;** *seh pioh THee • ktee • oh ee • seh*

Is it 3G?	**Είναι 3G;**
	ee • neh 3G
I have run out of credit/minutes.	**Δεν έχω μονάδες/λεπτά.**
	THehn eh • khoh moh • nah • THehs/ leh • ptah
Can I buy some credit?	**Μπορώ να αγοράσω μονάδες;**
	boh • roh nah ah • ghoh • rah • soh moh • nah • THehs
Do you have a phone charger?	**Έχετε φορτιστή για τηλέφωνο;**
	eh • kheh • teh foh • rtee • stee yah tee • leh • foh • noh
Can I have your number?	**Μπορώ να έχω τον αριθμό τηλεφώνου σας;**
	boh • roh nah eh • khoh tohn ah • reeth • moh tee • leh • foh • noo sahs
Here's my number.	**Ορίστε ο αριθμός τηλεφώνου μου.**
	oh • ree • steh oh ah • reeth • mohs tee • leh • foh • noo moo
Please text me.	**Παρακαλώ, στείλτε μου μήνυμα.**
	pah • rah • kah • loh steel • teh moo mee • nee • mah
I'll call you.	**Θα σας πάρω τηλέφωνο.**
	thah sahs pah • rohtee • leh • foh • noh

For Numbers, see page 20.

YOU MAY HEAR...

Παρακαλώ συμπληρώστε αυτήν την τελωνειακή δήλωση.	Please fill out the customs declaration form.
pah • rah • kah • loh seem • blee • rohs • teh ahf • teen teen teh • loh • nee • ah • kee THee • loh • see	
Ποια είναι η αξία;	What's the value?
piah ee • neh ee ah • ksee • ah	
Τι είναι μέσα;	What's inside?
tee ee • neh meh • sah	

TELEPHONE ETIQUETTE

Hello. This is…	**Εμπρός. Είμαι ο** m / **η** f …
	ehm • <u>brohs</u> ee • meh oh/ee…
I'd like to speak to…	**Θα ήθελα να μιλήσω με τον** m /**την** f…
	thah <u>ee</u> • theh • lah nah mee • <u>lee</u> • soh meh tohn/teen…
Extension…	**Εσωτερική γραμμή…**
	eh • soh • teh • ree • <u>kee</u> ghrah • mee…
Speak louder/more slowly.	**Μιλείστε πιο δυνατά/πιο αργά.**
	mee • <u>lees</u> • the pioh THee • nah • <u>tah</u>/ahr • <u>ghah</u>
Repeat that, please.	**Επαναλάβετέ το, παρακαλώ.**
	eh • pah • nah • <u>lah</u> • veh • <u>teh</u> toh pah • rah • kah • <u>loh</u>
I'll call back later.	**Θα έρθω σε επαφή μαζί σας αργότερα.**
	thah <u>ehr</u> • thoh seh eh • pah • <u>fee</u> mah • <u>zee</u> sahs ahr • <u>ghoh</u> • teh • rah
Bye.	**Αντίο.**
	ah • <u>dee</u> • oh

FAX

Can I send/receive a fax here?	**Μπορώ να στείλω/λάβω φαξ από εδώ;**
	boh • <u>roh</u> nah <u>stee</u> • loh/<u>lah</u> • voh fahks ah • <u>poh</u> eh • <u>THoh</u>
What's the fax number?	**Ποιος είναι ο αριθμός φαξ;**
	piohs ee • neh oh ah • reeth • <u>mohs</u> fahks
Please fax this to…	**Παρακαλώ στείλτε αυτό το φαξ σε…**
	pah • rah • kah • <u>loh</u> <u>steel</u> • teh ahf • <u>toh</u> toh fahks seh…

POST

Where's the post office/mailbox?	**Πού είναι το ταχυδρομείο/το γραμματοκιβώτιο;**
	poo <u>ee</u> • neh toh tah • khee • roh • <u>mee</u> • oh/ toh ghrah • mah • toh kee • <u>voh</u> • tee • oh
A stamp for this postcard/letter.	**Ένα γραμματόσημο γι' αυτή την κάρτα/ αυτό το γράμμα.**
	<u>eh</u> • nah ghrah • mah • <u>toh</u> • see • moh yah ahf • <u>teen</u> teen <u>kahr</u> • tah/ahf • <u>toh</u> toh <u>ghrah</u> • mah
How much?	**Πόσο;**
	<u>poh</u> • soh
I want to send this package by airmail/express.	**Θέλω να στείλω αυτό το πακέτο αεροπορικώς/ εξπρές.**
	<u>theh</u> • lohnah <u>stee</u> • loh ahf • <u>toh</u> toh pah <u>keh</u> • toh • ah • <u>eh</u> • roh • poh • ree • <u>kohs</u>/ ehks • <u>prehs</u>
Can I have a receipt?	**Μπορώ να έχω μια απόδειξη;**
	boh • <u>roh</u> nah <u>eh</u> • khoh miah ah • <u>poh</u> • THee • ksee

The post office is open from 8:00 a.m. to 8:00 p.m., except on Wednesday and Saturday when it closes at around 1:00 p.m. Main post offices are open Sunday morning. Mailboxes are yellow and bear the initials **ΕΛΤΑ** (ehl • <u>tah</u>).

SIGHTSEEING

NEED TO KNOW

Where's the tourist information office?	**Πού είναι το γραφείο τουρισμού;**
	poo ee • neh toh ghrah • fee • oh too • reez • moo
What are the main points of interest?	**Ποια είναι τα κυριότερα αξιοθέατα;**
	piah ee • neh tah kee • ree • oh • teh • rah ah • ksee • oh • theh • ah • tah
Do you have tours in English?	**Γίνονται ξεναγήσεις στα αγγλικά;**
	ghee • nohn • deh kseh • nah • ghee • sees stah ahng • lee • kah
Could I have a map/guide?	**Μπορώ να έχω έναν χάρτη/οδηγό;**
	boh • roh nah eh • khoh eh • nahn khahr • tee/oh • THee • ghoh

TOURIST INFORMATION

Do you have any information on...?	**Έχετε πληροφορίες για...;** _eh_ • kheh • the plee • roh • foh • _ree_ • ehs yah...
Can you recommend...?	**Μπορείτε να συστήσετε έναν/μία/ένα...;** boh • _ree_ • teh nah sees • _tee_ • seh • teh _eh_ • nahn/_mee_ • ah/_eh_ • nah...
a bus tour	**περιήγηση με λεωφορείο** peh • ree • _ee_ • ghee • see meh leh • oh • foh • _ree_ • oh
a boat trip	**μια εκδρομή με βάρκα** _mee_ • ah ehk • THroh • _mee_ meh _vahr_ • kah
an excursion	**μια εκδρομή** _mee_ • ah ehk • THroh • _mee_
a sightseeing tour	**μια ξενάγηση στα αξιοθέατα** _mee_ • ah kseh • _nah_ • yee • see stah ah • ksee • oh • _theh_ • ah • tah

For Asking Directions, see page 69.

(i)

The official, government-run tourist information offices are known as **EOT** (eh • _oht_), **Ελληνικός Οργανισμός Τουρισμού** (eh • lee • nee • _kohs_ ohr • ghah • nees • _mohs_ too • rees • _moo_), in Greece and **KOT** (koht), **Κυπριακός Οργανισμός Τουρισμού** (keep • ree • ah • _kohs_ ohr • ghah • nees • _mohs_ too • rees • _moo_) in Cyprus. They can be found in most tourist resorts and major towns.

ON TOUR

I'd like to go on the tour to…	**Θα ήθελα να πάω στην ξενάγηση στο…** *thah ee • theh • lah nah pah • oh steen kseh • nah • yee • see stoh…*
When's the next tour?	**Πότε είναι η επόμενη περιήγηση;** *poh • teh ee • neh ee eh • poh • meh • nee peh • ree • ee • ghee • see*
Are there tours in English?	**Γίνονται ξεναγήσεις στα αγγλικά;** *ghee • nohn • deh kseh • nah • yee • sees stah ahng • lee • kah*
What time do we leave/return?	**Τι ώρα αναχωρούμε/επιστρέφουμε;** *tee oh • rah ah • nah • khoh • roo • meh/ eh • pees • treh • foo • meh*
We'd like to have a look at the…	**Θα θέλαμε να ρίξουμε μια ματιά…** *thah theh • lah • meh nah ree • ksoo • meh miah mah • tiah…*
Can we stop here…?	**Μπορούμε να σταματήσουμε εδώ…;** *boh • roo • meh nah stah • mah • tee • soo • meh eh • THoh…*
to take photographs	**για να βγάλουμε φωτογραφίες** *yah nah vghah • loo • meh foh • toh • ghrah • fee • ehs*

to buy souvenirs	**για να αγοράσουμε σουβενίρ**
	yah nah ah • ghoh • <u>rah</u> • soo • meh
	soo • veh • <u>neer</u>
to use the	**για τουαλέτα**
restroom [toilet]	*yah too • ah • <u>leh</u> • tah*
Is there access for	**Υπάρχει πρόσβαση για άτομα με ειδικές**
the disabled?	**ανάγκες;**
	ee • <u>pahr</u> • khee <u>prohz</u> • vah • see yah
	<u>ah</u> • toh • mah meh ee • THee • <u>kehs</u>
	ah • <u>nahn</u> • gehs

For Tickets, see page 50.

SEEING THE SIGHTS

Where is...?	**Πού είναι...;**
	poo <u>ee</u> • neh...
the battleground	**το πεδίο μάχης**
	toh peh • <u>THee</u> • oh mah • khees
the botanical	**ο βοτανικός κήπος**
garden	*oh voh • tah • nee • <u>kohs</u> <u>kee</u> • pohs*
the castle	**το κάστρο**
	toh <u>kahs</u> • troh

Where is...?	**Πού είναι...;**
	poo <u>ee</u> • neh...
the downtown area	**το κέντρο της πόλης**
	toh <u>kehn</u> • droh tees <u>poh</u> • lees
the fountain	**το συντριβάνι**
	toh seen • dree • <u>vah</u> • nee
the library	**η βιβλιοθήκη**
	ee veev • lee • oh • <u>thee</u> • kee
the market	**η αγορά**
	ee ah • ghoh • <u>rah</u>
the museum	**το μουσείο**
	toh moo • <u>see</u> • oh
the old town	**η παλιά πόλη**
	ee pah • <u>liah</u> <u>poh</u> • lee
the opera house	**το μέγαρο μουσικής**
	toh meh • <u>ghah</u> • roh moo • see • kees
the palace	**τα ανάκτορα**
	tah ah • <u>nahk</u> • toh • rah
the park	**το πάρκο**
	toh <u>pahr</u> • koh
the ruins	**τα αρχαία**
	tah ahr • <u>kheh</u> • ah
the shopping area	**η εμπορική περιοχή**
	ee ehm • boh • ree • <u>kee</u> peh • ree • oh • <u>khee</u>

the town hall	**το Δημαρχείο** *toh THee • mahr • khee • oh*
Can you show me on the map?	**Μπορείτε να μου δείξετε στο χάρτη;** *boh • ree • teh nah moo THee • kseh • teh stoh khahr • tee*
It's…	**Είναι…** *ee • neh…*
amazing	**καταπληκτικό** *kah • tah • plee • ktee • koh*
beautiful	**όμορφο** *oh • mohr • foh*
boring	**βαρετός** *vah • reh • toh*
interesting	**ενδιαφέρον** *ehn • THee • ah • feh • rohn*
magnificent	**μεγαλοπρεπές** *meh • ghah • lohp • reh • pehs*
romantic	**ρομαντικό** *roh • mahn • dee • koh*
strange	**παράξενο** *pah • rah • kseh • noh*
terrible	**απαίσιο** *ah • peh • see • oh*
ugly	**άσχημο** *ahs • khee • moh*
I (don't) like it.	**(Δεν) Μου αρέσει.** *(THen) moo ah • reh • see*

RELIGIOUS SITES

Where is…?	**Πού είναι…;** *poo ee • neh…*
the cathedral	**ο καθεδρικός** *oh kah • theh • THree • kohs*

the Catholic/ Protestant church	**η καθολική/ προτεσταντική εκκλησία** *ee kah•thoh • lee•kee/* *proh•teh•stahn•dee•<u>kee</u>* *ehk•lee•<u>see</u>•ah*
the mosque	**το τζαμί** *toh jah•<u>mee</u>*
the shrine	**ο ιερός χώρος** *oh ee•eh•<u>rohs khoh</u>•rohs*
the synagogue	**η συναγωγή** *ee see•nah•ghoh•<u>yee</u>*
the temple	**ο ναός** *oh nah•<u>ohs</u>*
What time is mass/ the service?	**Τι ώρα είναι η λειτουργία;** *tee <u>oh</u>•rah ee•neh* *ee lee•toor•<u>yee</u>•ah*

ACTIVITIES

SHOPPING

NEED TO KNOW

Where is the market/mall?	**Πού είναι η αγορά/το εμπορικό κέντρο;** poo <u>ee</u> • neh ee ah • ghoh • <u>rah</u>/toh ehm • boh • ree • <u>koh kehn</u> • droh
I'm just looking.	**Απλώς κοιτάω.** ahp • <u>lohs</u> kee • <u>tah</u> • oh
Can you help me?	**Μπορείτε να με βοηθήσετε;** boh • <u>ree</u> • teh nah meh voh • ee • <u>thee</u> • seh • teh
I'm being helped.	**Με εξυπηρετούν.** meh eh • ksee • pee • reh • <u>toon</u>
How much?	**Πόσο;** poh • soh
This/That one, thanks.	**Αυτό/Εκείνο, παρακαλώ.** ahf • <u>toh</u>/eh • <u>kee</u> • noh pah • rah • kah • <u>loh</u>
That's all, thanks.	**Τίποτε άλλο, ευχαριστώ.** <u>tee</u> • poh • teh <u>ah</u> • loh ehf • khah • rees • <u>toh</u>
Where do I pay?	**Πού πληρώνω;** poo plee • <u>roh</u> • noh
I'll pay in cash/by credit card.	**Θα πληρώσω τοις μετρητοίς/με πιστωτική κάρτα.** thah plee • <u>roh</u> • soh tees meht • ree • <u>tees</u>/meh pees • toh • tee • <u>kee kahr</u> • tah
A receipt, please.	**Μια απόδειξη, παρακαλώ.** miah ah • <u>poh</u> • THee • ksee pah • rah • kah • <u>loh</u>

Shopping can be a great pleasure in Greece. Apart
from the standard department stores, you can wander
through flea markets and seek out the small handicraft stores
that line the narrow alleys of most islands and old towns.

AT THE SHOPS

Where is…?	**Πού είναι…;**
	poo ee • neh…
the antiques store	**το κατάστημα με αντίκες**
	toh kah • tahs • tee • mah meh ahn • tee • kehs
the bakery	**το αρτοποιείο**
	toh ahr • toh • pee • ee • oh
the bank	**η τράπεζα**
	ee • trah • peh • zah
the bookstore	**το βιβλιοπωλείο**
	toh veev • lee • oh • poh • lee • oh
the clothing store	**το κατάστημα ρούχων**
	toh kah • tahs • tee • mah roo • khohn
the delicatessen	**τα τυριά-αλλαντικά**
	tah teer • yah ah • lahn • dee • kah
the department store	**το πολυκατάστημα**
	toh poh • lee • kah • tahs • tee • mah
the gift shop	**το κατάστημα σουβενίρ**
	toh kah • tah • stee • mah soo • veh • neer
the health food store	**το κατάστημα με υγιεινές τροφές**
	toh kah • tahs • tee • mah meh ee • yee • ee • nehs troh • fehs
the jeweler	**το κοσμηματοπωλείο**
	toh kohz • mee • mah • toh • poh • lee • oh
the liquor store [off-licence]	**η κάβα**
	ee kah • vah

the market	**η αγορά**
	ee ah • ghoh • _rah_
the music store	**το κατάστημα μουσικής**
	toh kah • _tah_ • stee • mah moo • see • _kees_
the pastry store	**το ζαχαροπλαστείο**
	toh zah • khah • rohp • lahs • _tee_ • oh
Where is...?	**Πού είναι...;**
	poo _ee_ • neh...
the pharmacy	**το φαρμακείο**
	toh fahr • mah • _kee_ • oh
the produce [grocery] store	**το παντοπωλείο**
	toh pahn • doh • poh • _lee_ • oh
the shoe store	**το κατάστημα υποδημάτων**
	toh kah • _tahs_ • tee • mah ee • poh • THee • _mah_ • tohn
the shopping mall	**το εμπορικό κέντρο**
	toh ehm • boh • ree • _koh kehn_ • droh
the souvenir store	**το κατάστημα σουβενίρ**
	toh kah • _tahs_ • tee • mah soo • veh • _neer_
the supermarket	**το σουπερμάρκετ**
	toh _soo_ • pehr _mahr_ • keht
the tobacconist	**το καπνοπωλείο**
	toh kahp • noh • poh • _lee_ • oh
the toy store	**το κατάστημα παιχνιδιών**
	toh kah • _tahs_ • tee • mah pehkh • neeTH • _yohn_

ASK AN ASSISTANT

When do you open/ close?	**Τι ώρα ανοίγετε/κλείνετε;**
	tee _oh_ • rah ah • _nee_ • gheh • teh/ _klee_ • neh • teh
Where is...?	**Πού είναι...;**
	poo _ee_ • neh...

the cashier	**το ταμείο**
	toh tah • mee • oh
the escalator	**οι κυλιόμενες σκάλες**
	ee kee • lee • oh • meh • nehs skah • lehs
the elevator [lift]	**το ασανσέρ**
	toh ah • sahn • sehr
the fitting room	**το δοκιμαστήριο**
	toh THoh • kee • mahs • tee • ree • oh
the store directory	**ο οδηγός καταστήματος**
	oh oh • THee • ghohs kah • tahs • tee • mah • tohs
Can you help me?	**Μπορείτε να με βοηθήσετε;**
	boh • ree • teh nah meh voh • ee • thee • seh • teh
I'm just looking.	**Απλώς κοιτάω.**
	ahp • lohs kee • tah • oh
I'm being helped.	**Εξυπηρετούμαι.**
	eh • ksee • pee • reh • too • meh
Do you have any…?	**Έχετε καθόλου…;**
	eh • kheh • teh kah • thoh • loo…
Could you show me…?	**Μπορείτε να μου δείξετε…;**
	boh • ree • teh nah moo THee • kseh • teh…
Can you ship/wrap it?	**Μπορείτε να το στείλετε/τυλίξετε;**
	boh • ree • teh nah toh stee • leh • teh/ tee • lee • kseh • teh
How much?	**Πόσο;**
	poh • soh
That's all, thanks.	**Τίποτε άλλο, ευχαριστώ.**
	tee • poh • teh ah • loh ehf • khahr • ees • toh

For Souvenirs, see page 127.

YOU MAY HEAR...

Μπορώ να σας βοηθήσω;	Can I help you?
boh • <u>roh</u> nah sahs voh • ee • <u>thee</u> • soh	
Μισό λεπτό.	Just a moment.
mee • <u>soh</u> lehp • <u>toh</u>	
Τί θα θέλατε;	What would you
tee thah <u>theh</u> • lah • teh	like?
Τίποτε άλλο;	Anything else?
<u>tee</u> • poh • teh <u>ah</u> • loh	

YOU MAY SEE...

ανοιχτό/κλειστό	open/closed
ah • nee • <u>khtoh</u>/klee • <u>stoh</u>	
κλειστό για το μεσημέρι	closed for lunch
klee • stoh yah toh meh • see • <u>meh</u> • ree	
δοκιμαστήριο	fitting room
THoh • kee • mah • <u>stee</u> • ree • oh	
ταμείο	cashier
tah • <u>mee</u> • oh	
μόνο μετρητά	cash only
<u>moh</u> • noh meh • tree • tah	
δεκτές πιστωτικές κάρτες	credit cards
THeh • <u>ktehs</u> pee • stoh • tee • <u>kehs</u>	accepted
<u>kahr</u> • tehs	
εργάσιμες ώρες	business hours
ehr • <u>ghah</u> • see • mehs <u>oh</u> • rehs	
έξοδος	exit
<u>eh</u> • ksoh • THohs	

PERSONAL PREFERENCES

I want something…	**Θέλω κάτι…** _theh_ • loh <u>kah</u> • tee…
cheap	**φτηνό** ftee • <u>noh</u>
expensive	**ακριβό** ahk • ree • <u>voh</u>
larger	**μεγαλύτερο** meh • ghah • <u>lee</u> • teh • roh
smaller	**μικρότερο** meek • <u>roh</u> • teh • roh
from this region	**από αυτό το μέρος** ah • <u>poh</u> ahf • <u>toh</u> toh meh • rohs
Around…euros.	**Γύρω στα…ευρώ.** <u>yee</u> • roh stah…ehv • <u>roh</u>
Is it real?	**Είναι αληθινό;** ee • neh ah • lee • thee • <u>noh</u>
Could you show me this/that?	**Μπορείτε να μου δείξετε αυτό/εκείνο;** boh • <u>ree</u> • teh nah moo <u>THee</u> • kseh • teh ahf • <u>toh</u>/eh • <u>kee</u> • noh
That's not quite what I want.	**Δεν είναι ακριβώς αυτό που θέλω.** THehn <u>ee</u> • neh ahk • ree • <u>vohs</u> ahf • <u>toh</u> poo <u>theh</u> • loh
I don't like it.	**Δεν μου αρέσει.** THehn moo ah • <u>reh</u> • see
That's too expensive.	**Είναι πολύ ακριβό.** <u>ee</u> • neh poh • <u>lee</u> ahk • ree • <u>voh</u>
I'd like to think about it.	**Θα ήθελα να το σκεφτώ.** thah <u>ee</u> • theh • lah nah toh skehf • <u>toh</u>
I'll take it.	**Θα το πάρω.** thah toh <u>pah</u> • roh

PAYING & BARGAINING

How much?	**Πόσο;**
	poh • soh
I'll pay...	**Θα πληρώσω...**
	thah plee • roh • soh...
by cash	**τοις μετρητοίς**
	tees meht • ree • tees
by credit card	**με πιστωτική κάρτα**
	meh pees • toh • tee • kee kahr • tah
by traveler's check	**με ταξιδιωτική επιταγή**
	meh tah • ksee • THyo • tee • kee
	eh • pee • tah • yee
A receipt, please.	**Μια απόδειξη, παρακαλώ.**
	miah ah • poh • THee • ksee
	pah • rah • kah • loh
That's too much.	**Είναι πολλά.**
	ee • neh poh • lah
I'll give you...	**Θα σας δώσω...**
	thah sahs THoh • soh...
I only have...euros.	**Έχω μόνο...ευρώ.**
	eh • khoh moh • noh...ehv • roh
Is that your best price?	**Αυτή είναι η καλύτερη τιμή σας;**
	ahf • tee ee • neh ee kah • lee • teh • ree
	tee • mee sahs
Can you give me a discount?	**Μπορείτε να μου κάνετε έκπτωση;**
	boh • ree • teh nah moo kah • neh • teh
	ehkp • toh • see

For Numbers, see page 20.

YOU MAY HEAR...

Πώς θα πληρώσετε;
pohs thah plee • <u>roh</u> • seh • teh

How are you paying?

Η πιστωτική σας κάρτα απορρίφθηκε.
ee pee • stoh • tee • <u>kee</u> sahs <u>kahr</u> • tah ah • poh • ree • fthee • keh

Your credit card has been declined.

Ταυτότητα, παρακαλώ.
tahf • <u>toh</u> • tee • tah, pah • rah • kah • <u>loh</u>

ID, please.

Δεν δεχόμαστε πιστωτικές κάρτες.
THehn THe • <u>khoh</u> • mah • steh pee • stoh • tee • <u>kehs</u> <u>kahr</u> • tehs

We don't accept credit cards.

Μόνο μετρητά, παρακαλώ.
<u>moh</u> • noh meht • ree • <u>tah</u> pah • rah • kah • <u>loh</u>

Cash only, please.

Εχετε ψιλά;
<u>eh</u> • kheh • teh psee • <u>lah</u>

Do you have any smaller change?

MAKING A COMPLAINT

I'd like...

Θα ήθελα...
thah <u>ee</u> • theh • lah...

to exchange this
να αλλάξω αυτό
nah ah • <u>lah</u> • ksoh ahf • <u>toh</u>

to return this
να επιστρέψω αυτό
nah eh • pees • <u>treh</u> • psoh ahf • <u>toh</u>

a refund
επιστροφή των χρημάτων μου
eh • pees • troh • <u>fee</u> tohn khree • <u>mah</u> • tohn moo

to see the manager
να δω τον διευθυντή
nah THoh tohn THee • ehf • theen • <u>dee</u>

SERVICES

Can you recommend...?	**Μπορείτε να συστήσετε...;** *boh • ree • teh nah sees • tee • seh • teh...*
a barber	**έναν κουρέα** *eh • nahn koo • reh • ah*
a dry cleaner	**ένα καθαριστήριο** *eh • nah kah • thah • rees • tee • ree • oh*
a hairdresser	**ένα κομμωτήριο** *eh • nah koh • moh • tee • ree • oh*
a laundromat [launderette]	**πλυντήριο ρούχων** *plee • dee • ree • oh roo • khohn*
a nail salon	**ένα σαλόνι νυχιών** *eh • nah sah • loh • nee nee • khiohn*
a spa	**ένα σπα** *eh • nah spah*
a travel agency	**ένα ταξιδιωτικό γραφείο** *eh • nah tah • ksee • THee • oh • tee • koh ghrah • fee • oh*
Can you...this?	**Μπορείτε να...αυτό;** *boh • ree • teh nah...ahf • toh*
alter	**μεταποιήσετε** *meh • tah • pee • ee • seh • teh*
clean	**καθαρίσετε** *kah • thah • ree • seh • teh*
mend	**επιδιορθώσετε** *eh • pee • THee • ohr • thoh • seh • teh*
press	**σιδερώσετε** *see • THeh • roh • seh • teh*
When will it/they be ready?	**Πότε θα είναι έτοιμο/έτοιμα;** *poh • teh thah ee • neh eh • tee • moh/ eh • tee • mah*

HAIR & BEAUTY

I'd like…	**Θα ήθελα…** *thah ee • theh • lah…*
an appointment	**να κλείσω ένα ραντεβού για σήμερα/αύριο**
for today/ tomorrow	*nah klee • soh eh • nah rahn • deh • voo yah see • meh • rah/ahv • ree • oh*
some colour/ highlights	**βαφή/ανταύγειες** *vah • fee/ah • dahv • yehs*
my hair styled/ blow-dried	**ένα χτένισμα/στέγνωμα με πιστολάκι** *eh • nah khteh • nee • smah/ steh • ghnoh • mah meh pee • stoh • lah • kee*
a haircut	**ένα κούρεμα** *eh • nah koo • reh • mah*
I'd like…	**Θα ήθελα…** *thah ee • theh • lah…*
an eyebrow/ bikini wax	**χαλάουα στα φρύδια/στο μπικίνι** *khah • lah • oo • ah stah free • yah/ stoh bee • kee • nee*
a facial	**έναν καθαρισμό προσώπου** *eh • nahn kah • thah • reez • moh proh • soh • poo*
a manicure/ pedicure	**ένα μανικιούρ/πεντικιούρ** *eh • nahmah • nee • kee • oor/ pehn • dee • kee • oor*
a (sports) massage	**ένα (αθλητικό) μασάζ** *eh • nah (ahth • lee • tee • koh) mah • sahz*
A trim, please.	**Κόψιμο, παρακαλώ.** *koh • psee • moh, pah • rah • kah • loh*
Don't cut it too short.	**Μην τα κόψετε πολύ κοντά.** *meen tah koh • pseh • teh poh • lee kohn • dah*

Shorter here.	**Πιο κοντά εδώ.**
	pioh kohn • dah eh • THoh
Do you do...?	**Κάνετε...;**
	kah • neh • teh...
acupuncture	**βελονισμό**
	veh • loh • neez • moh
aromatherapy	**αρωματοθεραπεία**
	ah • roh • mah • toh • theh • rah • pee • ah
oxygen treatment	**οξυγονοθεραπεία**
	oh • ksee • ghoh • noh • theh • rah • pee • ah
Is there a sauna?	**Υπάρχει σάουνα;**
	ee • pahr • kee sah • oo • nah

ⓘ

You will find spas and wellness centers, particularly
at luxury hotels, in every major city and on most islands
in Greece. You can visit these spas for a full day or for
one treatment, without being a guest at the hotel. You will
usually have to make an appointment in advance. Tipping is
customary, particularly in hair salons, where customers may
choose to tip the assistants or trainees.

ANTIQUES

How old is this?	**Πόσο παλιό είναι αυτό;**
	poh • soh pah • lioh ee • neh ahf • toh
Do you have anything from the...period?	**Έχετε τίποτα από την...περίοδο;**
	eh • kheh • teh tee • poh • tah ah • poh teen....peh • ree • oh • THoh
Do I have to fill out any forms?	**Πρέπει να συμπληρώσω έντυπα;**
	preh • pee nah see • blee • roh • soh eh • ndee • pah

Will I have problems with customs?	**Θα έχω προβλήματα με το τελωνείο;**
	thah eh • khoh prohv • lee • mah • tah meh
	toh teh • loh • nee • oh
Is there a certificate of authenticity?	**Υπάρχει πιστοποιητικό γνησιότητας;**
	ee • pahr • khee
	pees • toh • pee • ee • tee • koh
	ghnee • see • oh • tee • tahs
Can you ship/ wrap it?	**Μπορείτε να το στείλετε/τυλίξετε;**
	boh • ree • teh nah toh stee • leh • teh/
	tee • lee • kseh • teh

CLOTHING

I'd like…	**Θα ήθελα…**
	thah ee • theh • lah…
Can I try this on?	**Μπορώ να το δοκιμάσω;**
	boh • roh nah toh THoh • kee • mah • soh
It doesn't fit.	**Δεν μου κάνει.**
	THehn moo kah • nee
It's too…	**Είναι πολύ…**
	ee • neh poh • lee…
big	**μεγάλο**
	meh • ghah • loh
small	**μικρό**
	meek • roh
short	**κοντό**
	kon • doh
long	**μακρύ**
	mak • ree
tight	**στενό**
	steh • noh
loose	**φαρδύ**
	fahr • THee
Do you have this in size…?	**Το έχετε στο μέγεθος…;**
	toh eh • kheh • teh stoh
	meh • yeh • thohs…

Do you have this in a bigger/smaller size?	**Το έχετε σε μεγαλύτερο/μικρότερο μέγεθος;** toh _kheh_ • teh seh meh • ghah • _lee_ • teh • roh/ meek • _roh_ • teh • roh _meh_ • gheh • thohs

For Numbers, see page 20.

YOU MAY SEE...

ΑΝΔΡΙΚΑ
ahn • THree • _kah_ — men's clothing

ΓΥΝΑΙΚΕΙΑ
yee • neh • _kee_ • a — women's clothing

ΠΑΙΔΙΚΑ
peh • THee • _kah_ — children's clothing

YOU MAY HEAR...

Σας πηγαίνει.
sahs pee • _gheh_ • nee — That looks great on you.

Πώς σας είναι;
pohs sahs • _ee_ • neh — How does it fit?

Δεν έχουμε το μέγεθός σας.
THen _eh_ • khoo • meh toh _meh_ • gheh • _thohs_ sahs — We don't have your size.

COLORS

I'm looking for something in...	**Ψάχνω κάτι σε...** _psahkh_ • noh _kah_ • tee seh...
beige	**μπεζ** _behz_
black	**μαύρο** _mahv_ • roh

blue	**μπλε**
	bleh
brown	**καφέ**
	kah • feh
green	**πράσινο**
	prah • see • noh
gray	**γκρι**
	gree
orange	**πορτοκαλί**
	pohr • toh • kah • lee
pink	**ροζ**
	rohz
purple	**μωβ**
	mohv
red	**κόκκινο**
	koh • kee • noh
white	**άσπρο**
	ahs • proh
yellow	**κίτρινο**
	keet • ree • noh

CLOTHES & ACCESSORIES

a backpack	**το σακκίδιο**
	toh sah • kee • THee • oh
a belt	**η ζώνη**
	ee zoh • nee
a bikini	**το μπικίνι**
	toh bee • kee • nee
a blouse	**η μπλούζα**
	ee bloo • zah
a bra	**το σουτιέν**
	toh soo • tiehn
briefs [underpants] (women's)	**το κυλοτάκι**
	toh kee • loh • tah • kee

briefs [underpants] (men's and women's)	**το σλιπ** *toh sleep*
a coat	**το παλτό** *toh pahl • toh*
a dress	**το φόρεμα** *toh foh • reh • mah*
a hat	**το καπέλλο** *toh kah • peh • loh*
a jacket	**το σακάκι** *toh sah • kah • kee*
jeans	**το μπλου-τζην** *toh bloo • jeen*
pajamas	**πιτζάμες** *pee • tzah • mehs*
pants [trousers]	**το παντελόνι** *toh pahn • deh • loh • nee*
pantyhose [tights]	**το καλσόν** *toh kahl • sohn*
a purse [handbag]	**η τσάντα** *ee tsahn • dah*
a raincoat	**το αδιάβροχο** *toh ah • THee • ahv • roh • khoh* *sah • kah • kee*
a scarf	**το κασκώλ** *toh kahs kohl*
a shirt	**το πουκάμισο** *toh poo • kah • mee • soh*
shorts	**το σόρτς** *toh sohrts*
a skirt	**η φούστα** *ee foos • tah*
socks	**οι κάλτσες** *ee kahl • tsehs*
a suit (men's/women's)	**το κουστούμι/ταγιέρ** *toh koos • too • mee/ tah • yehr*

sunglasses	**τα γυαλιά ηλίου**
	tah yah • liah ee • lee • oo
a sweater	**το πουλόβερ**
	toh poo • loh • vehr
a sweatshirt	**το φούτερ**
	toh foo • ter
swimming trunks/	**το μαγιό**
a swimsuit	*toh mah • yoh*
a T-shirt	**το μπλουζάκι**
	toh bloo • zah • kee
a tie	**η γραβάτα**
	ee ghrah • vah • tah
underwear	**τα εσώρουχα**
	tah eh • soh • roo • khah

FABRIC

I'd like...	**Θα ήθελα...**
	thah ee • theh • lah...
cotton	**βαμβακερό**
	vahm • vah • keh • roh
denim	**τζιν**
	deh • neem jeen
lace	**δαντέλα**
	THahn • teh • lah
leather	**δερμάτινο**
	THehr • mah • tee • noh
linen	**λινό**
	lee • noh
silk	**μεταξωτό**
	meh • tah • ksoh • toh
wool	**μάλλινο**
	mah • lee • noh

Is it machine washable?	**Πλένεται στο πλυντήριο;**
	pleh • neh • teh stoh
	pleen • dee • ree • oh

SHOES

I'd like...	**Θα ήθελα...**
	thah ee • theh • lah...
high-heeled/ flat shoes	**τα ψηλοτάκουνα/επίπεδα παπούτσια**
	tah psee • loh • tah • koo • nah/ee • siah
	pah • poo • tsiah
boots	**οι μπότες**
	ee boh • tehs
loafers	**τα μοκασίνια**
	tah moh • kah • see • niah
sandals	**τα πέδιλα**
	tah peh • THee • lah
shoes	**τα παπούτσια**
	tah pah • poo • tsiah
slippers	**οι παντόφλες**
	ee pahn • dohf • lehs
sneakers	**τα αθλητικά παπούτσια**
	tah ahth • lee • tee • kah pah • poo • tsiah
In size...	**Στο νούμερο...**
	stoh noo • meh • roh...

For Numbers, see page 20.

SIZES

small (S)	**μικρό**
	meek • roh
medium (M)	**μεσαίο**
	meh • seh • oh
large (L)	**μεγάλο**
	meh • gha • loh

extra large (XL)	**extra large**
	eh • xtrah lahrj
petite	**μικρό νούμερο**
	mee • kroh noo • meh • roh
plus size	**μεγάλο νούμερο**
	meh • ghah • loh noo • meh • roh

NEWSAGENT & TOBACCONIST

Do you sell English-language books/ newspapers?	**Πουλάτε αγγλικές εφημερίδες/περιοδικά;**
	poo • lah • teh ahng • lee • kehs
	eh • fee • meh • ree • THes/
	peh • rioh • THee • kah
I'd like...	**Θα ήθελα...**
	thah ee • theh • lah...
candy [sweets]	**γλυκά**
	ghlee • kah
chewing gum	**τσίχλες**
	tseekh • lehs
a chocolate bar	**σοκολάτα**
	soh • koh • lah • tah
cigars	**πούρα**
	poo • rah
a pack/carton of cigarettes	**ένα πακέτο/μια κούτα τσιγάρα**
	eh • nah pah • keh • toh/miah koo • tah
	tsee • ghah • rah
a lighter	**έναν αναπτήρα**
	eh • nahn ah • nahp • tee • rah
a magazine	**ένα περιοδικό**
	eh • nah peh • ree • oh • THee • koh
matches	**σπίρτα**
	speer • tah
a newspaper	**μια εφημερίδα**
	miah eh • fee • meh • ree • THah

a pen	**ένα στυλό**
	eh • nah stee • loh
a postcard	**μια καρτ ποστάλ**
	miah kahrt poh • stahl
a road/town map of…	**έναν οδικό χάρτη/έναν χάρτη της πόλης για…**
	eh • nahn oh • THee • koh khahr • tee/
	eh • nahn khahr • tee tees poh • lees yah…
stamps	**γραμματόσημα**
	ghrah • mah • toh • see • mah

PHOTOGRAPHY

I'm looking for…camera.	**Ψάχνω για…φωτογραφική μηχανή.**
	psahkh • noh yah…
	foh • tohgh • rah • fee • kee
	mee • khah • nee
an automatic	**μια αυτόματη**
	miah ahf • toh • mah • tee
a digital	**μια ψηφιακή**
	miah psee • fee • ah • kee
a disposable	**μια μιας χρήσεως**
	miah miahs khree • seh • ohs
I'd like…	**Θα ήθελα…**
	thah ee • theh • lah…
a battery	**μια μπαταρία**
	miah bah • tah • ree • ah
digital prints	**ψηφιακές εκτυπώσεις**
	psee • fee • ah • kehs ehk • tee • poh • sees
a memory card	**μια κάρτα μνήμης**
	miah • kahr • tah mnee • mees
Can I print digital photos here?	**Μπορώ να εκτυπώσω ψηφιακές φωτογραφίες εδώ;**
	boh • roh nah ehk • tee • poh • soh
	psee • fee • ah • kehs
	foh • toh • ghrah • fee • ehs eh • THoh

SOUVENIRS

bottle of wine	**μπουκάλι κρασί**
	boo • <u>kah</u> • lee krah • <u>see</u>
box of pastries	**κουτί γλυκά**
	koo • <u>tee</u> ghlee • <u>kah</u>
dried Corinthian	**κορινθιακή σταφίδα**
currants	*koh • reen • thee • ah • <u>kee</u> stah • <u>fee</u> • THah*
ground Greek coffee	**ελληνικός καφές**
	eh • lee • nee • <u>kohs</u> kah • <u>fehs</u>
halva	**χαλβά**
	khahl • <u>vahs</u>
key ring	**μπρελόκ**
	breh • <u>lohk</u>
olives	**ελιές**
	eh • <u>liehs</u>
olive oil	**λάδι**
	<u>lah</u> • THee
pistachio nuts	**φυστίκια**
	fees • <u>tee</u> • kiah
postcard	**καρτποστάλ**
	kahrt • pohs • <u>tahl</u>
T-shirt	**μπλουζάκι**
	bloo • <u>zah</u> • kee

thyme honey	**θυμαρίσιο μέλι**
	thee • mah • ree • sioh meh • lee
Turkish delight	**λουκούμι**
	loo • koo • mee
Can I see this/ that?	**Μπορώ να δω αυτό/εκείνο;**
	boh • roh nah THoh
	ahf • toh/eh • kee • noh
The one in the window/display case.	**Αυτό στη βιτρίνα.**
	ahf • toh stee veet • ree • nah
I'd like…	**Θα ήθελα…**
	thah ee • theh • lah…
a battery	**μια μπαταρία**
	miah bah • tah • ree • ah
a bracelet	**ένα βραχιόλι**
	eh • nah vrah • khioh • lee
a brooch	**μια καρφίτσα**
	miah kahr • fee • tsah
earrings	**ένα ζευγάρι σκουλαρίκια**
	eh • nah zehv • gah • ree
	skoo • lah • ree • kiah
a necklace	**ένα κολλιέ**
	eh • nah koh • lieh

a ring	**ένα δαχτυλίδι**
	eh • nah THahkh • tee • lee • THee
a watch	**ένα ρολόι**
	eh • nah roh • loh • ee
copper	**χαλκό**
	khahl • koh
crystal	**κρύσταλλο**
	krees • tah • loh
diamond	**διαμάντι**
	THiah • mahn • dee
(white/yellow)	**λευκόχρυσο/χρυσό**
gold	*lehf • koh • khree • soh/khree • soh*
pearl	**μαργαριτάρι**
	mahr • ghah • ree • tah • ree
pewter	**κασσίτερο**
	kah • see • teh • roh
platinum	**πλατίνα**
	plah • tee • nah
sterling silver	**ασήμι**
	ah • see • mee
Is this real?	**Είναι αληθινό;**
	ee • neh ah • lee • thee • noh
Can you engrave it?	**Μπορείτε να το χαράξετε;**
	boh • ree • teh nah toh
	khah • rah • kseh • teh

(i)

There is a vast choice of souvenirs to buy in Greece.
In all major tourist locations, you will find shops
selling jewelry, handmade goods and other typical souvenirs.
In Athens, there are some very nice jewelry shops in
Monastiraki. You can find anything from ancient Greek-
style jewelry to pieces made by contemporary designers.
Handicrafts range from re-creations of ancient Greek pottery
to textiles, and handmade backgammon sets.

SPORT & LEISURE

NEED TO KNOW

When's the game?	**Πότε είναι ο αγώνας;**
	poh • teh ee • neh oh ah • ghoh • nahs
Where's...?	**Πού είναι...;**
	poo ee • neh...
the beach	**η παραλία**
	ee pah • rah • lee • ah
the park	**το πάρκο**
	toh pahr • koh
the pool	**η πισίνα**
	ee pee • see • nah
Is it safe to swim/ dive here?	**Είναι ασφαλές εδώ για κολύμπι/ κατάδυση;**
	ee • neh ahs • fah • lehs eh • THoh yah koh • leem • bee/kah • tah • THee • see
Can I hire golf clubs?	**Μπορώ να νοικιάσω μπαστούνια του γκόλφ;**
	boh • roh nah nee • kiah • soh bahs • too • niah too gohlf
How much per hour?	**Πόσο χρεώνεται η ώρα;**
	poh • soh khreh • oh • neh • teh ee oh • rah
How far is it to...?	**Πόσο μακριά είναι για...;**
	poh • soh mahk • ree • ah ee • neh yah...
Can you show me on the map?	**Μπορείτε να μου δείξετε στο χάρτη;**
	boh • ree • teh nah moo THee • kseh • teh stoh khahr • tee

WATCHING SPORT

When's…	**Πότε είναι…**
	poh • teh ee • neh…
the baseball game	**ο αγώνας μπέιζμπολ**
	oh ah • ghoh • nahs beh • ee • zbohl
the basketball game	**ο αγώνας μπάσκετ**
	oh ah • ghoh • nahs bahs • keht
the boxing match	**ο αγώνας μποξ**
	oh ah • ghoh • nahs bohks
the cricket game	**ο αγώνας κρίκετ**
	oh ah • ghoh • nahs kree • keht
the cycling race	**ο αγώνας ποδηλασίας**
	oh ah • ghoh • nahs poh • THee • lah • see • ahs
the golf tournament	**το τουρνουά γκολφ**
	toh toor • noo • ah gohlf
the soccer [football] game	**ο αγώνας ποδοσφαίρου**
	oh ah • ghoh • nahs poh • THohs • feh • roo
the tennis match	**ο αγώνας τέννις**
	oh ah • ghoh • nahs teh • nees
the volleyball game	**ο αγώνας βόλεϊ**
	oh ah • ghoh • nahs voh • leh • ee
Which teams are playing?	**Ποιες ομάδες παίζουν;**
	pee • ehs oh • mah • THehs peh • zoon
Where's…?	**Πού είναι…;**
	poo ee • neh…
the horse track	**το ιπποδρόμιο**
	toh ee • poh • THroh • mee • oh
the racetrack	**ο ιππόδρομος**
	oh ee • poh • THroh • mohs
the stadium	**το στάδιο**
	toh stah • THee • oh

Where can I place a bet?	**Πού μπορώ να βάλω στοίχημα;** *poo boh • roh nah vah • loh stee • khee • mah*

ⓘ

The most popular sport in Greece is **καλαθοσφαίρηση** *(kah • lah • thohs • feh • ree • see)*, basketball; even the smallest towns have their own basketball teams. **Ποδόσφαιρο** *(poh • THohs • feh • roh)*, soccer, is also popular, and matches are usually played on Sunday.
Water sports are very popular on the islands and in coastal areas. However, you need a special permit to dive with oxygen tanks.
Winter skiing has gained popularity in the last few years – there are more than 15 ski resorts on the mainland. Contact the tourist information office for details on locations and snow conditions.

PLAYING SPORT

Where's…?	**Πού είναι...;** *poo ee • neh…*
the golf course	**το γήπεδο του γκόλφ** *toh yee • peh • THoh too gohlf*
the gym	**το γυμναστήριο** *toh gheem • nahs • tee • ree • oh*
the park	**το πάρκο** *toh pahr • koh*
Where are the tennis courts?	**Πού είναι τα γήπεδα του τέννις;** *poo ee • neh tah ghee • peh • THah too teh • nees*
How much per…?	**Ποιο είναι το κόστος για...;** *pioh ee • neh toh kohs • tohs yah…*

day	**την ημέρα**
	teen ee • meh • rah
hour	**την ώρα**
	teen oh • rah
game	**το παιχνίδι**
	toh peh • khnee • THee
round	**το παιχνίδι**
	toh peh • khnee • THee
Can I hire…?	**Μπορώ να νοικιάσω…;**
	boh • roh nah nee • kiah • soh…
golf clubs	**μπαστούνια του γκόλφ**
	bahs • too • niah too gohlf
equipment	**εξοπλισμό**
	eh • ksohp • leez • moh
a racket	**μια ρακέτα**
	miah rah • keh • tah

AT THE BEACH/POOL

Where's the beach/ pool?	**Πού είναι η παραλία/πισίνα;**
	poo ee • neh ee pah • rah • lee • ah/ pee • see • nah
Is there…?	**Υπάρχει…;**
	ee • pahr • khee…
a kiddie pool	**παιδική πισίνα**
	peh • THee • kee pee • see • nah
an indoor/ outdoor pool	**εσωτερική/εξωτερική πισίνα**
	eh • soh • teh • ree • kee/ eh • ksoh • teh • ree • kee pee • see • nah
a lifeguard	**ναυαγοσώστης**
	nah • vah • ghoh • sohs • tees
Is it safe…?	**Είναι ασφαλές…;**
	ee • neh ahs • fah • lehs…
to swim	**εδώ για κολύμπι**
	eh • THoh yah koh • leem • bee

to dive	**εδώ για κατάδυση** *eh • THoh yah kah • tah • THee • see*
for children	**για παιδιά** *yah peh • THyah*
I want to hire...	**Θέλω να νοικιάσω...** *theh • loh nah nee • kiah • soh...*
a deck chair	**μια σεζ-λονγκ** *miah sehz • lohng*
diving equipment	**εξοπλισμό καταδύσεων** *eh • ksoh • plee • smoh kah • tah • THee • seh • ohn*
a jet-ski	**ένα τζετ-σκι** *eh • nah jeht skee*
a motorboat	**μια εξωλέμβιο** *miah eh • ksoh • lehm • vee • oh*
a rowboat	**βάρκα** *vahr • kah*
a sailing boat	**ένα ιστιοπλοϊκό** *eh • nah ees • tee • oh • ploh • ee • koh*
snorkeling equipment	**εξοπλισμό κατάδυσης με αναπνευστήρα** *eh • ksoh • plee • smoh kah • tah • THee • sees meh ah • nah • pnehf • stee • rah*
a surfboard	**μιασανίδα του σέρφινγκ** *miah sah • nee • THah too sehrf*
a towel	**μια πετσέτα** *miah peh • tseh • tah*
an umbrella	**μια ομπρέλλα θαλάσσης** *miah ohm • breh • lah thah • lah • sees*
water skis	**πέδιλα θαλάσσιου σκι** *peh • THee • lah thah • lah • see • oo skee*
For...hours.	**Για...ώρες.** *yah... oh • rehs*

Greek beaches, which are usually free of charge, often offer a range of water sports. Beaches that are run by **EOT** require an entrance fee, but they tend to have more facilities. The use of jet-skis is restricted to a few beaches only, at a certain distance from the land and at specific times. Topless and nude sunbathing is acceptable at many island and mainland resorts, though it might be worth checking with a local beforehand if you're the only one!

YOU MAY SEE...

ΤΕΛΕΣΚΙ	ski lift
teh • leh • skee	
ΤΕΛΕΣΕΖ	chair lift
teh • leh • sehz	
ΤΕΛΕΦΕΡΙΚ	cable car
teh • leh • feh • reek	
ΠΙΣΤΑ ΑΡΧΑΡΙΩΝ	baby slope
pees • tah ahr • khahr • ee • ohn	
ΜΕΣΑΙΑ ΠΙΣΤΑ	intermediate slope
meh • seh • ah pees • tah	
ΠΙΣΤΑ ΠΡΟΧΩΡΗΜΕΝΩΝ	advanced slope
pees • tah proh • khoh • ree • meh • nohn	
ΠΙΣΤΑ ΚΛΕΙΣΤΗ	trail closed
pees • tah klees • tee	

WINTER SPORTS

A lift pass for a day/ few days, please.

Μια άδεια για μια ημέρα/μερικές ημέρες, παρακαλώ.

miah ah • THee • ah yah miah
ee • meh • rah/meh • ree • kehs
ee • meh • rehs pah • rah • kah • loh

I'd like to hire…	**Θα ήθελα να νοικιάσω…**
	thah <u>ee</u> • theh • lah nah
	nee • <u>kiah</u> • soh…
boots	**μπότες του σκι**
	<u>boh</u> • tehs too skee
a helmet	**ένα κράνος**
	eh • nah <u>krah</u> • nohs
poles	**μπαστούνια του σκι**
	bahs • <u>too</u> • niah too skee
skis	**πέδιλα του σκι**
	<u>peh</u> • THee • lah too skee
a snowboard	**μια σανίδα snowboard**
	miah sah • <u>nee</u> • THah snoh • oo • <u>bohrd</u>
snowshoes	**παπούτσια χιονιού**
	pah • <u>poo</u> • tsiah khioh • <u>nioo</u>
These are too big/small.	**Αυτά είναι πολυ μεγάλα/μικρά.**
	ahf • <u>tah</u> ee • neh poh • <u>lee</u>
	meh • <u>ghah</u> • lah/meek • <u>rah</u>
Are there lessons?	**Γίνονται μαθήματα;**
	<u>yee</u> • nohn • deh mah • <u>thee</u> • mah • tah
I'm a beginner.	**Είμαι αρχάριος.**
	<u>ee</u> • meh ahr • <u>khah</u> • ree • ohs
I'm experienced.	**Είμαι έμπειρος** m **/έμπειρη** f.
	<u>ee</u> • meh <u>ehm</u> • bee • rohs/<u>ehm</u> • bee • ree

A trail [piste] map, please.	**Έναν χάρτη της πίστας.** _eh • nahn khahr • tee tees pees • tahs_

OUT IN THE COUNTRY

I'd like a map of…	**Θα ήθελα ένα χάρτη…** _thah ee • theh • lah eh • nah khahr • tee…_
this region	**αυτής της περιοχής** _ahf • tees tees peh • ree • oh • khees_
walking routes	**των διαδρομών περιήγησης** _tohn THee • ah • THroh • mohn_ _peh • ree • ee • yee • sees_
cycle routes	**των ποδηλατόδρομων** _tohn poh • THee • lah • toh • THroh • mohn_
the trails	**των μονοπατιών** _tohn moh • noh • pah • tiohn_
Is it easy/difficult?	**Είναι εύκολο/δύσκολο;** _ee • neh ehf • koh • loh/ees • koh • loh_
Is it far/steep?	**Είναι μακριά/απότομο;** _ee • neh mahk • ree • ah/_ _ah • poh • toh • moh_
How far is it to…?	**Πόσο μακριά είναι για…;** _poh • soh mahk • ree • ah ee • neh yah…_
Can you show me on the map?	**Μπορείτε να μου δείξετε στο χάρτη;** _boh • ree • teh nah moo THee • kseh • teh_ _stoh khahr • tee_
I'm lost.	**Έχω χαθεί.** _eh • khoh khah • thee_
Where's…?	**Πού είναι…;** _poo ee • neh…_
the ancient temple	**ο αρχαίος ναός** _oh ahr • kheh • ohs nah • ohs_
the ancient theater	**το αρχαίο θέατρο** _toh ahr • kheh • oh theh • ah • troh_

the bridge	**η γέφυρα**
	ee <u>yeh</u> • fee • rah
the cave	**το σπήλαιο**
	toh <u>spee</u> • leh • oh
the desert	**η έρημος**
	ee <u>eh</u> • ree • mohs
the cliff	**ο γκρεμός**
	oh greh • <u>mohs</u>
the farm	**η φάρμα**
	ee <u>fahr</u> • mah
the field	**το χωράφι**
	toh khoh • <u>rah</u> • fee
the forest	**το δάσος**
	toh <u>THah</u> • sohs
the gorge	**το φαράγγι**
	toh fah • <u>rah</u> • gee
the hill	**ο λόφος**
	oh <u>loh</u> • fohs
the lake	**η λίμνη**
	ee <u>leem</u> • nee
the mountain	**το βουνό**
	toh voo • <u>noh</u>
the nature reserve	**ο εθνικός δρυμός**
	oh ehth • nee • <u>kohs</u> THree • <u>mohs</u>

the viewpoint	**η πανοραμική θέση**
	ee pah • noh • rah • mee • kee theh • see
the park	**το πάρκο**
	toh pahr • koh
the path	**το μονοπάτι**
	toh moh • noh • pah • tee
the peak	**η κορυφή**
	ee koh • ree • fee
the picnic area	**η περιοχή για πικ-νικ**
	ee peh • ree • oh • khee yah peek • neek
the pond	**η λίμνη**
	ee lee • mnee
the river	**ο ποταμός**
	oh poh • tah • mohs
the sea	**η θάλασσα**
	ee thah • lah • sah
the thermal bath	**τα ιαματικά λουτρα**
	tah ee • ah • mah • tee • kah loot • rah
the hot spring	**τα ιαματικά λουτρα**
	tah ee • ah • mah • tee • kah loot • rah
the stream	**το ρέμα**
	toh reh • mah
the valley	**η κοιλάδα**
	ee kee • lah • THah
the vineyard	**ο αμπελώνας**
	oh ah • beh • loh • nahs
the volcano	**το ηφαίστειο**
	toh ee • feh • stee • oh
the waterfall	**ο καταρράκτης**
	oh kah • tah • rahk • tees

For Asking Directions, see page 69.

TRAVELING WITH CHILDREN

NEED TO KNOW

Is there a discount for children?	**Υπάρχει μειωμένο εισιτήριο για παιδιά;** *ee • pahr • khee mee • oh • meh • noh* *ee • see • tee • ree • oh yah peh • THyah*
Can you recommend a babysitter?	**Μπορείτε να συστήσετε μια υπεύθυνη μπέιμπυ-σίτερ;** *boh • ree • teh nah sees • tee • seh • teh* *miah ee • pehf • thee • nee* *beh • ee • bee see • tehr*
Could I have a child's seat/highchair?	**Μπορούμε να έχουμε ένα παιδικό καθισματάκι/μια καρέκλα μωρού;** *boh • roo • meh nah eh • khoo • meh* *eh-nah peh • THee • koh* *kah • theez • mah • tah • kee/miah* *kah • reh • klah moh • roo*
Where can I change the baby?	**Πού μπορώ να αλλάξω το μωρό;** *poo boh • roh* *nah ah • lah • ksoh toh moh • roh*

OUT & ABOUT

Can you recommend something for the kids?	**Μπορείτε να μας συστήσετε κάτι για τα παιδιά;**
	boh • ree • teh nah mahs
	sees • tee • seh the kah • tee yah tah
	peh • THyah
Where's…?	**Πού είναι…;**
	poo ee • neh…
the amusement park	**το πάρκο ψυχαγωγίας**
	toh pahr • koh psee • khah • ghoh • yee • ahs
the arcade	**η αίθουσα ψυχαγωγίας**
	ee eh • thoo • sah
	psee • khah • ghoh • yee • ahs
the kiddie pool	**η παιδική πισίνα**
	ee peh • THee • kee pee • see • nah
the park	**το πάρκο**
	toh pahr • koh
the playground	**η παιδική χαρά**
	ee peh • THee • kee khah • rah
the zoo	**ο ζωολογικός κήπος**
	oh zoh • oh • loh • yee • kohs kee • pohs
Are kids allowed?	**Επιτρέπονται τα παιδιά;**
	eh • pee • treh • pohn • deh tah peh • THyah
Is it safe for kids?	**Είναι ασφαλές για παιδιά;**
	ee • neh ahs • fah • lehs yah tah
	peh • THyah
Is it suitable for…year olds?	**Είναι κατάλληλο για παιδιά…ετών;**
	ee • neh kah • tah • lee • loh yah
	peh • THyah…eh • tohn

For Numbers, see page 20.

YOU MAY HEAR...

Τι όμορφο! *tee oh • mohr • foh*	How cute!
Πως τον/την λένε; *pohs tohn/teen leh • neh*	What's his/her name?
Πόσο χρονών είναι; *poh • soh khroh • nohn ee • neh*	How old is he/she?

BABY ESSENTIALS

Do you have...?	**Έχετε...;** *eh • kheh • teh...*
a baby bottle	**ένα μπιμπερό** *eh • nah bee • beh • roh*
baby food	**παιδικές τροφές** *peh • THee • kehs troh • fehs*
baby wipes	**υγρά μαντηλάκια** *eegh • rah mahn • dee • lah • kiah*
a car seat	**ένα παιδικό κάθισμα** *eh • nah peh • THee • koh kah • thee • smah*
a children's menu	**έναν παιδικό κατάλογο** *eh • nahn peh • THee • koh kah • tah • loh • ghoh*
a child's portion	**μια παιδική μερίδα** *miah peh • THee • kee meh • ree • THah*
a child's seat/ highchair	**ένα παιδικό κάθισμα/καρεκλάκι** *eh • nah peh • ee • koh kah • theez • mah/ kah • rehk • lah • kee moh • roo*
a crib/cot	**μια κούνια/ένα παιδικό κρεβάτι** *miah koo • niah/eh • nah peh • THee • koh kreh • vah • tee*

diapers [nappies]	**πάνες μωρού**
	ee pah • nehs moh • roo
formula	**βρεφικό γάλα**
	vreh • fee • koh ghah • lah
a pacifier [dummy]	**μια πιπίλα**
	miah pee • pee • lah
a playpen	**ένα παιδικό παρκάκι**
	eh • nah peh • THee • koh pahr • kah • kee
a stroller [pushchair]	**ένα καροτσάκι**
	eh • nah kah • roh • tsah • kee
Can I breastfeed the baby here?	**Μπορώ να θηλάσω το μωρό εδώ;**
	boh • roh nah thee • lah • soh toh moh • roh eh • THoh
Where can I change the baby?	**Πού μπορώ να αλλάξω το μωρό;**
	poo boh • roh nah ah • lah • ksoh toh moh • roh

For Dining with Children, see page 178.

BABYSITTING

Can you recommend a reliable babysitter?	**Μπορείτε να συστήσετε μια υπεύθυνη μπέιμπυ-σίτερ;**
	boh • ree • teh nah sees • tee • seh • teh miah ee • pehf • thee • nee beh • ee • bee see • tehr
What's the charge?	**Ποιό είναι το κόστος;**
	pioh ee • neh toh kohs • tohs
I'll pick them up at...	**Θα τα πάρω στις...**
	thah tah pah • roh stees...
I can be reached at...	**Θα με βρείτε στο...**
	thah meh vree • teh stoh...

HEALTH & SAFETY

EMERGENCIES

NEED TO KNOW

Help!	**Βοήθεια!**
	voh • ee • thee • ah
Go away!	**Φύγετε!**
	fee • yeh • teh
Stop, thief!	**Σταματήστε τον κλέφτη!**
	stah • mah • tees teh tohn klehf • tee
Get a doctor!	**Φωνάξτε ένα γιατρό!**
	foh • nahks • teh eh • nah yaht • roh
Fire!	**Φωτιά!**
	foh • tiah
I'm lost.	**Έχω χαθεί.**
	eh • khoh khah • thee
Can you help me?	**Μπορείτε να με βοηθήσετε;**
	boh • ree • teh nah meh
	voh • ee • thee • seh • the

YOU MAY HEAR...

Παρακαλώ συμπληρώστε αυτό το έντυπο.
pah • rah • kah • loh
sehm • blee • rohs • teh
ahf • toh toh ehn • tee • poh

Please fill
out this form.

Την ταυτότητά σας, παρακαλώ.
teen tahf • toh • tee • tah sahs
pah • rah • kah • loh

Your identification,
please.

Πότε/Πού έγινε;
poh • teh/poo eh • yee • neh

When/Where did it
happen?

Πώς είναι εμφανισιακά;
pohs ee • neh
ehm • fah • nee • see • ah • kah

What does he/she
look like?

In an emergency, dial: **100** for the police, **199** for the fire
brigade and **166** for the ambulance. Or you can also dial the
European SOS number: **112**

POLICE

NEED TO KNOW

Call the police!	**Φωνάξτε την αστυνομία!**
	foh • nahks • teh teen
	ahs • tee • noh • mee • ah
Where's the nearest police station?	**Πού είναι το κοντινότερο αστυνομικό τμήμα;**
	poo ee • neh toh
	kohn • dee • noh • teh • roh
	ahs • tee • noh • mee • koh tmee • mah
There has been an accident.	**Έγινε ένα ατύχημα.**
	eh • yee • neh eh • nah
	ah • tee • khee • mah
My child is missing.	**Λείπει το παιδί μου.**
	lee • pee toh peh • THee moo
I need...	**Χρειάζομαι...**
	khree • ah • zoh • meh...
an interpreter	**έναν διερμηνέα**
	eh • nahn THee • ehr • mee • neh • ah
I need...	**Χρειάζομαι...**
	khree • ah • zoh • meh...
to contact my lawyer	**να επικοινωνήσω με τον δικηγόρο μου**
	nah eh • pee • kee • noh • nee • soh meh
	tohn THee • kee • ghoh • roh moo
to make a phone call	**να κάνω ένα τηλέφωνο**
	nah kah • noh eh • nah
	tee • leh • foh • noh
I'm innocent.	**Είμαι αθώος m /αθώα f.**
	ee • meh ah • thoh • ohs/ah • thoh • ah

CRIME & LOST PROPERTY

I want to report…	**Θέλω να αναφέρω…**
	theh • loh nah ah nah • feh • roh…
a mugging	**μια ληστεία**
	miah lehs • tee • ah
a rape	**έναν βιασμό**
	eh • nahn vee • ahs • moh
a theft	**μια κλοπή**
	miah kloh • pee
I've been robbed/	**Με έκλεψαν/λήστεψαν.**
mugged.	*meh ehk • leh • psahn/lees • teh • psahn*
My…has/have	**Μου έκλεψαν…μου.**
been stolen.	*moo ehk • leh • psahn…moo*
I've lost my…	**Έχασα…**
	eh • khah • sah…
knapsack	**τον σάκκο**
	tohn sah • koh
bicycle	**το ποδήλατο**
	toh poh • THee • lah • toh
camera	**τη φωτογραφική μηχανή**
	tee foh • tohgh • rah • fee • kee
	mee • khah • nee
car	**το αυτοκίνητο**
	toh ahf • toh • kee • nee • toh
computer	**τον υπολογιστή**
	tohn ee • poh • loh • yees • tee
credit cards	**τις πιστωτικές κάρτες**
	tees pees • toh • tee • kehs kahr • tehs
jewelry	**τα κοσμήματα**
	tah kohs • mee • mah • tah
money	**τα χρήματα**
	tah khree • mah • tah
passport	**το διαβατήριο**
	toh THiah • vah • tee • ree • oh

purse	**την τσάντα** *teen tsahn • dah*
traveler's checks	**τις ταξιδιωτικές επιταγές** *tees tah • ksee • THee • oh • tee • kehs* *eh • pee • tah • yehs*
wallet	**το πορτοφόλι** *toh pohr • toh • foh • lee*
I need a police report.	**Θέλω να κάνω αναφορά στην αστυνομία.** *theh • loh nah kah • noh ah • nah • foh • rah* *steen ah • stee • noh • mee • ah*
Where is the British/ American/Irish embassy?	**Πού είναι η αγγλική/αμερικάνικη/ ιρλανδική πρεσβεία;** *poo ee • neh ee ag • lee • kee* *ah • meh • ree • kah • nee • kee/* *eer • lahn • THee • kee preh • svee • ah*

HEALTH

NEED TO KNOW

I'm sick [ill].	**Είμαι άρρωστος.** *ee • meh ah • rohs • tohs*
I need an English-speaking doctor.	**Χρειάζομαι έναν γιατρό που να μιλάει αγγλικά.** *khree • ah • zoh • meh eh • nahn* *yaht • roh poo nah mee • lah • ee* *ang • lee • kah*
It hurts here.	**Με πονάει εδώ.** *meh poh • nah • ee eh • THoh*
I have a stomachache.	**Έχω στομαχόπονο.** *eh • khoh stoh • mah • khoh • poh • noh*

FINDING A DOCTOR

Can you recommend a doctor/dentist?	**Μπορείτε να συστήσετε έναν γιατρό/ οδοντίατρο;** *boh • ree • teh nah sees • tee • seh • the eh • nahn yaht • roh* *oh • THohn • dee • aht • roh*
Could the doctor come to see me here?	**Μπορεί να έρθει να με δει εδώ ο γιατρός;** *boh • ree nah ehr • thee nah meh THee eh • THoh oh yaht • rohs*
I need an English-speaking doctor.	**Χρειάζομαι έναν γιατρό που να μιλάει αγγλικά.** *khree • ah • zoh • meh eh • nahn yaht • roh poo nah mee • lah • ee ahng lee • kah*
What are the office hours?	**Ποιες ώρες δέχεται;** *piehs oh • rehs THeh • kheh • teh*
Can I make an appointment for…?	**Μπορώ να κλείσω ένα ραντεβού για…;** *boh • roh nah klee • soh eh • nah rahn • deh • voo yah…*
today	**σήμερα** *see • meh • rah*
tomorrow	**αύριο** *ahv • ree • oh*
as soon as possible	**όσο το δυνατό πιο σύντομα** *oh • soh toh THee • nah • toh pioh seen • doh • mah*
It's urgent.	**Είναι επείγον.** *ee • neh eh • pee • ghohn*

SYMPTOMS

I'm...	**Έχω...**
	_eh_ • khoh...
bleeding	**αιμορραγία**
	eh • moh • rah • _yee_ • ah
constipated	**δυσκοιλιότητα**
	THees • kee • lee • _oh_ • tee • tah
dizzy	**ζαλάδες**
	zah • _lah_ • THehs
nauseous	**ναυτία**
	nahf • _tee_ • ah
vomiting	**εμετούς**
	eh • meh • _toos_
It hurts here.	**Με πονάει εδώ.**
	meh poh • _nah_ • ee eh • _THoh_
I have...	**Έχω...**
	_eh_ • khoh...
an allergic reaction	**αλλεργική αντίδραση**
	ah • lehr • yee • _kee_ ahn • dee • THrah • see
a chest pain	**πόνο στο στήθος**
	poh • noh stoh _stee_ • thohs
cramps	**κράμπες**
	krah • behs
diarrhea	**διάρροια**
	THee • _ah_ • ree • ah
an earache	**πόνο στο αυτί**
	poh • noh stoh ahf • _tee_
a fever	**πυρετό**
	pee • reh • _toh_
a pain	**πόνο**
	poh • noh
a rash	**εξάνθημα**
	eh • _ksahn_ • thee • mah

a sprain	**διάστρεμμα**
	THee • <u>ahs</u> • treh • mah
some swelling	**πρήξιμο**
	<u>pree</u> • ksee • moh
a sore throat	**πονόλαιμο**
	poh • <u>noh</u> • leh • moh
a stomachache	**στομαχόπονο**
	stoh • mah • <u>khoh</u> • poh • noh
sunstroke	**ηλίαση**
	ee • <u>lee</u> • ah • see
I've been sick [ill] for...days.	**Αισθάνομαι άρρωστος εδώ και...ημέρες.**
	ehs • <u>thah</u> • noh • meh <u>ah</u> • rohs • tohs
	eh • <u>THoh</u> keh ee • <u>meh</u> • rehs

For Numbers, see page 20.

CONDITIONS

I'm...	**Έχω...**
	<u>eh</u> • khoh...
anemic	**αναιμία**
	ah • neh • <u>mee</u> • ah
asthmatic	**άσθμα**
	<u>ahs</u> • thmah
diabetic	**διαβήτη**
	THiah • <u>vee</u> • tee
epileptic	**επιληψία**
	eh • pee • lee • <u>psee</u> • ah
I'm allergic to antibiotics/ penicillin.	**Είμαι αλλεργικός στα αντιβιωτικά/στην πενικιλίνη.**
	<u>ee</u> • meh ah • lehr • yee • <u>kohs</u> stah
	ahn • dee • vee • oh • tee • <u>kah</u>/
	steen peh • nee • kee • <u>lee</u> • nee

YOU MAY HEAR...

Τι συμβαίνει; *tee seem • veh • nee*	What's wrong?
Πού πονάει; *poo poh • nah • ee*	Where does it hurt?
Πονάει εδώ; *poh • nah • ee eh • THoh*	Does it hurt here?
Παίρνετε άλλα φάρμακα; *pehr • neh • teh ah • lah fahr • mah • kah*	Are you taking any other medication?
Είστε αλλεργικός m /**αλλεργική** f **σε κάτι;** *ees • teh ah • lehr • yeek • ohs/* *ah • lehr • yeek • ee seh kah • tee*	Are you allergic to anything?
Ανοίξτε το στόμα σας. *ah • nee • ksteh toh stoh • mah sahs*	Open your mouth.
Πάρτε μια βαθιά αναπνοή. *pahr • teh miah vah • thiah* *ah • nahp • noh • ee*	Breathe deeply.
Βήξτε, παρακαλώ. *vee • ksteh, pah • rah • kah • loh*	Cough, please.
Θέλω να πάτε στο νοσοκομείο. *theh • loh nah pah • teh stoh* *noh • soh • koh • mee • oh*	I want you to go to the hospital.

I have arthritis/ (high/low) blood pressure.	**Έχω αρθρίτιδα/(υψηλή/χαμηλή) πίεση.** *eh • khoh ahr • three • tee • THah/* *(ee • psee • lee/ khah • mee • lee)* *pee • eh • see*
I have a heart condition.	**Έχω πρόβλημα καρδιάς.** *eh • khoh prohv • lee • mah kahrTH • yahs*
I'm on...	**Παίρνω...** *pehr • noh...*

TREATMENT

Do I need a prescription/ medicine?	**Χρειάζομαι συνταγή/φάρμακο;** khree•_ah_•zoh•meh see•ntah•_ghee_/ _fahr_•mah•koh
Can you prescribe a generic drug [unbranded medication]?	**Μπορείτε να γράψετε ένα γένιο φάρμακο;** boh•_ree_•teh nah _ghrah_•pseh•teh _eh_•nah _fahr_•mah•koh
Where can I get it?	**Από πού μπορώ να το πάρω;** ah•_poh_ poo boh•_roh_ nah toh _pah_•roh

For Dietary Requirements, see page 176.

HOSPITAL

Please notify my family.	**Παρακαλώ ειδοποιήστε την οικογένειά μου.** pah•rah•kah•_loh_ ee•THoh•pee•_ees_•teh teen ee•koh•_yeh_•nee•_ah_ moo
I'm in pain.	**Πονάω.** poh•_nah_•oh
I need a doctor/ nurse.	**Χρειάζομαι έναν γιατρό/μια νοσοκόμα.** khree•_ah_•zoh• meh _eh_•nahn yaht•_roh_/ miah noh•soh•_koh_•mah
When are visiting hours?	**Ποιες είναι οι ώρες επισκεπτηρίου;** pee•_ehs_ _ee_•neh ee _oh_•rehs eh•pees•kehp•tee•_ree_•oo
I'm visiting…	**Επισκέπτομαι…** eh•pees•_kehp_•toh•meh…

DENTIST

I've broken a tooth.	**Έσπασα ένα δόντι.** _ehs • pah • sah eh • nah THohn • dee_
I'm lost a filling.	**Μου έφυγε ένα σφράγισμα.** _moo eh • fee • gheh eh • nah sfrah • yees • mah_
This tooth hurts.	**Αυτό το δόντι με πονάει.** _ahf • toh toh THohn • dee meh poh • nah • ee_
Can you fix this denture?	**Μπορείτε να φτιάξετε αυτή την τεχνητή οδοντοστοιχία;** _boh • ree • teh nah ftee • ah • kseh • teh ahf • tee teen tehkh • nee • tee oh • THohn • dohs • tee • khee • ah_

GYNECOLOGIST

I have menstrual cramps/a vaginal infection.	**Έχω πόνους περιόδου/κολπική μόλυνση.** _eh • khoh poh • noos peh • ree • oh • THoo/ kohl • pee • kee moh • leen • see_
I missed my period.	**Έχω καθυστέρηση.** _eh • khoh kah • thees • teh • ree • see_
I'm on the Pill.	**Παίρνω αντισυλληπτικό χάπι.** _pehr • noh ahn • dee • see • leep • tee • koh khah • pee_
I'm (...months) pregnant.	**Είμαι (...μηνών) έγκυος.** _ee • meh (...mee • nohn) eh • gee • ohs_
I'm (not) pregnant.	**(Δεν) Είμαι έγκυος.** _(THehn) ee • meh ehn • gee • ohs_
I haven't had my period for...months.	**Δεν έχω περίοδο εδώ και...μήνες.** _THehn eh • khoh peh • ree • oh • THoh eh • THoh keh...mee • nehs_

For Numbers, see page 20.

OPTICIAN

I've lost...	**Έχασα...**
	_eh_ • khah • sah...
a contact lens	**έναν φακό επαφής**
	_eh_ • nahn fah • _koh_ eh • pah • _fees_
my glasses	**τα γυαλιά μου**
	tah yah • lee • _ah_ moo
a lens	**έναν φακό**
	_eh_ • nahn fah • _koh_

PAYMENT & INSURANCE

How much?	**Πόσο;**
	poh • soh
Can I pay by credit card?	**Μπορώ να πληρώσω με αυτή την πιστωτική κάρτα;**
	boh • _roh_ nah plee • _roh_ • soh meh ahf • _tee_ teen pees • toh • tee • _kee kahr_ • tah
I have insurance.	**Έχω ασφάλεια.**
	_eh_ • khoh ahs • _fah_ • lee • ah
Can I have a receipt for my insurance?	**Μπορώ να έχω μια απόδειξη για την ασφάλεια υγείας μου;**
	boh • _roh_ nah eh • khoh miah ah • _poh_ • THee • ksee yah teen ahs • _fah_ • lee • ah ee • _yee_ • ahs moo

For Money, see page 33

PHARMACY

NEED TO KNOW

Where's the nearest pharmacy?	**Πού είναι το κοντινότερο φαρμακείο;** *poo ee • neh toh kohn • dee • noh • teh • roh fahr • mah • kee • oh*
What time does the pharmacy [chemist] open/close?	**Τι ώρα ανοίγει/κλείνει το φαρμακείο;** *tee oh • rah ah • nee • yee/klee • nee toh fahr • mah • kee • oh*
What would you recommend for…?	**Τι συνιστάτε για…;** *tee see • nees • tah • teh yah…*
How much should I take?	**Πόσο πρέπει να πάρω;** *poh • soh preh • pee nah pah • roh*
Can you fill [make up] this prescription for me?	**Μπορείτε να μου φτιάξετε αυτή τη συνταγή;** *boh • ree • teh nah moo ftiah • kseh • teh ahf • tee tee seen • dah • yee*
I'm allergic to…	**Είμαι αλλεργικός** *m*/**αλλεργική** *f* **σε …** *ee • meh ah • lehr • yeek • ohs/ ah • lehr • yeek • ee seh…*

Many medications that are prescription-only in other countries can be bought over the counter in Greece. Pharmacies are open during normal working hours and on a rotating basis at all other times, so that there will always be one open 24 hours a day in any given area. Read the list on display in all pharmacy windows to find the one nearest to you.

WHAT TO TAKE

How much should I take?	**Πόσο πρέπει να πάρω;** _poh • soh <u>preh</u> • pee nah <u>pah</u> • roh_
How many times a day should I take it?	**Πόσες φορές την ημέρα πρέπει να το παίρνω;** _poh • sehs foh • <u>rehs</u> teen ee • <u>meh</u> • rah <u>preh</u> • pee nah toh <u>pehr</u> • noh_
Is it suitable for children?	**Είναι κατάλληλο για παιδιά;** _<u>ee</u> • neh kah • <u>tah</u> • lee • loh yah peh • <u>THyah</u>_
I'm taking…	**Παίρνω…** _<u>pehr</u> • noh…_
Are there side effects?	**Έχει παρενέργειες;** _<u>eh</u> • khee pah • reh • <u>nehr</u> • yee • ehs_
I'd like some medicine for…	**Θα ήθελα ένα φάρμακο για…** _thah <u>ee</u> • theh • lah <u>eh</u> • nah <u>fahr</u> • mah • koh yah…_
a cold	**το κρυολόγημα** _toh kree • oh • <u>loh</u> • yee • mah_
a cough	**το βήχα** _toh <u>vee</u> • khah_
diarrhea	**τη διάρροια** _tee THee • <u>ah</u> • ree • ah_
a headache	**πονοκέφαλο** _poh • noh • <u>keh</u> • fah • loh_
hay fever	**την αλλεργία σε γύρη** _teen ah • lehr • <u>yee</u> • ah seh <u>yee</u> • ree_
insect bites	**το τσίμπημα από έντομο** _toh <u>tseem</u> • bee • mah ah • <u>poh</u> <u>ehn</u> • doh • moh_
motion sickness	**τη ναυτία** _tee nahf • <u>tee</u> • ah_
a sore throat	**τον πονόλαιμο** _tohn poh • <u>noh</u> • leh • moh_

sunburn	**τα εγκαύματα από τον ήλιο**
	tah eh • gkahv • mah • tah ahpoh tohn
	ee • lioh
a toothache	**πονόδοντο**
	poh • noh • THoh • doh
an upset stomach	**το στομαχόπονο**
	toh stoh • mah • khoh • poh • noh

YOU MAY SEE...

ΧΑΠΙ(Α)	tablet(s)
khah • pee(ah)	
ΣΤΑΓΟΝΕΣ	drops
stah • ghoh • nehs	
ΠΡΙΝ/ΜΕΤΑ/ΜΕ ΤΟ ΓΕΥΜΑ	before/after/with
preen/me • tah/meh toh yehv • mah	meals
ΜΕ ΑΔΕΙΟ ΣΤΟΜΑΧΙ	on an empty
meh ah • THioh stoh • mah • khee	stomach
ΜΟΝΟ ΓΙΑ ΕΞΩΤΕΡΙΚΗ ΧΡΗΣΗ	for external use
moh • noh ya eh • ksoh • teh • ree • kee	only
khree • see	
ΜΙΑ/ΔΥΟ/ΤΡΕΙΣ ΦΟΡΕΣ	once/twice/three
ΤΗΝ ΗΜΕΡΑ	times a day
miah/ee • oh/trees foh • rehs teen	
ee • meh • rah	

BASIC SUPPLIES

I'd like...	**Θα ήθελα...**
	thah ee • theh • lah...
acetaminophen	**παρακεταμόλη**
[paracetamol]	*pah • rah • keh • tah • moh • lee*

antiseptic cream	**μια αντισηπτική κρέμα**
	miah ahn • dee • seep • tee • _kee kreh_ • mah
aspirin	**ασπιρίνη**
	ahs • pee • _ree_ • nee
bandages	**επιδέσμους**
	eh • pee • _THehz_ • moos
a comb	**μια χτένα**
	miah _khteh_ • nah
condoms	**προφυλακτικά**
	proh • fee • lahk • tee • _kah_
contact lens	**ένα υγρό καθαρισμού φακών επαφής**
solution	eegh • _roh_ kah • thah • rees • _moo_
	fah • _kohn_ eh • pah • _fees_
deodorant	**ένα αποσμητικό**
	_eh_ • nah ah • pohz • mee • tee • _koh_
a hairbrush	**μια βούρτσα**
	miah _voor_ • tsah
hair spray	**μια λακ**
	miah lahk
ibuprofen	**ιμπουπροφέν**
	ee • boo • proh • _fehn_
insect repellent	**εντομοαπωθητικό**
	ehn • doh • moh • ah • poh • thee • tee • _koh_
a nail file	**μια λίμα για τα νύχια**
	miah _lee_ • mah yah tah _nee_ • khiah
a (disposable)	**ένα ξυραφάκι (μιας χρήσης)**
razor	_eh_ • nah ksee • rah • _fah_ • kee (miahs
	khree • sees)
razor blades	**ξυραφάκια**
	ksee • rah • _fah_ • kiah
sanitary napkins	**σερβιέτες**
[towels]	sehr • vee • _eh_ • tehs
shampoo/	**σαμπουάν/γαλάκτωμα για τα μαλλιά**
conditioner	sahm • poo • _ahn_/ghah • _lahk_ • toh • mah
	yah tah mah • _liah_

soap	**ένα σαπούνι**
	eh • nah sah • poo • nee
I'd like...	**Θα ήθελα...**
	thah ee • theh • lah...
sunscreen	**αντιηλιακό**
	ahn • dee • ee • lee • ah • koh
tampons	**ταμπόν**
	tahm • bohn
tissues	**χαρτομάντηλα**
	khahr • toh • mahn • dee • lah
toilet paper	**χαρτί υγείας**
	khahr • tee ee • yee • ahs
a toothbrush	**οδοντόβουρτσα**
	oh • THoh • ndoh • voor • tsah
toothpaste	**μια οδοντόπαστα**
	miah oh • THohn • doh • pah • stah

For Baby Essentials, see page 142.

CHILD HEALTH & EMERGENCY

Can you recommend a pediatrician?	**Μπορείτε να συστήσετε έναν παιδίατρο;**
	boh • ree • teh nah sees • tee • seh • teh eh • nahn peh • THee • aht • roh
My child is allergic to...	**Το παιδί μου είναι αλλεργικό σε...**
	toh peh • THee moo ee • neh ah • lehr • ghee • koh seh...
My child is missing.	**Λείπει το παιδί μου.**
	lee • pee toh peh • THee moo
Have you seen a boy/girl?	**Είδατε ένα αγόρι/κορίτσι;**
	ee • THah • the eh • nah ah • ghoh • ree/ koh • ree • tsee

For Police, see page 148.

DISABLED TRAVELERS

NEED TO KNOW

Is there...?	**Υπάρχει...;** *ee • pahr • khee...*
access for the disabled	**πρόσβαση για άτομα με ειδικές ανάγκες** *prohz • vah • see yah ah • toh • mah meh ee • THee • kehs ah • nahn • gehs*
a wheelchair ramp	**ράμπα για αναπηρικό καρότσι** *rahm • bah yah ah • nah • pee • ree • koh kah • roh • tsee*
a disabled-accessible toilet	**προσβάσιμη τουαλέτα για ανάπηρους** *prohs • vah • see • mee too • ah • leh • tah yah ah • nah • pee • roos*
I need...	**Χρειάζομαι...** *khree • ah • zoh • meh...*
assistance	**βοήθεια** *voh • ee • thiah*
an elevator [lift]	**ασανσέρ** *ah • sahn • sehr*
a ground-floor room	**ισόγειο** *ee • soh • yee • oh*

ASKING FOR ASSISTANCE

I'm disabled.	**Είμαι ανάπηρος.**
	ee • meh ah • nah • pee • rohs
I'm deaf.	**Είμαι κουφός.**
	ee • meh koo • fohs
I'm visually/	**Έχω προβλήματα όρασης/ακοής.**
hearing impaired.	*eh • khoh prohv • lee • mah • tah*
	oh • rah • sees/ah • koh • ees
I'm unable to walk	**Δεν μπορώ να περπατήσω/χρησιμοποιήσω**
far/use the stairs.	**τις σκάλες.**
	thehn boh • roh nah pehr • pah • tee • soh/
	khree • see • moh • pee • ee • soh tees
	skah • lehs
Please speak louder.	**Μιλήστε πιο δυνατά.**
	mee • lee • steh pioh THee • nah • tah
Can I bring my	**Μπορώ να φέρω την αναπηρική μου**
wheelchair?	**καρέκλα;**
	boh • roh nah feh • roh teen
	ah • nah • pee • ree • kee moo
	kah • rehk • lah

Are guide dogs permitted?	**Επιτρέπονται οι σκύλοι οδηγοί;**
	eh • peet • <u>reh</u> • pohn • deh ee skee • lee oh • THee • <u>ghee</u>
Can you help me?	**Μπορείτε να με βοηθήσετε;**
	boh • <u>ree</u> • teh nah meh voh • ee • <u>thee</u> • seh • teh
Please open/hold the door.	**Παρακαλώ ανοίξτε/κρατείστε την πόρτα.**
	pah • rah • kah • <u>loh</u> ah • <u>nee</u> • ksteh/ krah • <u>tee</u> • steh teen <u>pohr</u> • tah

For Emergencies, see page 146.

FOOD & DRINK

EATING OUT

NEED TO KNOW

Can you recommend a good restaurant/ bar?	**Μπορείτε να συστήσετε ένα καλό εστιατόριο/μπαρ;**
	boh • ree • teh nah
	sees • tee • seh • teh eh • nah kah • loh
	ehs • tee • ah • toh • ree • oh/bahr
Is there a traditional Greek/ an inexpensive restaurant near here?	**Υπάρχει κανένα ελληνικό/φθηνό εστιατόριο εδώ κοντά;**
	ee • pahr • khee kah • neh • nah
	eh • lee • nee • koh/fthee • noh
	ehs • tee • ah • toh • ree • oh eh • THoh kohn • dah
A table for..., please.	**Ένα τραπέζι για..., παρακαλώ.**
	eh • nah trah • peh • zee yah...
	pah • rah • kah • loh
Could we sit...?	**Μπορούμε να καθήσουμε...;**
	boh • roo • meh nah
	kah • thee • soo • meh...
here/there	**εδώ/εκεί**
	eh • THoh/eh • kee
outside	**έξω**
	eh • ksoh
in a non-smoking area	**σε έναν χώρο για μη καπνίζοντες**
	seh eh • nahn khoh • roh yah mee kahp • nee • zohn • dehs
I'm waiting for someone.	**Περιμένω κάποιον.**
	peh • ree • meh • noh kah • piohn
Where are the toilets?	**Πού είναι η τουαλέτα;**
	poo ee • neh ee too • ah • leh • tah

A menu, please.	**Έναν κατάλογο, παρακαλώ.** *eh • nahn kah • tah • loh • ghoh* *pah • rah • kah • loh*
What do you recommend?	**Τι προτείνετε;** *tee proh • tee • neh • the*
I'd like…	**Θα ήθελα…** *thah ee • theh • lah…*
Some more…, please.	**Λίγο ακόμη…, παρακαλώ.** *lee • ghoh ah • koh • mee…* *pah • rah • kah • loh*
Enjoy your meal!	**Καλή όρεξη!** *kah • lee oh • reh • ksee*
The check [bill], please.	**Τον λογαριασμό, παρακαλώ.** *tohn loh • ghah • riahs • moh* *pah • rah • kah • loh*
Is service included?	**Συμπεριλαμβάνεται και το φιλοδώρημα;** *seem • beh • ree • lahm • vah • neh • teh* *keh toh fee • loh • THoh • ree • mah*
Can I pay by credit card?	**Μπορώ να πληρώσω με πιστωτική κάρτα;** *boh • roh nah plee • roh • soh meh* *pee • stoh • tee • kee kahr • tah*
Can I have a receipt?	**Μπορώ να έχω απόδειξη;** *boh • roh nah eh • khoh* *ah • poh • THee • ksee*
Thank you.	**Ευχαριστώ.** *ehf • hah • ree • stoh*

WHERE TO EAT

Can you recommend...?	**Μπορείτε να συστήσετε...;**
	boh • ree • teh nah sees • tee • seh • teh...
a restaurant	**ένα εστιατόριο**
	eh • nah ehs • tee • ah • toh • ree • oh
a bar	**ένα μπαρ**
	eh • nah bahr
a cafe	**μια καφετέρια**
	miah kah • feh • teh • ree • ah
a fast-food place	**ένα φάστ φουντ**
	eh • nah fahst food
a cheap restaurant	**ένα φτηνό εστιατόριο**
	eh • nah ftee • noh
	eh • stee • ah • toh • ree • oh
an expensive restaurant	**ένα ακριβό εστιατόριο**
	eh • nah ah • kree • voh
	eh • stee • ah • toh • ree • oh
a restaurant with a good view	**ένα εστιατόριο με καλή θέα**
	eh • nah eh • stee • ah • toh • ree • oh
	meh kah • lee theh • ah
an authentic/a non-touristy restaurant	**ένα αυθεντικό/όχι τουριστικό εστιατόριο**
	eh • nah ahf • then • ntee • koh/oh • khee
	too • ree • stee • koh
	eh • stee • ah • toh • ree • oh
a souvlaki/gyros stand	**ένα σουβλατζίδικο**
	eh • nah soov • la • jee • THee • koh

RESERVATIONS & PREFERENCES

I'd like to reserve a table...	**Θα ήθελα να κλείσω ένα τραπέζι...**
	thah ee • theh • lah nah klee • soh eh • nah
	trah • peh • zee...
for two	**για δύο**
	yah THee • oh

YOU MAY HEAR...

Έχετε κάνει κράτηση;
eh • kheh • teh kah • nee krah • tee • see

Do you have a reservation?

Πόσα άτομα;
poh • sah ah • toh • mah

How many?

Καπνίζοντες ή μη καπνίζοντες;
kah • pnee • zohn • dehs ee mee kah • pnee • zohn • dehs

Smoking or non-smoking?

Είσαστε έτοιμοι να παραγγείλετε;
ee • sahs • teh eh • tee • mee nah pah • rah • gee • leh • teh

Are you ready to order?

Τι θα πάρετε;
tee thah pah • reh • teh

What would you like?

Σας συστήνω...
sahs sees • tee • noh...

I recommend...

Καλή όρεξη.
kah • lee oh • reh • ksee

Enjoy your meal.

for this evening	**γι' απόψε** *yah ah • poh • pseh*
for tomorrow at...	**για αύριο στις...** *yah ahv • ree • oh stees...*
A table for two, please.	**Ένα τραπέζι για δύο, παρακαλώ.** *eh • nah trah • peh • zee yah THee • oh pah • rah • kah • loh*
We have a reservation.	**Έχουμε κλείσει τραπέζι.** *eh • khoo • meh klee • see trah • peh • zee*
My name is...	**Λέγομαι...** *leh • ghoh • meh...*
Can we sit...?	**Μπορούμε να καθίσουμε...;** *boh • roo • meh nah kah • thee • soo • meh*

here/there	**εδώ/εκεί**
	eh • <u>THoh</u>/eh • <u>kee</u>
outside	**έξω**
	<u>eh</u> • ksoh
in a non-smoking area	**στους μη καπνίζοντες**
	stoos mee kah • <u>pnee</u> • zoh • dehs
by the window	**δίπλα στο παράθυρο**
	<u>THee</u> • plah stoh pah • <u>rah</u> • thee • roh
in the shade	**στη σκιά**
	stee skee • <u>ah</u>
in the sun	**στον ήλιο**
	stohn <u>ee</u> • lioh
Where is the restroom [toilet]?	**Πού είναι η τουαλέτα;**
	poo <u>ee</u> • neh ee
	too • ah • <u>leh</u> • tah

HOW TO ORDER

Waiter!/Waitress!	**Γκαρσόν!/Δεσποινίς!**
	gahr • <u>sohn</u>/THehs • pee • <u>nees</u>
We're ready to order.	**Είμαστε έτοιμοι να παραγγείλουμε.**
	<u>ee</u> • mahs • teh <u>eh</u> • tee • mee nah
	pah • rah • <u>gee</u> • loo • meh

May I see the wine list?	**Μπορώ να δω τον κατάλογο κρασιών;**
	boh • <u>roh</u> nah THoh tohn
	kah • <u>tah</u> • loh • ghoh krah • <u>siohn</u>
I'd like…	**Θα ήθελα…**
	thah <u>ee</u> • theh • lah…
a bottle of…	**ένα μπουκάλι…**
	<u>eh</u> • nah boo • <u>kah</u> • lee…
carafe of…	**μια καράφα…**
	miah kah • <u>rah</u> • fah…
glass of…	**ένα ποτήρι…**
	<u>eh</u> • nah poh • <u>tee</u> • ree…
The menu, please.	**Τον κατάλογο, παρακαλώ.**
	tohn kah • <u>tah</u> • loh • ghoh
	pah • rah • kah • <u>loh</u>
Do you have…?	**Έχετε…;**
	<u>eh</u> • kheh • teh…
a menu in English	**έναν κατάλογο στα Αγγλικά**
	<u>eh</u> • nahn kah • <u>tah</u> • loh • ghoh stah
	ahng • lee • <u>kah</u>
a fixed-price menu	**έναν κατάλογο με σταθερές τιμές**
	<u>eh</u> • nahn kah • <u>tah</u> • loh • ghoh meh
	stah • theh • <u>rehs</u> tee • <u>mehs</u>
a children's menu	**παιδικό μενού**
	peh • THee • <u>koh</u> meh • <u>noo</u>
What do you recommend?	**Τι προτείνετε;**
	tee proh • <u>tee</u> • neh • the
What's this?	**Τι είναι αυτό;**
	tee <u>ee</u> • neh ahf • <u>toh</u>
What's in it?	**Τι περιέχει;**
	tee peh • ree • <u>eh</u> • khee
Is it spicy?	**Είναι πικάντικο;**
	<u>ee</u> • neh pee • <u>kahn</u> • dee • koh
I'd like…	**Θα ήθελα…**
	thah <u>ee</u> • theh • lah…

174 • FOOD & DRINK

More..., please.	**Λίγο ακόμη..., παρακαλώ.**
	lee • ghoh ah • _koh_ • mee...
	pah • rah • kah • _loh_
With/Without...	**Με/Χωρίς...**
	meh/khoh • _rees_...
I can't have...	**Δεν πρέπει να φάω φαγητό που περιέχει...**
	THehn _preh_ • pee nah _fah_ • oh
	fah • yee • _toh_ poo peh • ree • _eh_ • khee...
rare	**με το αίμα του, σενιάν**
	meh toh _eh_ • mah too seh • _nian_
medium	**μέτρια ψημένο**
	meht • ree • ah psee • _meh_ • noh
well-done	**καλοψημένο**
	kah • loh • psee • _meh_ • noh
It's to go [take away].	**Είναι για το σπίτι.**
	_ee_ • neh yah toh _spee_ • tee

For Drinks, see page 200.

YOU MAY SEE...

ΚΟΥΒΕΡ	cover charge
koo • _vehr_	
ΣΤΑΘΕΡΗ ΤΙΜΗ	fixed-price
stah • theh • _ree_ tee • _mee_	
ΚΑΤΑΛΟΓΟΣ	menu
kah • _tah_ • loh • ghohs	
ΜΕΝΟΥ ΤΗΣ ΗΜΕΡΑΣ	menu of the day
meh • _noo_ tees ee • _meh_ • rahs	
Η ΕΞΥΠΗΡΕΤΗΣΗ (ΔΕΝ)	service (not)
ΠΕΡΙΛΑΜΒΑΝΕΤΑΙ	included
ee eh • ksee • pee _reh_ • tee • see	
(THehn) peh • ree • lahm • _vahn_ • eh • the	
ΠΙΑΤΑ ΤΗΣ ΗΜΕΡΑΣ	specials
pee • _ah_ • tah tees ee • _meh_ • rahs	

COOKING METHODS

baked	**του φούρνου**
	too <u>foor</u> • noo
barbecued, grilled	**της σχάρας**
	tees <u>skhah</u> • rahs
boiled	**βραστό**
	vrah • <u>stoh</u>
braised	**κατσαρόλας**
	kah • tsah • <u>roh</u> • lahs
breaded	**πανέ**
	pah • <u>neh</u>
cooked in olive oil	**λαδερό**
	lah • THeh • <u>roh</u>
creamed	**με κρέμα γάλακτος**
	meh <u>kreh</u> • mah <u>ghah</u> • lah • ktohs
diced	**σε κύβους**
	seh <u>kee</u> • voos
filleted	**φιλέτο**
	fee • <u>leh</u> • toh
fried	**τηγανητό**
	tee • ghah • nee • <u>toh</u>
marinated	**μαρινάτο**
	mah • ree • <u>nah</u> • toh

poached	ποσέ
	poh • seh
roasted	ψητό
	psee • toh
sautéed	σωτέ
	soh • teh
smoked	καπνιστό
	kah • pnee • stoh
steamed	στον ατμό
	stohn aht • moh
stewed	μαγειρευτό
	mah • yee • rehf • toh
stewed in tomato sauce	γιαχνί
	yahkh • nee
stewed in wine	κρασάτο
	krah • sah • toh
stuffed	γεμιστό
	yeh • mees • toh

DIETARY REQUIREMENTS

I'm...	Είμαι...
	ee • meh...
diabetic	διαβητικός *m* /διαβητική *f*
	THee • ah • vee • teek • ohs/
	THee • ah • vee • tee • kee
lactose intolerant	έχω ευαισθησία στα γαλακτοκομικά
	eh • khoh eh • vehs • thee • see • ah stah
	ghah • lahk • toh • koh • mee • kah
vegetarian	χορτοφάγος
	khohr • toh • fah • ghohs
vegan	χορτοφάγος
	khoh • rtoh • fah • ghos

I'm allergic to…	**είμαι αλλεργικός** *m* **/αλλεργική** *f* **σε…**
	ee • meh ah • lehr • yeek • <u>ohs</u>/
	ah • lehr • yeek • <u>ee</u> seh…
I can't eat…	**Δεν πρέπει να φάω φαγητό που περιέχει…**
	THehn <u>preh</u> • pee nah <u>fah</u> • oh fah • yee • <u>toh</u>
	poo peh • ree • <u>eh</u> • khee…
dairy	**γαλακτοκομικά**
	ghah • lahk • toh • koh • mee • <u>kah</u>
gluten	**γλουτένη**
	ghloo • <u>teh</u> • nee
nuts	**ξηρούς καρπούς**
	ksee • <u>roos</u> kahr • <u>poos</u>
pork	**χοιρινό**
	khee • ree • <u>noh</u>
shellfish	**οστρακοειδή**
	ohs • trah • koh • ee • <u>THee</u>
I can't eat…	**Δεν πρέπει να φάω φαγητό που περιέχει…**
	THehn <u>preh</u> • pee nah <u>fah</u> • oh fah • yee • <u>toh</u>
	poo peh • ree • <u>eh</u> • khee…
spicy foods	**πικάντικα τρόφιμα**
	pee • <u>kahn</u> • dee • kah troh • fee • mah
wheat	**σιτάρι**
	see • <u>tah</u> • ree

Is it halal/kosher?	**Αυτό είναι χαλάλ/κόσερ;**
	ahf <u>toh</u> ee • neh khah • <u>lahl</u>/<u>koh</u> • sehr
Do you have...?	**Έχετε...;**
	<u>eh</u> • kheh • teh
skimmed milk	**αποβουτυρωμένο γάλα**
	ah • poh • voo • tee • roh • <u>meh</u> • noh
	<u>ghah</u> • lah
whole milk	**πλήρες γάλα**
	<u>plee</u> • rehs ghah • lah
soya milk	**γάλα σόγιας**
	<u>ghah</u> • lah soh • yahs

DINING WITH CHILDREN

Do you have a children's menu?	**Έχετε παιδικό μενού;**
	<u>eh</u> • kheh • teh peh • THee • <u>koh</u> meh • <u>noo</u>
Can we have a child's seat?	**Μπορούμε να έχουμε ένα παιδικό κάθισμα;**
	boh • <u>roo</u> • meh nah <u>eh</u> • khoo • meh <u>eh</u> • nah
	peh • THee • <u>koh</u> kah • theez • mah
Where can I feed/ change the baby?	**Πού μπορώ να ταΐσω/αλλάξω το μωρό;**
	poo boh • <u>roh</u> nah tah • <u>ee</u> • soh/
	ah • <u>lah</u> • ksoh toh moh • <u>roh</u>
Can you warm this?	**Μπορείτε να το ζεστάνετε;**
	boh • <u>ree</u> • teh nah toh zehs • <u>tah</u> • neh • teh

For Traveling with Children, see page 140.

HOW TO COMPLAIN

How much longer will our food be?	**Πόση ώρα ακόμη θα κάνει το φαγητό;**
	<u>poh</u> • see <u>oh</u> • rah ah • <u>koh</u> • mee thah
	kah • nee toh fah • yee • <u>toh</u>
We can't wait any longer.	**Δεν μπορούμε να περιμένουμε άλλο.**
	THehn boh • <u>roo</u> • meh nah
	peh • ree • <u>meh</u> • noo • meh <u>ah</u> • loh

We're leaving.	**Φεύγουμε.**
	fehv • ghoo • meh
That's not what I ordered.	**Δεν παρήγγειλα αυτό.**
	THehn pah • ree • ngee • lah ahf • toh
I asked for…	**Ζήτησα…**
	zee • tee • sah…
I can't eat this.	**Δεν μπορώ να το φάω.**
	THehn boh • roh nah toh fah • oh
This is too…	**Αυτό είναι πολύ…**
	ahf • toh ee • neh poh • lee…
cold/hot	**κρύο/ζεστό**
	kree • oh/zehs • toh
salty/spicy	**αλμυρό/πικάντικο**
	ahl • mee • roh/pee • kahn • dee • koh
tough/bland	**σκληρό/ανάλατο**
	sklee • roh/ahl • mee • roh
This isn't clean/fresh.	**Αυτό δεν είναι καθαρό/φρέσκο.**
	ahf • toh THehn ee • neh kah • thah • roh/ frehs • koh

PAYING

The check [bill], please.	**Τον λογαριασμό, παρακαλώ.**
	tohn loh • ghahr • yahs • moh pah • rah • kah • loh
We'd like to pay separately.	**Θα πληρώσουμε ξεχωριστά.**
	thah plee • roh • soo • meh kseh • khoh • rees • tah
It's all together.	**Όλοι μαζί.**
	oh • lee mah • zee
Is service included?	**Συμπεριλαμβάνεται και το σέρβις;**
	seem • beh • ree • lahm • vah • neh • teh keh toh sehr • vees
What's this amount for?	**Τί είναι αυτό το ποσό;**
	tee ee • neh ahf • toh toh poh • soh

I didn't have that. I had…	**Δεν πήρα αυτό. Πήρα…** *THehn <u>pee</u> • rah ahf • <u>toh pee</u> • rah…*
Can I pay by credit card?	**Μπορώ να πληρώσω με αυτήν την πιστωτική κάρτα;** *boh • <u>roh</u> nah plee • <u>roh</u> • soh meh ahf • <u>teen</u> teen pees • toh • tee • <u>kee kahr</u> • tah*
Can I have an itemized bill/ a receipt?	**Μπορώ να έχω έναν αναλυτικό λογαριασμό/μια αναλυτική απόδειξη;** *boh • <u>roh</u> nah <u>eh</u> • khoh <u>eh</u> • nahn ah • nah • lee • tee • <u>koh</u> loh • ghahr • yahs • <u>moh</u>/ miah ah • nah • lee • tee • <u>kee</u> ah • <u>poh</u> • ee • ksee*
That was a delicious meal.	**Ήταν ένα πολύ νόστιμο γεύμα.** *<u>ee</u> • tahn <u>eh</u> • nah poh • <u>lee nohs</u> • tee • moh yehv • mah*
I've already paid.	**Πλήρωσα ήδη.** *plee • roh • sah <u>ee</u> • THee*

For Numbers, see page 20.

(i)

In Greek restaurants the service charge is included in
the price. However, it is still customary to leave a little extra if
you are satisfied with the service.

MEALS & COOKING

Greeks rarely eat breakfast (**πρωινό**/proh • ee • noh).
They usually have a strong coffee with sugar (**βαρύ γλυκό**/
vah • ree ghlee • koh) in the morning, followed by another
one between 10:00 and 11:00 a.m., maybe with a pastry.
Lunch (**μεσημεριανό**/meh • see • meh • riah • noh) is the
main meal, although because of the summer heat some
Greeks eat lighter at lunchtime and have their main meal in
the evening. It is usually eaten from 2:00 to 3:00 p.m., but
most restaurants will serve it until 4:00 p.m.
Dinner (**βραδυνό**/vrah • THee • noh) is often eaten
late — normally at 9:00 or 10:00 p.m. It is not unusual
to find restaurants serving food until midnight or later.
Snacks can be bought at souvlaki stalls (**σουβλατζήδικα**/
soov • lah • jee • THee • kah) or snack bars (**σνακ μπαρ**/
snahk bahr) until the early hours of the morning. You can
also buy tasty snacks, such as cheese pie (**τυρόπιτα**/
tee • rhoh • pee • tah), at bakeries, which are open from very
early in the morning until the afternoon.

BREAKFAST

bacon	**μπέικον**
	beh • ee • kohn
bread	**ψωμί**
	psoh • mee
butter	**βούτυρο**
	voo • tee • roh
cereal (cold/hot)	**δημητριακά με (ζεστό/κρύο) γάλα**
	THee • meet • ree • ah • kah meh
	(zehs • toh/kree • oh) ghah • lah

cheese	**τυρί**
	tee • <u>ree</u>
coffee/tea	**καφέ/τσάι**
	kah • <u>feh</u>/<u>tsah</u> • ee
cold cuts	**αλλαντικά**
[charcuterie]	ah • lah • ndee • <u>kah</u>
scrambled eggs	**ομελέτα**
	oh • meh • <u>leh</u> • tah
juice	**χυμός**
	khee • <u>mohs</u>
granola [muesli]	**μούσλι**
	<u>moo</u> • slee
honey	**μέλι**
	<u>meh</u> • lee
muffin	**μάφιν**
	<u>mah</u> • feen
milk	**γάλα**
	<u>ghah</u> • lah
oatmeal	**κουάκερ**
	koo • <u>ah</u> • kehr
omelet	**ομελέτα**
	oh • meh • <u>leh</u> • tah
roll	**ψωμάκι**
	psoh • <u>mah</u> • kee
sausage	**λουκάνικο**
	loo • <u>kah</u> • nee • koh
toast	**ψωμί φρυγανιά**
	psoh • <u>mee</u> free • ghah • <u>niah</u>
yogurt (with honey)	**γιαούρτι (με μέλι)**
	yah • <u>oor</u> • tee (meh <u>meh</u> • lee)

APPETIZERS

cold meat	**κρύο κρέας**
	<u>kree</u> • oh <u>kreh</u> • ahs

...eggs	**αυγά...**
	ahv • ghah...
soft-boiled	**μελάτα**
	meh • lah • tah
hard-boiled	**σφικτά**
	sfeekh • tah
fried	**τηγανητά μάτια**
	tee • ghah • nee • tah mah • tiah
poached	**ποσέ**
	poh • seh
fish roe dip	**ταραμοσαλάτα**
	tah • rah • moh • sah • lah • tah
fried baby squid	**καλαμαράκια**
	kah • lah • mah • rah • kiah
fried meatballs	**κεφτεδάκια**
	kef • teh • THah • kiah
fried whitebait	**μαρίδα τηγανητή**
	mah • ree • THah tee • ghah • nee • tee
herring (smoked)	**ρέγγα (καπνιστή)**
	rehn • gah (kahp • nees • tee)
olive (stuffed)	**ελιά (γεμιστή)**
	eh • liah (yeh • mees • tee)
cheese omelet	**ομελέττα με τυρί**
	oh • meh • leh • tah meh tee • ree
ham omelet	**ομελέττα με ζαμπόν**
	oh • meh • leh • tah meh zahm • bohn
pâté	**πατέ**
	pah • teh

(i)

Μεζέδες *(meh • zeh • dehs)*, appetizers, can be a meal alone. Greeks will often go out for a glass of **ούζο** *(oo • zoh)*, an anise-flavored liqueur, accompanied by appetizers.

spinach and feta in	**σπανακόπιττα**
pastry dough	*spah • nah • <u>koh</u> • pee • tah*
stuffed grape leaves	**ντολμαδάκι**
	dohl • mah • <u>THah</u> • kee
yogurt, garlic and	**τζατζίκι**
cucumber dip	*jah • <u>jee</u> • kee*

> ℹ️
>
> A traditional and very tasty egg dish in Greece
> is **στραπατσάδα** *(strah • pah • <u>tsah</u> • THah)*,
> scrambled eggs with fresh tomato, but sometimes with
> other ingredients depending on the region. Another
> traditional method of using egg is in **αυγολέμονο**
> *(ahv • ghoh • <u>leh</u> • moh • noh)*: egg yolk and lemon are added
> to a sauce or soup. This sauce usually accompanies warm
> stuffed grape leaves and other vegetable dishes or stews.

SOUP

bean soup with	**φασολάδα**
tomatoes and	*fah • soh • <u>lah</u> • THah*
parsley	

chicken soup	**κοτόσουπα**
	koh • <u>toh</u> • soo • pah
chickpea soup	**ρεβύθια σούπα**
	reh • <u>vee</u> • thiah <u>soo</u> • pah
cracked wheat soup	**τραχανάς**
	trah • khah • <u>nahs</u>
fish soup thickened	**ψαρόσουπα αυγολέμονο**
with egg and lemon	psah • <u>roh</u> • soo • pah
	ahv • ghoh • <u>leh</u> • moh • noh
fish stew with	**κακαβιά**
tomatoes	kah • kahv • <u>yah</u>
lentil soup	**φακές σούπα**
	fah • <u>kehs</u> soo • pah
meat soup	**κρεατόσουπα**
	kreh • ah • <u>toh</u> • soo • pah
soup with rice, eggs	**σούπα αυγολέμονο**
and lemon juice	<u>soo</u> • pah ahv • ghoh • <u>leh</u> • moh • noh
tripe soup	**πατσάς**
	pah • <u>tsahs</u>
tahini (sesame	**ταχινόσουπα**
paste) soup	tah • khee • <u>noh</u> • soo • pah
tomato soup	**τοματόσουπα**
	toh • mah • <u>toh</u> • soo • pah
vegetable soup	**χορτόσουπα**
	khohr • <u>toh</u> • soo • pah

FISH & SEAFOOD

anchovy	**αντσούγια**
	ahn • <u>joo</u> • yahs
crab	**καβούρι**
	kah • <u>voo</u> • ree
cuttlefish	**σουπιά**
	soo • <u>piah</u>

eel	**χέλι**
	kheh • lee
fresh cod	**μπακαλιάρος**
	bah • kah • _liah_ • rohs
grouper	**σφυρίδα**
	sfee • _ree_ • THah
mullet	**κέφαλος**
	keh • fah • lohs
lobster	**αστακός**
	ahs • tah • _kohs_
marinated mullet,	**ψάρι μαρινάτο**
sole or mackerel	_psah_ • ree mah • ree • _nah_ • toh
mussels	**μύδι**
	mee • THee
octopus	**χταπόδι**
	khtah • _poh_ • THee
oyster	**στρείδι**
	stree • THee
red mullet	**μπαρμπούνι**
	bahr • _boo_ • nee
salted cod	**μπακαλιάρος παστός**
	bah • kah • _liah_ • rohs pahs • _tohs_
sardine	**σαρδέλα**
	sahr • _THeh_ • lah
shrimp [prawn]	**γαρίδα**
	ghah • ree • THah
sole	**γλώσσα**
	ghloh • sah
squid	**καλαμάρι**
	kah • lah • _mah_ • ree
swordfish	**ξιφίας**
	ksee • _fee_ • ahs
tuna	**τόννος**
	toh • nohs

MEAT & POULTRY

beef	**βοδινό** *voh • THee • <u>noh</u>*
beef or veal stewed with tomatoes and eggplant [aubergine]	**μελιτζανάτο** *meh • lee • jah • <u>nah</u> • toh*
brains	**μυαλό** *miah • <u>loh</u>*
Greek burger	**μπιφτέκι** *beef • <u>teh</u> • kee*
chicken	**κοτόπουλο** *koh • <u>toh</u> • poo • loh*
cutlet	**κοτολέτα** *koh • toh • <u>leh</u> • tah*
duck	**πάπια** *<u>pah</u> • piah*
fillet	**φιλέτο** *fee • <u>leh</u> • toh*
goat	**κατσικάκι** *kah • tsee • <u>kah</u> • kee*
goose	**χήνα** *<u>khee</u> • nah*

ham	**ζαμπόν** *zahm • bohn*
kidney	**νεφρό** *neh • froh*
lamb	**αρνί** *ahr • nee*
liver	**συκώτι** *see • koh • tee*
layers of eggplant [aubergine], meat and white sauce	**μουσακάς** *moo • sah • kahs*
meat with orzo pasta baked with tomatoes	**γιουβέτσι** *yoo • veh • tsee*
pheasant	**φασιανός** *fah • siah • nohs*
pork	**χοιρινό** *khee • ree • noh*
rabbit	**κουνέλι** *koo • neh • lee*
sausage	**λουκάνικο** *loo • kah • nee • koh*
skewered pork or lamb, cooked over charcoal	**κοντοσούβλι** *koh • ndoh • soov • lee dohs*
spiced lamb and potatoes baked in parchment or in filo pastry	**αρνάκι εξοχικό** *ahr • nah • kee eh • ksoh • khee • koh*
turkey	**γαλοπούλα** *ghah • loh • poo • lah*
veal	**μοσχάρι** *mohs • khah • ree*
veal/pork steak	**μπριζόλα μοσχαρίσια/χοιρινή** *bree • zoh • lah mohs • khah • ree • siah/ khee • ree • nee*

VEGETABLES & STAPLES

artichokes	**αγκινάρες** ahn • gkee • <u>nah</u> • rehs
asparagus	**σπαράγγια** spah • <u>rahn</u> • giah
bay leaf	**δαφνόφυλλο** THah • <u>fnoh</u> • fee • loh
basil	**βασιλικός** vah • see • lee • <u>kohs</u>
bread	**ψωμί** psoh • <u>mee</u>
broad beans	**κουκί** koo • <u>kee</u>
butter bean	**φασόλι γίγαντας** fah • <u>soh</u> • lee <u>yee</u> • ghahn • dahs
cabbage	**λάχανο** <u>lah</u> • khah • noh
carrot	**καρότο** kah • <u>roh</u> • toh
cauliflower	**κουνουπίδι** koo • noo • <u>pee</u> • THee
celery	**σέλερι** <u>seh</u> • leh • ree
cinnamon	**κανέλλα** kah • <u>neh</u> • lah
cucumber	**αγγούρι** ahn • <u>goo</u> • ree
dill	**άνηθος** <u>ah</u> • nee • thohs
eggplant [aubergine]	**μελιτζάνα** meh • lee • <u>jah</u> • nah
garlic	**σκόρδο** <u>skohr</u> • THoh

green bean	**φασολάκι**
	fah • soh • <u>lah</u> • kee
green peppers	**πιπεριές πράσινες**
	pee • pehr • <u>yehs</u> <u>prah</u> • see • nehs
leek	**πράσο**
	<u>prah</u> • soh
mastic	**μαστίχα**
	mahs • <u>tee</u> • khah
mint	**δυόσμος**
	THee • <u>ohz</u> • mohs
mushroom	**μανιτάρι**
	mah • nee • <u>tah</u> • ree
okra	**μπάμια**
	<u>bah</u> • miah
onion	**κρεμμύδι**
	kreh • <u>mee</u> • Thee
oregano	**ρίγανη**
	<u>ree</u> • ghah • nee
parsley	**μαϊντανός**
	mah • ee • dah • <u>nohs</u>
pasta	**ζυμαρικά**
	zee • mah • ree • <u>kah</u>
peas	**αρακάς**
	ah • rah • <u>kahs</u>

peppers	**πιπεριές**
	pee • pehr • yehs
potato	**πατάτα**
	pah • tah • tah
red cabbage	**κόκκινο λάχανο**
	koh • kee • noh lah • khah • noh
rosemary	**δεντρολίβανο**
	THehn • droh • lee • vah • noh
sage	**φασκόμηλο**
	fahs • koh • mee • loh
spinach	**σπανάκι**
	spah • nah • kee
sugar	**ζάχαρη**
	zah • khah • ree
thyme	**θυμάρι**
	thee • mah • ree
toast	**ψωμί φρυγανιά**
	psoh • mee free • ghah • niah
tomato	**ντομάτα**
	ndoh • mah • tah
unleavened bread	**λαγάνα**
	lah • ghah • nah
zucchini [courgette]	**κολοκυθάκι**
	koh • loh • kee • thah • kee

FRUIT

apple	**μήλο**
	mee • loh
apricot	**βερύκοκο**
	veh • ree • koh • koh
banana	**μπανάνα**
	bah • nah • nah
cherry	**κεράσι**
	keh • rah • see

date	**χουρμάς**
	khoor • <u>mahs</u>
fig	**σύκο**
	<u>see</u> • koh
grape	**σταφύλι**
	stah • <u>fee</u> • lee
grapefruit	**γκρέιπφρουτ**
	<u>greh</u> • eep • froot
lemon	**λεμόνι**
	leh • <u>moh</u> • nee
melon	**πεπόνι**
	peh • <u>poh</u> • nee
orange	**πορτοκάλι**
	pohr • toh • <u>kah</u> • lee
peach	**ροδάκινο**
	roh • <u>THah</u> • kee • noh
pear	**αχλάδι**
	akh • <u>lah</u> • THee
plum	**δαμάσκηνο**
	THah • <u>mahs</u> • kee • noh
pineapple	**ανανάς**
	ah • nah • <u>nahs</u>
tangerine	**μανταρίνι**
	mahn • dah • <u>ree</u> • nee

| watermelon | **καρπούζι** |
| | *kahr • poo • zee* |

CHEESE

feta cheese	**φέτα**
	feh • tah
Gruyere cheese	**γραβιέρα**
	ghrah • vieh • rah
Kaseri, yellow cheese	**κασέρι**
	kah • seh • ree
cottage cheese	**τυρί κότατζ**
	tee • ree koh • tahtz

DESSERT

apple pie	**μηλόπιτα**
	mee • loh • pee • tah
baklava, flaky pastry with nut filling	**μπακλαβάς**
	bah • klah • vahs
candy [sweets]	**καραμέλα**
	kah • rah • meh • lah
caramel custard	**κρέμα καραμελέ**
	kreh • mah kah • rah • meh • leh

filo pastry filled with almonds, orange juice and cinnamon	**κοπεγχάγη** *koh • pehn • <u>khah</u> • ghee*
flaky pastry filled with custard and steeped in syrup	**γαλακτομπούρεκο** *ghah • lah • ktoh • <u>boo</u> • reh • koh*
fruit salad	**φρουτοσαλάτα** *froo • toh • sah • <u>lah</u> • tah*
halva, sweet sesame seed paste	**χαλβάς** *khahl • <u>vahs</u>*
ice cream	**παγωτό** *pah • ghoh • <u>toh</u>*
rice pudding	**ρυζόγαλο** *ree • <u>zoh</u> • ghah • loh*
shredded pastry roll filled with nuts and steeped in syrup	**καταΐφι** *kah • tah • <u>ee</u> • fee*
Turkish delight	**λουκούμι** *loo • <u>koo</u> • mee*
walnut cake	**καρυδόπιτα** *kah • ree • <u>THoh</u> • pee • tah*

SAUCES & CONDIMENTS

salt	**Αλάτι** *ah • <u>lah</u> • tee*
pepper	**Πιπέρι** *pee • <u>peh</u> • ree*
mustard	**Μουστάρδα** *moo • <u>stahr</u> • THah*
ketchup	**Κέτσαπ** *<u>keh</u> • tsahp*

Large-scale supermarkets can be found on the outskirts of most towns; smaller supermarkets are located near city centers. There are several large chains, including: **AB Βασιλόπουλος** *(ahl • fah <u>vee</u> • tah vah • see • <u>loh</u> • poo • lohs)*, **Dia** *(<u>dee</u> • ah)*, **Champion** *(<u>chahm</u> • pee • ohn)*, **ΣΚΛΑΒΕΝΙΤΗΣ** *(sklah • veh • <u>nee</u> • tees)* and **Spar** *(spahr)*.

AT THE MARKET

Where are the trolleys/baskets?	**Πού είναι τα καροτσάκια/καλάθια;** *poo <u>ee</u> • neh tah kah • roh • <u>tsah</u> • kiah/ kah • <u>lah</u> • thiah*
Where is/are…?	**Πού είναι...;** *poo <u>ee</u> • neh...*
I'd like some of that/those.	**Θα ήθελα μερικά από αυτά/εκείνα.** *thah <u>ee</u> • theh • lah meh • ree • <u>kah</u> ah • <u>poh</u> ahf <u>tah</u>/eh • <u>kee</u> • nah*
Can I taste it?	**Μπορώ να το δοκιμάσω;** *boh • <u>roh</u> nah toh THoh • kee • <u>mah</u> • soh*

Measurements in Europe are metric — and that applies to the weight of food too. If you tend to think in pounds and ounces, it's worth brushing up on what the metric equivalent is before you go shopping for fruit and veg in markets and supermarkets. Five hundred grams, or half a kilo, is a common quantity to order, and that converts to just over a pound (17.65 ounces, to be precise).

YOU MAY HEAR...

Μπορώ να σας βοηθήσω;
boh • _roh_ nah sahs voh • ee • _thee_ • soh

Can I help you?

Τι θα πάρετε;
tee thah _pah_ • reh • teh

What would you like?

Τίποτε άλλο;
tee • poh • teh _ah_ • loh

Anything else?

Αυτά είναι...ευρώ.
ahf • _tah_ ee • _neh_... ehv • _roh_

That's...euros.

YOU MAY SEE...

ΑΝΑΛΩΣΗ ΚΑΤΑ **ΠΡΟΤΙΜΗΣΗ ΠΡΙΝ ΑΠΟ...** *ah • nah • loh • see kah • tah* *proh • tee • mee • see preen ah • poh*	best before...
ΘΕΡΜΙΔΕΣ *thehr • mee • THehs*	calories
ΧΩΡΙΣ ΛΙΠΑΡΑ *khoh • rees lee • pah • rah*	fat free
ΔΙΑΤΗΡΕΙΤΑΙ ΣΤΟ ΨΥΓΕΙΟ *THee • ah • tee • ree • teh stoh* *psee • yee • oh*	keep refrigerated
ΜΠΟΡΕΙ ΝΑ ΠΕΡΙΕΧΕΙ **ΙΧΝΗ ΑΠΟ...** *boh • ree nah peh • ree • eh • khee* *eekh • nee ah • poh...*	may contain traces of...
για φούρνο μικροκυμάτων *yah foo • rnoh* *mee • kroh • kee • mah • tohn*	microwaveable
πώληση μέχρι... *poh • lee • see meh • khree*	sell by...
κατάλληλο για χορτοφάγους *kah • tah • lee • loh yah* *khoh • rtoh • fah • ghoos*	suitable for vegetarians

I'd like...	**Θα ήθελα...** *thah ee • theh • lah...*
a kilo/half-kilo of...	**ένα/μισό κιλό...** *eh • nah/mee • soh kee • loh...*
a liter/half-liter of...	**ένα/μισό λίτρο...** *eh • nah/mee • soh leet • roh...*
a piece of...	**ένα κομμάτι...** *eh • nah koh • mah • tee...*

a slice of…	**μια φέτα…**
	miah feh • tah…
More/Less.	**Περισσότερο/Λιγότερο.**
	peh • ree • soh • teh • roh/
	lee • ghoh • teh • roh
How much?	**Πόσο;**
	poh • soh
Where do I pay?	**Πού πληρώνω;**
	poo plee • roh • noh
A bag, please.	**Μια σακούλα, παρακαλώ.**
	miah sah • koo • lah pah • rah • kah • loh
I'm being helped.	**Εξυπηρετούμαι.**
	eh • ksee • pee • reh • too • meh

For Money, see page 33.

IN THE KITCHEN

bottle opener	**τιρμπουσόν**
	teer • mboo • sohn
bowls	**τα μπωλ**
	tah bohl
can opener	**ανοιχτήρι**
	ah • neekh • tee • ree
corkscrew	**τιρμπουσόν**
	teer • boo • sohn
cups	**τα φλυτζάνια**
	tah flee • jah • niah
forks	**τα πηρούνια**
	tah pee • roo • niah
frying pan	**τηγάνι**
	tee • ghah • nee
glasses	**τα ποτήρια**
	tah poh • teer • yah

knives	**τα μαχαίρια**
	tah mah • khehr • yah
measuring cup/	**μεζούρα φλυτζάνι/κουτάλι**
spoon	*meh • zoo • rah*
	flee • jah • nee/koo • tah • lee
napkin	**χαρτοπετσέτα**
	khahr • toh • peh • tseh • tah
plates	**τα πιάτα**
	tah piah • tah
pot	**κανάτα**
	kah • nah • tah
saucepan	**κατσαρόλα**
	kah • tsah • roh • lah
spatula	**σπάτουλα**
	spah • too • lah
spoons	**κουτάλια**
	koo • tah • liah

For Domestic Items, see page 85.

DRINKS

NEED TO KNOW

May I see the wine list/drinks menu?	**Μπορώ να δω τον κατάλογο με τα κρασιά/ποτά;** *boh • roh nah THoh tohn kah • tah • loh • ghoh meh tah krah • siah/poh • tah*
What do you recommend?	**Τι συστήνετε;** *tee see • stee • neh • the*
I'd like a bottle/ glass of red/white wine.	**Θα ήθελα ένα μπουκάλι/ποτήρι κόκκινο/λευκό κρασί.** *thah ee • theh • lah eh • nah boo • kah • lee/poh • tee • ree koh • kee • noh/lehf • koh krah • see*
The house wine, please.	**Το κρασί του καταστήματος, παρακαλώ.** *toh krah • see too kah • tah • stee • mah • tohs pah • rah • kah • loh*
Another bottle/ glass, please.	**Άλλο ένα μπουκάλι/ποτήρι, παρακαλώ.** *ah • loh eh • nah boo • kah • lee/poh • tee • ree pah • rah • kah • loh*
I'd like a local beer.	**Θα ήθελα μια τοπική μπύρα.** *thah ee • theh • lah miah toh • pee • kee bee • rah*
Let me buy you a drink.	**Να σας κεράσω ένα ποτό.** *nah sahs keh • rah • soh eh • nah poh • toh*
Cheers!	**Στην υγειά σας!** *steen ee • ghiah sahs*

A sparkling water.	**Ena ανθρακούχο νερό**
	eh • nah ahn • thrah • koo • khoh neh • roh
A still water.	**Ena νερό χωρίς ανθρακικό**
	eh • nah neh • roh khoh • rees
	ahn • thrah • kee • koh
Is the tap water safe to drink?	**Είναι το νερό βρύσης πόσιμο;**
	ee • neh toh neh • roh vree • sees
	poh • see • moh

(i)

The most popular drinks in the summer are **φραπέ**
(_frah • peh_), iced instant coffee shaken to produce a thick
coffee froth, with or without milk and sugar, and **φρέντο**
(_frehd • doh_), iced espresso with or without milk, found
at most coffee shops and bars. Freshly squeezed juices
are also widely consumed. Tap water is drinkable almost
everywhere, but if you prefer you can get **εμφιαλωμένο νερό**
(_ehm • fee • ah • loh • meh • noh neh • roh_), bottled water.

NON-ALCOHOLIC DRINKS

...coffee	**έναν καφέ...**
	eh • nahn kah • feh...
instant	**ένα Νεσκαφέ**
	eh • nah nehs • kah • feh
Greek	**ελληνικό**
	eh • lee • nee • koh
with cream/milk	**με κρέμα/γάλα**
	meh kreh • mah/ghah • lah
...juice	**χυμός...**
	khee • mohs...

apple	**μήλο**
	mee • loh
grapefruit	**γκρέιπφρουτ**
	greh • eep • froot
orange	**πορτοκάλι**
	poh • rtoh • _kah_ • lee
iced tea	**παγωμένο τσάι**
	pah • ghoh • _meh_ • noh _tsah_ • ee
tea with milk/	**τσάι με γάλα/λεμόνι**
lemon	_tsah_ • ee meh _ghah_ • lah/
	leh • _moh_ • nee
mineral water	**μεταλλικό νερό**
	meh • tah • lee • _koh_ neh • _roh_
hot chocolate	**ζεστή σοκολάτα**
	zeh • _stee_ soh • koh • _lah_ • tah

YOU MAY HEAR...

Θέλετε κάτι να πιείτε;
theh • leh • teh kah • tee
nah pee • _ee_ • teh

Can I get you a drink?

Με γάλα/ζάχαρη;
meh _ghah_ • lah/_zah_ • khah • ree

With milk/ sugar?

Νερό ανθρακούχο/χωρίς ανθρακικό;
neh • _roh_ ahn • thrah _koo_ • khoh/
khoh • _rees_ ahn • thrah • kee • _koh_

Sparkling/Still water?

APERITIFS, COCKTAILS & LIQUEURS

Greek brandy	**Μεταξά**
	meh • tah • _ksah_
kumquat liqueur	**κουμ-κουάτ**
(Corfu)	koom • koo • _aht_

straight [neat]	**σκέτο**
	skeh • toh
on the rocks	**με πάγο**
	meh _pah_ • ghoh
ouzo	**ούζο**
	_oo_ • zoh

BEER

beer	**μπύρα**
	bee • rah
bottled	**εμφιαλωμένη**
	ehm • fee • ah • loh • _meh_ • nee
draft	**βαρελίσια**
	vah • reh • _lee_ • siah
light/dark	**ξανθή/μαύρη**
	ksahn • _thee/mahv_ • ree
local/imported	**τοπικό/εισαγόμενο**
	toh • pee • _koh/_
	ee • sah • _ghoh_ • meh • noh

WINE

blush [rosé]	**ροζέ**
	roh • _zeh_
chilled	**παγωμένο**
	pah • ghoh • _meh_ • noh
dry	**ξηρό**
	ksee • _roh_
red	**μπουκάλι κόκκινο**
	boo • _kah_ • lee koh • _kee_ • noh
sweet	**γλυκό**
	ghlee • _koh_
white	**λευκό**
	lehf • koh
wine	**κρασί**
	krah • _see_

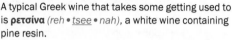

A typical Greek wine that takes some getting used to is **ρετσίνα** (reh • <u>tsee</u> • nah), a white wine containing pine resin.

Wine is usually produced and consumed locally – a restaurant owner will often bring you a carafe of his or her very own wine if you ask for **κρασί βαρελίσιο** (krah • <u>see</u> vah • reh • <u>lee</u> • sioh), the house wine.

ON THE MENU

anchovy	**αντσούγια**
	ahn • <u>joo</u> • yah
apple	**μήλο**
	<u>mee</u> • loh
apple pie	**μηλόπιτα**
	mee • <u>loh</u> • pee • tah
apricot	**βερίκοκο**
	veh • <u>ree</u> • koh • koh
artichoke	**αγκινάρα**
	ahn • gkee • <u>nah</u> • rah
artificial sweetener	**ζαχαρίνη**
	zah • khah • <u>ree</u> • nee
asparagus	**σπαράγγι**
	spah • <u>rahn</u> • gee
bacon	**μπέικον**
	<u>beh</u> • ee • kohn
baklava, flaky pastry with nut filling	**μπακλαβάς**
	bah • klah • <u>vahs</u>
banana	**μπανάνα**
	bah • <u>nah</u> • nah
basil	**βασιλικός**
	vah • see • lee • <u>kohs</u>

bay leaf	**δαφνόφυλλο** *THah • fnoh • fee • loh*
bean soup with tomatoes and parsley	**φασολάδα** *fah • soh • lah • THah*
beef	**βοδινό** *voh • THee • noh*
beef or veal stewed with tomatoes and eggplant [aubergine]	**μελιτζανάτο** *meh • lee • jah • nah • toh*
beer	**μπίρα** *bee • rah*
brains	**μυαλό** *miah • loh*
bread	**ψωμί** *psoh • mee*
bread roll	**ψωμάκι** *psoh • mah • kee*
broad bean	**κουκί** *koo • kee*
butter	**βούτυρο** *voo • tee • roh*
butter bean	**φασόλι γίγαντας** *fah • soh • lee yee • ghahn • dahs*
cabbage	**λάχανο** *lah • khah • noh*
candy [sweets]	**καραμέλα** *kah • rah • meh • lah*
caramel custard	**κρέμα καραμελέ** *kreh • mah kah • rah • meh • leh*
carrot	**καρότο** *kah • roh • toh*
cauliflower	**κουνουπίδι** *koo • noo • pee • THee*

celery	**σέλερι**
	seh • leh • ree
cereal (cold/hot)	**δημητριακά με (ζεστό/κρύο) γάλα**
	THee • meet • ree • ah • kah meh
	(zehs • toh/kree • oh) ghah • lah
cheese	**τυρί**
	tee • ree
cheese omelet	**ομελέττα με τυρί**
	oh • meh • leh • tah meh tee • ree
cherry	**κεράσι**
	keh • rah • see
chicken	**κοτόπουλο**
	koh • toh • poo • loh
chicken soup	**κοτόσουπα**
	koh • toh • soo • pah
chickpea soup	**ρεβύθια σούπα**
	reh • vee • thiah soo • pah
chilled	**παγωμένο**
	pah • ghoh • meh • noh
cinnamon	**κανέλλα**
	kah • neh • lah
club soda	**σόδα**
	soh • THah

coffee	**καφέ**
	kah • fehs
cold cuts	**αλλαντικά**
[charcuterie]	*ah • lah • ndee • kah*
cold meat	**κρύο κρέας**
	kree • oh kreh • ahs
cottage cheese	**τυρί κότατζ**
	tee • ree koh • tahtz
crab	**καβούρι**
	kah • voo • ree
cracked wheat	**τραχανάς**
soup	*trah • khah • nahs*
cream	**κρέμα**
	kreh • mah
cucumber	**αγγούρι**
	ahn • goo • ree
cutlet	**κοτολέτα**
	koh • toh • leh • tah
cuttlefish	**σουπιά**
	soo • piah
date	**χουρμάς**
	khoor • mahs
dill	**άνηθος**
	ah • nee • thohs
draft	**βαρελίσια**
	vah • reh • lee • siah
duck	**πάπια**
	pah • piah
eel	**χέλι**
	kheh • lee
egg	**αυγό**
	ahv • ghoh
eggplant	**μελιτζάνα**
[aubergine]	*meh • lee • jah • nah*

fig	**σύκο**
	see • koh
fillet	**φιλέτο**
	fee • _leh_ • toh
filo pastry filled with almonds, orange juice and cinnamon	**κοπεγχάγη**
	koh • pehn • _khah_ • ghee
filo pastry filled with custard and steeped in syrup	**γαλακτομπούρεκο**
	ghah • lah • ktoh • _boo_ • reh • koh
fish	**ψάρι**
	psah • ree
fish soup thickened with egg and lemon	**ψαρόσουπα αυγολέμονο**
	psah • _roh_ • soo • pah ahv • ghoh • _leh_ • moh • noh
fish stew with tomatoes	**κακαβιά**
	kah • kahv • _yah_
fresh cod	**μπακαλιάρος**
	bah • kah • _liah_ • rohs
fried baby squid	**καλαμαράκια**
	kah • lah • mah • _rah_ • kiah
fried meatballs	**κεφτεδάκια**
	kef • teh • _THah_ • kiah
fried whitebait	**μαρίδα τηγανητή**
	mah • _ree_ • THah tee • ghah • nee • _tee_
fruit	**φρούτο**
	froo • toh
fruit juice	**χυμός φρούτων**
	khee • _mohs froo_ • tohn
fruit salad	**φρουτοσαλάτα**
	froo • toh • sah • _lah_ • tah
garlic	**σκόρδο**
	skohr • THoh
goat	**κατσικάκι**
	kah • tsee • _kah_ • kee

goose	χήνα
	khee • nah
granola [muesli]	μούσλι
	moos • lee
grape	σταφύλι
	stah • _fee_ • lee
grapefruit	γκρέιπφρουτ
	greh • eep • froot
Greek brandy	Μεταξά
	meh • tah • _ksah_
green bean	φασολάκι
	fah • soh • _lah_ • kee
green peppers	πιπεριές πράσινες
	pee • pehr • _yehs_ _prah_ • see • nehs
grouper	σφυρίδα
	sfee • _ree_ • THah
halva, sweet	χαλβάς
sesame seed paste	khahl • _vahs_
ham	ζαμπόν
	zahm • _bohn_
ham omelet	ομελέττα με ζαμπόν
	oh • meh • _leh_ • tah meh zahm • _bohn_
herring (smoked)	ρέγγα (καπνιστή)
	rehn • gah (kahp • nees • _tee_)

honey	**μέλι**
	meh • lee
ice cream	**παγωτό**
	pah • ghoh • _toh_
iced tea	**παγωμένο τσάι**
	pah • ghoh • _meh_ • noh tsah • ee
instant coffee	**Νεσκαφέ**
	nehs • kah • _feh_
juice	**χυμός**
	khee • _mohs_
kidney	**νεφρό**
	neh • _froh_
kumquat liqueur	**κουμ-κουάτ**
(Corfu)	koom • koo • _aht_
lamb	**αρνί**
	ahr • _nee_
layers of eggplant	**μουσακάς**
[aubergine], meat	moo • sah • _kahs_
and white sauce	
leek	**πράσο**
	prah • soh
lemon	**λεμόνι**
	leh • _moh_ • nee

lentil soup	**φακές σούπα**
	fah • kehs soo • pah
liqueur	**λικέρ**
	lee • kehr
liver	**συκώτι**
	see • koh • tee
lobster	**αστακός**
	ahs • tah • kohs
mackerel	**σκουμπρί**
	skoo • mbree
marinated mullet,	**ψάρι μαρινάτο**
sole or mackerel	*psah • ree mah • ree • nah • toh*
mastic	**μαστίχα**
	mahs • tee • khah
mayonnaise	**μαγιονέζα**
	mah • yoh • neh • zah
meat	**κρέας**
	kreh • ahs
meat soup	**κρεατόσουπα**
	kreh • ah • toh • soo • pah
meat with orzo pasta	**γιουβέτσι**
baked with tomatoes	*yoo • veh • tsee*
melon	**πεπόνι**
	peh • poh • nee
milk	**γάλα**
	ghah • lah
mint	**δυόσμος**
	THee • ohz • mohs
muffin	**μάφιν**
	mah • feen
mullet	**κέφαλος**
	keh • fah • lohs
mushroom	**μανιτάρι**
	mah • nee • tah • ree

mussels	**μύδι**
	mee • THee
nuts	**ξηροί καρποί**
	ksee • _ree_ kah • _rpee_
oatmeal	**κουάκερ**
	koo • _ah_ • kehr
octopus	**χταπόδι**
	khtah • _poh_ • THee
okra	**μπάμια**
	bah • miah
olive (stuffed)	**ελιά (γεμιστή)**
	eh • _liah_ (yeh • mees • _tee_)
olive oil	**ελαιόλαδο**
	eh • leh • _oh_ • lah • THoh
omelet	**ομελέτα**
	oh • meh • _leh_ • tah
on the rocks	**με πάγο**
	meh _pah_ • ghoh
onion	**κρεμμύδι**
	kreh • _mee_ • THee
orange	**πορτοκάλι**
	poh • rtoh • _kah_ • lee
oregano	**ρίγανη**
	ree • ghah • nee
ouzo	**ούζο**
	_oo_ • zoh
oyster	**στρείδι**
	stree • THee
parsley	**μαϊντανός**
	mah • ee • dah • _nohs_
pasta	**ζυμαρικά**
	zee • mah • ree • _kah_
paté	**πατέ**
	pah • _teh_

peach	ροδάκινο
	roh • THah • kee • noh
pear	αχλάδι
	akh • lah • THee
peas	αρακάς
	ah • rah • kahs
pheasant	φασιανός
	fah • siah • nohs
pineapple	ανανάς
	ah • nah • nahs
plum	δαμάσκηνο
	THah • mahs • kee • noh
poached	ποσέ
	poh • seh
pork	χοιρινό
	khee • ree • noh
porksteak	μπριζόλα χοιρινή
	bree • zoh • lah khee • ree • nee
potato	πατάτα
	pah • tah • tah
rabbit	κουνέλι
	koo • neh • lee
red cabbage	κόκκινο λάχανο
	koh • kee • noh lah • khah • noh

red mullet	**μπαρμπούνι**
	bahr • boo • nee
red wine	**κόκκινο κρασί**
	koh • kee • noh krah • see
rice	**ρύζι**
	ree • zee
rice pudding	**ρυζόγαλο**
	ree • zoh • ghah • loh
roast	**ψητό**
	psee • toh
roll	**ψωμάκι**
	psoh • mah • kee
rosemary	**δεντρολίβανο**
	THehn • droh • lee • vah • noh
sage	**φασκόμηλο**
	fahs • koh • mee • loh
salad	**σαλάτα**
	sah • lah • tah
salted cod	**μπακαλιάρος παστός**
	bah • kah • liah • rohs pahs • tohs
sardine	**σαρδέλα**
	sahr • THeh • lah
sauce	**σάλτσα**
	sah • ltsah
sausage	**λουκάνικο**
	loo • kah • nee • koh
scrambled eggs	**ομελέτα**
	oh • meh • leh • tah
shellfish	**όστρακα**
	oh • strah • kah
shredded pastry roll filled with nuts and steeped in syrup	**καταΐφι**
	kah • tah • ee • fee
shrimp [prawn]	**γαρίδα**
	ghah • ree • THah

skewered pork or lamb cooked over charcoal	**κοντοσούβλι** *koh • ndoh • <u>soov</u> • lee*
snack	**σνακ** *snahk*
soda	**αναψυκτικό** *ah • nah • psee • ktee • <u>koh</u>*
soft-boiled eggs	**μελάτα αυγά** *meh • <u>lah</u> • tah ahv • <u>gah</u>*
sole (fish)	**γλώσσα** *<u>ghloh</u> • sah*
soup	**σούπα** *<u>soo</u> • pah*
soup with rice, eggs and lemon juice	**σούπα αυγολέμονο** *<u>soo</u> • pah ahv • <u>ghoh</u> • <u>leh</u> • moh • noh*
spiced lamb and potatoes baked in parchment or in filo pastry	**αρνάκι εξοχικό** *ahr • <u>nah</u> • kee eh • ksoh • khee • <u>koh</u>*
spices	**μπαχαρικά** *bah • khah • ree • <u>kah</u>*
spinach	**σπανάκι** *spah • <u>nah</u> • kee*
spinach and feta in pastry dough	**σπανακόπιττα** *spah • nah • <u>koh</u> • pee • tah*
stuffed grape leaves	**ντολμαδάκι** *dohl • mah • <u>THah</u> • kee*
squid	**καλαμάρι** *kah • lah • <u>mah</u> • ree*
steak	**μπριζόλα** *bree • <u>zoh</u> • lah*
sugar	**ζάχαρη** *<u>zah</u> • khah • ree*
swordfish	**ξιφίας** *ksee • <u>fee</u> • ahs*

syrup	**σιρόπι**	
	see • <u>roh</u> • pee	
tahini (sesame paste) soup	**ταχινόσουπα**	
	tah • khee • <u>noh</u> • soo • pah	
tangerine	**μανταρίνι**	
	mahn • dah • <u>ree</u> • nee	
taramosalata, fish roe dip	**ταραμοσαλάτα**	
	tah • rah • moh • sah • <u>lah</u> • tah	
tea	**τσάι**	
	<u>tsah</u> • ee	
thyme	**θυμάρι**	
	thee • <u>mah</u> • ree	
toast	**ψωμί φρυγανιά**	
	psoh • <u>mee</u> free • ghah • <u>niah</u>	
tomato	**ντομάτα**	
	ndoh • <u>mah</u> • tah	
tomato soup	**τοματόσουπα**	
	toh • mah • <u>toh</u> • soo • pah	
tongue (meat)	**γλώσσα**	
	<u>ghloh</u> • sah	
tonic water	**τόνικ**	
	<u>toh</u> • neek	
tripe soup	**πατσάς**	
	pah • <u>tsahs</u>	

tuna	**τόννος**
	toh • nohs
turkey	**γαλοπούλα**
	ghah • loh • _poo_ • lah
Turkish delight	**λουκούμι**
	loo • _koo_ • mee
unleavened bread	**λαγάνα**
	lah • _ghah_ • nah
veal	**μοσχάρι**
	mohs • _khah_ • ree
veal steak	**μπριζόλα μοσχαρίσια**
	bree • _zoh_ • lah mohs • khah • _ree_ • siah
vegetable	**λαχανικό**
	lah • khah • nee • _koh_
vegetable soup	**χορτόσουπα**
	khohr • _toh_ • soo • pah
walnut cake	**καρυδόπιτα**
	kah • ree • _THoh_ • pee • tah
water	**νερό**
	neh • _roh_
watermelon	**καρπούζι**
	kahr • _poo_ • zee
wheat	**σιτάρι**
	see • _tah_ • ree
wine	**κρασί**
	krah • _see_
yogurt (with honey)	**γιαούρτι (με μέλι)**
	yah • _oor_ • tee (meh _meh_ • lee)
yogurt, garlic and cucumber dip	**τζατζίκι**
	jah • _jee_ • kee
zucchini [courgette]	**κολοκυθάκι**
	koh • loh • kee • _thah_ • kee

GOING OUT

GOING OUT

NEED TO KNOW

What's there to do in the evenings?	**Τι μπορώ να κάνω τα βράδια;**
	tee boh • roh nah
	kah • noh tah vrahTH • yah
Do you have a program of events?	**Έχετε ένα πρόγραμμα εκδηλώσεων;**
	eh • kheh • teh eh • nah
	prohgh • rah • mah
	ehk • THee • loh • seh • ohn
What's playing at the movies [cinema] tonight?	**Τι παίζει ο κινηματογράφος απόψε;**
	tee peh • zee oh
	kee • nee • mah • tohgh • rah • fohs
	ah • poh • pseh
Where's...?	**Πού είναι...;**
	poo ee • neh...
the downtown area	**το κέντρο της πόλης**
	toh kehn • droh tees poh • lees
the bar	**το μπαρ**
	toh bahr

the dance club	**η ντισκοτέκ** *ee dees • koh • <u>tehk</u>*
Is there a cover charge?	**Υπάρχει κουβέρ;** *ee • <u>pahr</u> • hee koo • <u>vehr</u>*

(i)

Nightlife in Greece is excellent. There are a great number of cafes, bars and dance and music clubs throughout cities and on the islands. Greeks will often start the evening around 10:00 p.m.; the evening will most likely go on well into the early hours at a nightclub or at **μπουζούκια** (*boo • <u>zoo</u> • kee • ah*), live music clubs. **Bouzoukia** are a big part of Greek nightlife, where Greeks often reserve a table and spend the evening listening, throwing flowers at their favorite singers and sometimes dancing on the tables. These clubs offer a range of musical genres: from traditional Greek music to contemporary pop. A typical evening there would end at around 5:00 a.m., when you will often encounter traffic jams along the main club strips. Clubbing is also very popular, with open-air summer clubs operating from about April to October.

ENTERTAINMENT

Can you recommend...?	**Μπορείτε να συστήσετε...;** *boh • <u>ree</u> • teh nah sees • <u>tee</u> • seh • teh...*
a concert	**μια συναυλία** *miah see • nahv • <u>lee</u> • ah*
a movie	**μια ταινία** *miah teh • <u>nee</u> • ah*
an opera	**μια όπερα** *miah <u>oh</u> • peh • rah*

a play	μια θεατρική παράσταση
	miah theh•aht•ree•<u>kee</u>
	pah•<u>rahs</u>•tah•see
When does it	**Πότε αρχίζει/τελειώνει;**
start/end?	*<u>poh</u>•the ahr•<u>khee</u>•zee/teh•<u>lioh</u>•nee*
What's the dress	**Πώς πρέπει να ντυθώ;**
code?	*pohs <u>preh</u>•pee nah dee•<u>thoh</u>*
I like...	**Μου αρέσει...**
	moo ah•<u>reh</u>•see...
classical music	**η κλασική μουσική**
	ee klah•see•<u>kee</u> moo•see•<u>kee</u>
folk music	**η δημοτική μουσική**
	ee THee•moh•tee•<u>kee</u> moo•see•<u>kee</u>
jazz	**η τζαζ**
	ee jahz
pop music	**η ποπ μουσική**
	ee pohp moo•see•<u>kee</u>
rap	**η ραπ**
	ee rahp

For Tickets, see page 50.

NIGHTLIFE

YOU MAY HEAR...

Παρακαλώ απενεργοποιήστε τα	Turn off
κινητά σας τηλέφωνα.	your mobile
pah•rah•kah•<u>loh</u>	phones, please.
ah•peh•nehr•ghoh•pee•<u>ees</u>•teh	
tah kee•nee•<u>tah</u> sahs tee•<u>leh</u>•foh•nah	

What's there to do in the evenings/ at night?	**Τι μπορώ να κάνω τα βράδια;/τη νύχτα;**
	tee boh • roh nah kah • noh tah vrahTH • yah/tee nee • khtah
Can you recommend...?	**Μπορείτε να συστήσετε...;**
	boh • ree • teh nah sees • tee • seh • teh...
a bar	**ένα μπαρ**
	eh • nah bahr
a cabaret	**ένα καμπαρέ**
	eh • nah kah • bah • reh
a casino	**ένα καζίνο**
	eh • nah kah • zee • noh
a dance club	**μια ντισκοτέκ**
	miah dees • koh • tehk
a gay club	**ένα κλαμπ για γκέι**
	eh • nah geh • ee klahb
a jazz club	**ένα κλαμπ με τζαζ μουσική**
	eh • nah klahb meh jahz moo • see • kee
a club with local music	**ένα κλαμπ με τοπική μουσική**
	eh • nah klahb meh toh • pee • kee moo • see • kee
Is there live music?	**Παίζει live μουσική;**
	peh • zee lah • eev moo • see • kee
How do I get there?	**Πώς πάω εκεί;**
	pohs pah • oh eh • kee

Is there a cover charge?	**Το κουβέρ χρεώνεται;** *toh koo • vehr khreh • oh • neh • teh*
Let's go dancing.	**Πάμε για χορό.** *pah • meh yah khoh • roh*
Is this area safe at night?	**Η περιοχή είναι ασφαλής τη νύχτα;** *ee peh • ree • oh • khee ee • neh ah • sfah • lees tee nee • khtah*

For The Dating Game, see page 225.

For The Dating Game, see page 225.

The Athens Festival takes place every summer and includes various concerts and theatrical performances particularly in the Odeion of Herod Atticus and the Epidaurus Ancient Theater, among other venues. Look out for feast days, especially on the islands. Some smaller villages or towns will often hold an amazing party with food, drink and music to celebrate the feast day of the patron saint of the local church or of the town.

Very useful information in English can be found in the Athens News, a newspaper which includes TV, movie, theater and other cultural listings. *Athens News* also includes information on where to buy tickets for various events.

ROMANCE

NEED TO KNOW

Would you like to go out for a drink/ dinner?	**Θέλετε να βγούμε για ποτό/φαγητό;** _theh • leh • teh nah vghoo • meh yah poh • toh/fah • yee • toh_
What are your plans for tonight/ tomorrow?	**Ποια είναι τα σχέδιά σας για απόψε/αύριο;** _piah ee • neh tah skheh • THee • ah sahs yah ah • poh • pseh/ahv • ree • oh_
Can I have your number?	**Μπορώ να έχω τον αριθμό τηλεφώνου σας;** _boh • roh nah eh • khoh tohn ah • reeth • moh tee • leh • foh • noo sahs_
May we join you?	**Να έρθουμε μαζί σας;** _nah ehr • thoo • meh mah • zee sahs_
Let me buy you a drink.	**Να σε κεράσω ένα ποτό.** _nah seh keh • rah • soh eh • nah poh • toh_
I like you.	**Μου αρέσεις.** _moo ah • reh • sees_
I love you.	**Σ' αγαπώ.** _sah • ghah • poh_

THE DATING GAME

Would you like to go out for coffee?	**Θα θέλατε να βγούμε για καφέ;** _thah theh • lah • teh nah vghoo • meh yah kah • feh_
Would you like to go out for a drink/to dinner?	**Θέλεις να βγεις για ποτό/φαγητό;** _theh • lees nah vghees yah poh • toh/ fah • ghee • toh_

What are your plans for…?	**Ποια είναι τα σχέδιά σας για…;**
	piah ee • neh tah skheh • THee • ah sahs yah…
tonight	**απόψε**
	ah • poh • pseh
tomorrow	**αύριο**
	ahv • ree • oh
this weekend	**αυτό το Σαββατοκύριακο**
	ahf • toh toh sah • vah • toh • kee • riah • koh
Where would you like to go?	**Πού θα θέλατε να πάμε;**
	poo thah theh • lah • the nah pah • meh
I'd like to go to…	**Θα ήθελα να πάω…**
	thah ee • theh • lah nah pah • oh…
Do you like…?	**Σου αρέσει…;**
	soo ah • reh • see…
Can I have your number/e-mail?	**Μου δίνετε το τηλέφωνο/e-mail σας;**
	moo THee • neh • teh toh tee • leh • foh • noh/ee • meh • eel sahs
Are you on Facebook/Twitter?	**Είσαι στο Facebook/Twitter;**
	ee • seh stoh Facebook/Twitter
Can I join you?	**Να έρθω κι εγώ στην παρέα σας;**
	nah ehr • thoh kee eh • ghoh steen pah • reh • ah sahs
You look great!	**Είστε πολύ όμορφος** m **/όμορφη** f **!**
	ee • steh poh • lee oh • mohr • fohs/ oh • mohr • fee
Shall we go somewhere quieter?	**Πάμε κάπου πιο ήσυχα;**
	pah • meh kah • poo pioh ee • see • khah

For Communications, see page 89.

ACCEPTING & REJECTING

Thank you.	**Ευχαριστώ. Θα το ήθελα πολύ.**
I'd love to.	ehf•khah•rees•<u>toh</u> thah toh <u>ee</u>•theh•lah poh•<u>lee</u>
Where should we meet?	**Πού θα συναντηθούμε;**
	poo thah see•nahn•dee•<u>thoo</u>•meh
I'll meet you at the bar/your hotel.	**Θα σε συναντήσω στο μπαρ/στο ξενοδοχείο σου.**
	thah seh see•nahn•<u>dee</u>•soh stoh bahr/ stoh kseh•noh•THoh•<u>khee</u>•oh soo
I'll come by at…	**Θα περάσω στις…**
	thah peh•<u>rah</u>•soh stees…
Thank you, but I'm busy.	**Σας ευχαριστώ, αλλά είμαι πολύ απασχολημένος** m /**απασχολημένη** f.
	sahs ehf•khah•rees•<u>toh</u> ah•lah <u>ee</u>•meh poh•<u>lee</u> ah•pahs•khoh•lee•<u>meh</u>•nohs/ ah•pahs•khoh•lee•<u>meh</u>•nee
I'm not interested.	**Δεν ενδιαφέρομαι.**
	THehn ehn•THee•ah•<u>feh</u>•roh•meh
Leave me alone, please!	**Σας παρακαλώ, αφήστε με ήσυχο** m / **ήσυχη** f!
	sahs pah•rah•kah•<u>loh</u> ah•<u>fees</u>•the meh <u>ee</u>•see•khoh/<u>ee</u>•see•khee
Stop bothering me!	**Σταματείστε να με ενοχλείτε!**
	stah•mah•<u>tee</u>•steh nah meh eh•noh•<u>khlee</u>•the

For Time, see page 24.

GETTING INTIMATE

Can I hug/kiss you?	**Μπορώ να σε αγκαλιάσω/φιλήσω;**
	boh • <u>roh</u> nah seh ahn • gah • <u>liah</u> • soh/
	fee • <u>lee</u> • soh
Yes.	**Ναι.**
	neh
No.	**Όχι.**
	<u>oh</u> • khee
Stop!	**Σταμάτα!**
	stah • <u>mah</u> • tah
I love you.	**Σ' αγαπώ.**
	sah • ghah • <u>poh</u>

SEXUAL PREFERENCES

Are you gay?	**Είσαι γκέι;**
	<u>ee</u> • seh <u>geh</u> • ee
I'm...	**Είμαι...**
	<u>ee</u> • meh...
heterosexual	**ετεροφυλόφιλος** *m* /**ετεροφυλόφιλη** *f*
	eh • teh • roh • fee • <u>loh</u> • fee • lohs/
	eh • teh • roh • fee • <u>loh</u> • fee • lee

homosexual	**ομοφυλόφιλος** m /**ομοφυλόφιλη** f
	oh • moh • fee • *loh* • fee • lohs/
	oh • moh • fee • *loh* • fee • lee
bisexual	**αμφιφυλόφιλος** m /**αμφιφυλόφιλη** f
	ahm • fee • fee • *loh* • fee • lohs/
	ahm • fee • fee • *loh* • fee • lee
Do you like men/women?	**Σου αρέσουν οι άνδρες/γυναίκες;**
	soo ah • *reh* • soon ee *ahn* • THrehs/
	ghee • *neh* • kehs

DICTIONARY

GREEK–ENGLISH

A

access n **πρόσβαση** <u>prohz</u>·vah·see
accessory **αξεσουάρ** ah·kseh·soo·<u>ahr</u>
accident **ατύχημα** ah·<u>tee</u>·khee·mah
accompany **συνοδεύω** see·noh·<u>THeh</u>·voh
account n **λογαριασμός**
   loh·ghahr·yahz·<u>mohs</u>
adaptor **προσαρμοστής**
   proh·sahr·moh·<u>stees</u>
address n **διεύθυνση** THee·<u>ehf</u>·theen·see
admission **είσοδος** <u>ee</u>·soh·Thohs
adult **ενήλικας** eh·<u>nee</u>·lee·kahs
advance **προκαταβολή**
   proh·kah·tah·voh·<u>lee</u>
after **μετά** meh·<u>tah</u>
afternoon **απόγευμα** ah·<u>poh</u>·yehv·mah
after-sun lotion **λοσιόν μετά την**
   ηλιοθεραπεία loh·<u>siohn</u> meh·<u>tah</u> teen
   ee·lioh·theh·rah·<u>pee</u>·ah
age n **ηλικία** ee·lee·<u>kee</u>·ah
agree **συμφωνώ** seem·foh·<u>noh</u>
air conditioning **κλιματισμός**
   klee·mah·teez·<u>mohs</u>
air pump n **αντλία αέρος** ahn·<u>dlee</u>·ah
   ah·<u>eh</u>·rohs
airline **αεροπορική εταιρία**
   ah·eh·roh·poh·ree·<u>kee</u> eh·the·<u>ree</u>·ah
airmail **αεροπορικώς**
   ah·eh·roh·poh·ree·<u>kohs</u>

airport **αεροδρόμιο**
   ah·eh·roh·<u>THroh</u>·mee·oh
aisle seat **διάδρομος**
   THee·<u>ah</u>·Throh·mohs
allergic **αλλεργικός** ahl·ehr·yee·<u>kohs</u>
allergy **αλλεργία** ah·lehr·<u>yee</u>·ah
alone **μόνος** <u>moh</u>·nohs
aluminum foil **αλουμινόχαρτο**
   ah·loo·mee·<u>noh</u>·khah·rtoh
amazing **καταπληκτικός**
   kah·tah·pleek·tee·<u>kohs</u>
ambassador **πρεσβευτής** prehz·vehf·<u>tees</u>
amber **κεχριμπάρι** kehkh·reem·<u>bah</u>·ree
ambulance **ασθενοφόρο**
   ahs·theh·noh·<u>foh</u>·roh
American adj **αμερικάνικος**
   ah·meh·ree·<u>kah</u>·nee·kohs; (nationality)
   Αμερικανός ah·meh·ree·kah·<u>nohs</u>
amount n **ποσό** poh·<u>soh</u>
amusement park **πάρκο ψυχαγωγίας**
   <u>pahr</u>·koh psee·khah·ghoh·<u>yee</u>·ahs
animal **ζώο** <u>zoh</u>·oh
another **άλλος** <u>ah</u>·lohs
antibiotic **αντιβιοτικό**
   ahn·dee·vee·oh·tee·<u>koh</u>
antiques store **κατάστημα με αντίκες**
   kah·<u>tah</u>·stee·mah meh ahn·<u>tee</u>·kehs
antiseptic cream **αντισηπτική κρέμα**
   ahn·dee·seep·tee·<u>kee</u> <u>kreh</u>·mah

---

adj adjective	**BE** British English	**prep** preposition
adv adverb	**n** noun	**v** verb

anything οτιδήποτε oh·tee·<u>THee</u>·poh·teh

apartment διαμέρισμα THee·ah·<u>meh</u>·reez·mah

apologize ζητώ συγγνώμη zee·<u>toh</u> seegh·<u>noh</u>·mee

appendix σκωληκοειδίτιδα skoh·lee·koh·ee·<u>THee</u>·tee·THah

appointment ραντεβού rahn·deh·<u>voo</u>

architecture αρχιτεκτονική ahr·khee·teh·ktoh·nee·<u>kee</u>

area code κωδικός περιοχής koh·THee·<u>kohs</u> peh·ree·oh·<u>khees</u>

arm n **χέρι** <u>kheh</u>·ree

arrange κανονίζω kah·noh·<u>nee</u>·zoh

arrest v **συλλαμβάνω** see·lahm·<u>vah</u>·noh

arrive φτάνω <u>ftah</u>·noh

art τέχνη <u>tekh</u>·nee

art gallery γκαλερί τέχνης gah·leh·<u>ree</u> <u>tekh</u>·nees

ashtray σταχτοδοχείο stakh·toh·THoh·<u>khee</u>·oh

ask ζητώ zee·<u>toh</u>

aspirin ασπιρίνη ahs·pee·<u>ree</u>·nee

asthmatic ασθματικός ahsth·mah·tee·<u>kohs</u>

ATM ATM ehee·tee·<u>ehm</u>

attack n **επίθεση** eh·<u>pee</u>·theh·see; v **επιτίθεμαι** eh·pee·<u>tee</u>·theh·meh

attractive ελκυστικός ehl·kees·tee·<u>kohs</u>

authenticity αυθεντικότητα ahf·thehn·dee·<u>koh</u>·tee·tah

B

baby μωρό moh·<u>roh</u>

baby food βρεφική τροφή vreh·fee·<u>kee</u> troh·<u>fee</u>

baby seat καρέκλα μωρού kah·<u>reh</u>·klah moh·<u>roo</u>

babysitter μπέιμπι σίτερ <u>beh</u>·ee·bee see·tehr

back n **πλάτη** <u>plah</u>·tee

back ache πόνος στην πλάτη <u>poh</u>·nohs steen <u>plah</u>·tee

backgammon τάβλι <u>tah</u>·vlee

bad κακός kah·<u>kohs</u>

baggage αποσκευές ah·pohs·keh·<u>vehs</u>

baggage check φύλαξη αποσκευών fee·lah·ksee ah·poh·skeh·<u>vohn</u>

baggage reclaim παραλαβή αποσκευών pah·rah·lah·<u>vee</u> ah·poh·skeh·<u>vohn</u>

bakery αρτοποιείο ah·rtoh·pee·<u>ee</u>·oh

balcony μπαλκόνι bahl·<u>koh</u>·nee

ballet μπαλέτο bah·<u>leh</u>·toh

bandage γάζα <u>ghah</u>·zah

bank τράπεζα <u>trah</u>·peh·zah

bank account λογαριασμός τραπέζης loh·ghahr·yahz·<u>mohs</u> trah·<u>peh</u>·zees

bank loan τραπεζικό δάνειο trah·peh·zee·<u>koh</u> <u>THah</u>·nee·oh

bar μπαρ bahr

barber κουρείο koo·<u>ree</u>·oh

basket καλάθι kah·<u>lah</u>·THee

basketball μπάσκετ <u>bah</u>·skeht

bathing suit μαγιό mah·<u>yoh</u>

bathroom μπάνιο <u>bah</u>·nioh

battery μπαταρία bah·tah·<u>ree</u>·ah

beach παραλία pah·rah·<u>lee</u>·ah

beautiful όμορφος <u>oh</u>·mohr·fohs

bed κρεβάτι kreh·<u>vah</u>·tee

bed and breakfast διαμονή με πρωινό THiah·moh·<u>nee</u> meh proh·ee·<u>noh</u>

bedding σεντόνια sehn·<u>doh</u>·niah

bedroom υπνοδωμάτιο
eep·noh·<u>THoh</u>·<u>mah</u>·tee·oh

before πριν preen

beginner αρχάριος ahr·<u>khah</u>·ree·ohs

belong ανήκω ah·<u>nee</u>·koh

belt ζώνη <u>zoh</u>·nee

bicycle ποδήλατο poh·<u>THee</u>·lah·toh

big μεγάλος meh·<u>ghah</u>·lohs

bikini μπικίνι bee·<u>kee</u>·nee

bird πουλί poo·<u>lee</u>

bite n (insect) **τσίμπημα** <u>tsee</u>·bee·mah

bladder ουροδόχος κύστη
oo·roh·<u>THoh</u>·khohs <u>kee</u>·stee

blanket κουβέρτα koo·<u>veh</u>·rtah

bleed αιμορραγία eh·moh·rah·<u>yee</u>·ah;
v **αιμορραγώ** eh·moh·rah·<u>yoh</u>

blinds περσίδες peh·<u>rsee</u>·THehs

blister φουσκάλα foo·<u>skah</u>·lah

blood αίμα <u>eh</u>·mah

blood group ομάδα αίματος
oh·<u>mah</u>·THah <u>eh</u>·mah·tohs

blood pressure πίεση <u>pee</u>·eh·see

blouse μπλούζα <u>bloo</u>·zah

boarding card κάρτα επιβίβασης
<u>kah</u>·rtah eh·pee·<u>vee</u>·vah·sees

boat βάρκα <u>vahr</u>·kah

boat trip ταξίδι με πλοίο tah·<u>ksee</u>·THee
meh <u>plee</u>·oh

body σώμα <u>soh</u>·mah

bone οστό oh·<u>stoh</u>

book n **βιβλίο** veev·<u>lee</u>·oh; v **κάνω
κράτηση** <u>kah</u>·noh <u>krah</u>·tee·see

bookstore βιβλιοπωλείο
veev·lee·oh·poh·<u>lee</u>·oh

boot μπότα <u>boh</u>·tah

border (country) **σύνορο** <u>see</u>·noh·roh

boring βαρετός vah·reh·<u>tohs</u>

borrow δανείζομαι THah·<u>nee</u>·zoh·meh

botanical garden βοτανικός κήπος
voh·tah·nee·<u>kohs</u> <u>kee</u>·pohs

bottle μπουκάλι boo·<u>kah</u>·lee

bottle opener τιρμπουσόν
teer·boo·<u>sohn</u>

bowel έντερο <u>ehn</u>·deh·roh

box office ταχυδρομική θυρίδα
tah·khee·THroh·mee·<u>kee</u> THee·<u>ree</u>·THah

boxing n **μποξ** bohks

boy αγόρι ah·<u>ghoh</u>·ree

boyfriend φίλος <u>fee</u>·lohs

bra σουτιέν soo·<u>tiehn</u>

break n **διάλειμμα** THee·<u>ah</u>·lee·mah; v
σπάω <u>spah</u>·oh

breakdown n (car) **βλάβη** <u>vlah</u>·vee

breakfast πρωινό proh·ee·<u>noh</u>

break-in n **διάρρηξη** THee·<u>ah</u>·ree·ksee

breast στήθος <u>stee</u>·THohs

breathe αναπνέω ah·nahp·<u>neh</u>·oh

breathtaking φαντασμαγορικός
fahn·dahz·mah·ghoh·ree·<u>kohs</u>

bridge n (over water) **γέφυρα** <u>yeh</u>·fee·rah;
(card game) **μπριτζ** breetz

briefcase χαρτοφύλακας
khah·rtoh·<u>fee</u>·lah·kahs

briefs (men's, women's) **σλιπ** sleep
(women's); **κυλοτάκι** kee·loh·<u>tah</u>·kee

bring φέρνω <u>fehr</u>·noh

Britain Βρετανία vreh·tah·<u>nee</u>·ah

British adj **βρετανικός** vreh·tah·nee·<u>kohs</u>;
(nationality) **Βρετανός** vreh·tah·<u>nohs</u>

brochure φυλλάδιο fee·<u>lah</u>·THee·oh

broken σπασμένος spahz·<u>meh</u>·nohs

broom n **σκούπα** <u>skoo</u>·pah

browse ξεφυλλίζω kseh·fee·<u>lee</u>·zoh

bruise n **μελανιά** meh·lah·<u>niah</u>

brush n **βούρτσα** <u>voor</u>·tsah; v **βουρτσίζω**
voor·<u>tsee</u>·zoh

build **κτίζω** ktee·zoh

building **κτίριο** ktee·ree·oh

burn n **έγκαυμα** eh·gahv·mah

bus **λεωφορείο** leh·oh·foh·ree·oh

bus route **διαδρομή λεωφορείων** THee·ah·THroh·mee leh·oh·foh·ree·ohn

bus station **σταθμός λεωφορείων** stahTH·mohs leh·oh·foh·ree·ohn

bus stop **στάση λεωφορείου** stah·see leh·oh·foh·ree·oo

business class **μπίζνες θέση** bee·znehs theh·see

business trip **επαγγελματικό ταξίδι** eh·pah·gehl·mah·tee·koh tah·ksee·THee

busy (occupied) **απασχολημένος** ah·pahs·khoh·lee·meh·nohs

but **αλλά** ah·lah

butane gas **υγραέριο** eegh·rah·eh·ree·oh

butcher shop **κρεοπωλείο** kreh·oh·poh·lee·oh

button **κουμπί** koo·bee

buy **αγοράζω** ah·ghoh·rah·zoh

C

cabaret **καμπαρέ** kah·bah·reh

cabin **καμπίνα** kah·bee·nah

cable car **τελεφερίκ** teh·leh·feh·reek

cafe **καφετέρια** kah·feh·teh·ree·ah

calendar **ημερολόγιο** ee·meh·roh·loh·yee·oh

call collect **με χρέωση του καλούμενου** meh khreh·oh·see too kah·loo·meh·noo

call n **κλήση** klee·see; v **καλώ** kah·loh

camcorder **φορητή βιντεοκάμερα** foh·ree·tee vee·deh·oh·kah·meh·rah

camera **φωτογραφική μηχανή** foh·tohgh·rah·fee·kee mee·khah·nee

camera case **θήκη μηχανής** thee·kee mee·khah·nees

camera store **κατάστημα με φωτογραφικά είδη** kah·tah·stee·mah meh foh·tohgh·rah·fee·kah ee·THee

camp bed **κρεβάτι εκστρατείας** kreh·vah·tee ehk·strah·tee·ahs

camping **κάμπινγκ** kah·mpeeng

camping equipment **εξοπλισμός κάμπινγκ** eh·ksohp·leez·mohs kah·mpeeng

campsite **χώρος κάμπινγκ** khoh·rohs kah·mpeeng

can opener **ανοιχτήρι** ah·neekh·tee·ree

Canada **Καναδάς** kah·nah·THahs

canal **κανάλι** kah·nah·lee

cancel v **ακυρώνω** ah·kee·roh·noh

cancer (disease) **καρκίνος** kahr·kee·nohs

candle **κερί** keh·ree

canoe **κανό** kah·noh

car **αυτοκίνητο** ahf·toh·kee·nee·toh

car park [BE] **χώρος στάθμευσης** khoh·rohs stahth·mehf·sees

car rental **ενοικίαση αυτοκινήτων** eh·nee·kee·ah·see ahf·toh·kee·nee·tohn

car wash **πλύσιμο αυτοκινήτου** plee·see·moh ahf·toh·kee·nee·too

carafe **καράφα** kah·rah·fah

caravan **τροχόσπιτο** troh·khohs·pee·toh

cards **χαρτιά** khahr·tiah

carpet (fitted) **μοκέτα** moh·keh·tah

carton **κουτί** koo·tee

cash desk [BE] **ταμείο** tah·mee·oh

cash n **μετρητά** meht·ree·tah; v **εξαργυρώνω** eh·ksahr·ghee·roh·noh

casino **καζίνο** kah·see·noh

castle **κάστρο** kahs·troh

catch v (bus) **παίρνω** pehr·noh

cathedral **καθεδρικός ναός**
kah·theh·THree·kohs nah·ohs

cave n **σπήλαιο** spee·leh·oh

CD **σι ντι** see dee

cell phone **κινητό** kee·nee·toh

change n **αλλαγή** ah·lah·yee; v **αλλάζω**
ah·lah·zoh

cheap **φτηνός** ftee·nohs

check n (bank) **επιταγή**
eh·pee·tah·yee; (bill) **λογαριασμός**
loh·ghahr·yahz·mohs

choose **διαλέγω** THiah·leh·ghoh

clean **καθαρός** kah·thah·rohs

cling film [BE] **διαφανή μεμβράνη**
THee·ah·fah·nee mehm·vrah·nee

clothing store **κατάστημα ρούχων**
kah·tahs·tee·mah roo·khohn

cold adj (temperature) **κρύος**
kree·ohs; n (chill) **κρυολόγημα**
kree·oh·loh·yee·mah

collapse v **καταρρέω** kah·tah·reh·oh

collect v **παίρνω** peh·rnoh

color n **χρώμα** khroh·mah

comb n **χτένα** khteh·nah; v **χτενίζω**
khteh·nee·zoh

come **έρχομαι** ehr·khoh·meh

come back v (return) **επιστρέφω**
eh·pees·treh·foh

commission n (agent fee) **προμήθεια**
proh·mee·thee·ah

company n (business) **εταιρία**
eh·teh·ree·ah; (companionship) **παρέα**
pah·reh·ah

complain **παραπονιέμαι**
pah·rah·poh·nieh·meh

computer **υπολογιστής**
ee·poh·loh·yee·stees

concert **συναυλία** see·nahv·lee·ah

concert hall **αίθουσα συναυλιών**
eh·thoo·sah see·nahv·lee·ohn

conditioner (hair) **γαλάκτωμα για τα
μαλλιά** ghah·lah·ktoh·mah yah tah
mah·liah

condom **προφυλακτικό**
proh·fee·lah·ktee·koh

conference **συνέδριο** see·neh·THree·oh

confirm **επιβεβαιώνω**
eh·pee·veh·veh·oh·noh

constipation **δυσκοιλιότητα**
thees·kee·lee·oh·tee·tah

Consulate **Προξενείο** proh·kseh·nee·oh

consult v **συμβουλεύομαι**
seem·voo·leh·voh·meh

contact v **επικοινωνώ**
eh·pee·kee·noh·noh

contact fluid **υγρό για φακούς επαφής**
eegh·roh yah fah·koos eh·pah·fees

contact lens **φακός επαφής** fah·kohs
eh·pah·fees

contagious **μεταδοτικός**
meh·tah·THoh·tee·kohs

contain **περιέχω** peh·ree·eh·khoh

contraceptive pill **αντισυλληπτικό χάπι**
ahn·dee·see·leep·tee·koh khah·pee

cook n (chef) **μάγειρας** mah·yee·rahs; v
μαγειρεύω mah·yee·reh·voh

copper **χαλκός** khahl·kohs

corkscrew **τιρμπουσόν** teer·boo·sohn

corner **γωνία** ghoh·nee·ah

correct v **διορθώνω** THee·ohr·thoh·noh

cosmetics **καλλυντικά** kah·leen·dee·kah

cot [BE] **παιδικό κρεβάτι** peh·THee·koh
kreh·vah·tee

cotton **βαμβάκι** vahm·vah·kee

cough n **βήχας** vee·khahs; v **βήχω** vee·khoh

counter **ταμείο** tah·mee·oh

country (nation) **χώρα** <u>khoh</u>·rah
countryside **εξοχή** eh·ksoh·<u>khee</u>
couple n (pair) **ζευγάρι** zehv·<u>ghah</u>·ree
courier n (messenger) **κούριερ**
koo·ree·ehr
court house **δικαστήριο**
THee·kahs·<u>tee</u>·ree·oh
cramp n **κράμπα** <u>krahm</u>·bah
credit card **πιστωτική κάρτα**
pees·toh·tee·<u>kee</u> kahr·tah
crib [cot BE] **παιδικό κρεβάτι**
peh·THee·<u>koh</u> kreh·<u>vah</u>·tee
crown n (dental, royal) **κορώνα**
koh·<u>roh</u>·nah
cruise n **κρουαζιέρα** kroo·ahz·<u>yeh</u>·rah
crutch n (walking support) **δεκανίκι**
THeh·kah·<u>nee</u>·kee
crystal n **κρύσταλλο** <u>kree</u>·stah·loh
cup **φλυτζάνι** flee·<u>jah</u>·nee
cupboard **ντουλάπα** doo·<u>lah</u>·pah
currency **νόμισμα** <u>noh</u>·meez·mah
currency exchange office **γραφείο**
ανταλλαγής συναλλάγματος
ghrah·<u>fee</u>·oh ahn·dah·lah·<u>yees</u>
see·nah·<u>lahgh</u>·mah·tohs
customs (tolls) **τελωνείο** teh·loh·<u>nee</u>·oh
customs declaration (tolls) **τελωνειακή**
δήλωση teh·loh·nee·ah·<u>kee</u>
<u>THee</u>·loh·see
cut n (wound) **κόψιμο** <u>koh</u>·psee·moh
cut glass n **σκαλιστό γυαλί** skah·lees·<u>toh</u>
yah·<u>lee</u>
cycle helmet **κράνος ποδηλάτη**
<u>krah</u>·nohs poh·THee·<u>lah</u>·tee
cyclist **ποδηλάτης** poh·THee·<u>lah</u>·tees
Cypriot adj **κυπριακός** keep·ree·ah·<u>kohs</u>;
(nationality) **Κύπριος** <u>kee</u>·pree·ohs
Cyprus **Κύπρος** <u>kee</u>·prohs

D

damage n **ζημιά** zee·<u>miah</u>; v
καταστρέφω kah·tah·<u>streh</u>·foh
dance v **χορεύω** khoh·<u>reh</u>·voh
dangerous **επικίνδυνος**
eh·pee·<u>keen</u>·THee·nohs
dark adj (color) **σκούρος** <u>skoo</u>·rohs
dawn n **ξημερώματα**
ksee·meh·<u>roh</u>·mah·tah
day trip **ημερήσια εκδρομή**
ee·meh·<u>ree</u>·see·ah ehk·THroh·<u>mee</u>
deaf **κουφός** koo·<u>fohs</u>
decide **αποφασίζω** ah·poh·fah·<u>see</u>·zoh
deck n **κατάστρωμα** kah·<u>tah</u>·stroh·mah
deck chair **σεζ-λονγκ** sehz <u>lohg</u>
declare **δηλώνω** THee·<u>loh</u>·noh
deduct (money) **αφαιρώ** ah·feh·<u>roh</u>
defrost **ξεπαγώνω** kseh·pah·<u>ghoh</u>·noh
degrees (temperature) **βαθμοί**
vahth·<u>mee</u>
delay n **καθυστέρηση**
kah·thee·<u>steh</u>·ree·see; v **καθυστερώ**
kah·thee·steh·<u>roh</u>
delicious **νόστιμος** <u>nohs</u>·tee·mohs
deliver **παραδίδω** pah·rah·<u>THee</u>·THoh
dental floss **οδοντικό νήμα**
oh·THohn·dee·<u>koh</u> <u>nee</u>·mah
dentist **οδοντίατρος**
oh·THohn·<u>dee</u>·ah·trohs
deodorant **αποσμητικό**
ah·pohz·mee·tee·<u>koh</u>
department store **πολυκατάστημα**
poh·lee·kah·<u>tahs</u>·tee·mah
departure (travel) **αναχώρηση**
ah·nah·<u>khoh</u>·ree·see
departure lounge **αίθουσα**
αναχωρήσεων <u>eh</u>·thoo·sah
ah·nah·khoh·<u>ree</u>·seh·ohn

depend **εξαρτώμαι** eh·ksahr·<u>toh</u>·meh

deposit n (down payment) **προκαταβολή**
proh·kah·tah·voh·<u>lee</u>

describe **περιγράφω** peh·reegh·<u>rah</u>·foh

designer **σχεδιαστής**
skheh·THee·ahs·<u>tees</u>

detergent **απορρυπαντικό**
ah·poh·ree·pahn·dee·<u>koh</u>

develop (photos) **εμφανίζω**
ehm·fah·<u>nee</u>·zoh

diabetes **διαβήτης** THee·ah·<u>vee</u>·tees

diabetic **διαβητικός**
THee·ah·vee·tee·<u>kohs</u>

diagnosis **διάγνωση** THee·<u>ahgh</u>·noh·see

dialing code **κωδικός** koh·THee·<u>kohs</u>

diamond n **διαμάντι** THiah·<u>mahn</u>·dee

diaper **πάνα μωρού** <u>pah</u>·nah moh·<u>roo</u>

diarrhea **διάρροια** THee·<u>ah</u>·ree·ah

dice n **ζάρια** <u>zah</u>·riah

dictionary **λεξικό** leh·ksee·<u>koh</u>

diesel **ντήζελ** <u>dee</u>·zehl

diet n **δίαιτα** THee·eh·tah

difficult **δύσκολος** THee·skoh·lohs

dining room **τραπεζαρία**
trah·peh·zah·<u>ree</u>·ah

dinner **βραδινό** vrah·<u>noh</u>

direct v **κατευθύνω** kah·tehf·<u>thee</u>·noh

direction n (instruction) **οδηγία**
oh·THee·<u>yee</u>·ah

dirty adj **βρώμικος** <u>vroh</u>·mee·kohs

disabled **άτομο με ειδικές ανάγκες**
<u>ah</u>·toh·moh meh ee·· ·<u>nahn</u> THee·<u>kehs</u>
ah ·gehs

discounted ticket **μειωμένο εισιτήριο**
mee·oh·<u>meh</u>·noh ee·see·<u>tee</u>·ree·oh

dishwashing liquid **λίγο υγρό πιάτων**
<u>lee</u>·ghoh ee·<u>ghroh</u> piah·tohn

district **περιφέρεια** peh·ree·<u>feh</u>·ree·ah

disturb **ενοχλώ** eh·noh·<u>khloh</u>

diving equipment **καταδυτικός
εξοπλισμός** kah·tah·THee·tee·<u>kohs</u>
eh·ksoh·pleez·<u>mohs</u>

divorced **διαζευγμένος**
THee·ah·zehv·<u>ghmeh</u>·nohs

dock **προκυμαία** proh·kee·<u>meh</u>·ah

doctor **γιατρός** yah·<u>trohs</u>

doll **κούκλα** <u>kook</u>·lah

dollar **δολάριο** THoh·<u>lah</u>·ree·oh

door **πόρτα** <u>pohr</u>·tah

dosage **δοσολογία** THoh·soh·loh·<u>yee</u>·ah

double adj **διπλός** THeep·<u>lohs</u>

double bed **διπλό κρεβάτι** THeep·<u>loh</u>
kreh·<u>vah</u>·tee

double room **δίκλινο δωμάτιο**
<u>THeek</u>·lee·noh THoh·<u>mah</u>·tee·oh

downtown area **κέντρο της πόλης**
kehn·droh tees <u>poh</u>·lees

dozen **ντουζίνα** doo·<u>zee</u>·nah

dress n **φόρεμα** <u>foh</u>·reh·mah

drink n **ποτό** poh·<u>toh</u>; v **πίνω** <u>pee</u>·noh

drive v **οδηγώ** oh·THee·<u>ghoh</u>

drugstore **φαρμακείο** fahr·mah·<u>kee</u>·oh

dry cleaner **καθαριστήριο**
kah·thah·rees·<u>tee</u>·ree·oh

dubbed **μεταγλωττισμένος**
meh·tahgh·loh·teez·<u>meh</u>·nohs

dusty **σκονισμένος** skoh·neez·<u>meh</u>·nohs

duty (customs) **φόρος** <u>foh</u>·rohs;
(obligation) **καθήκον** kah·<u>thee</u>·kohn

duty-free goods **αφορολόγητα είδη**
ah·foh·roh·<u>loh</u>·yee·tah ee·THee

duty-free shop **κατάστημα
αφορολόγητων** kah·<u>tahs</u>·tee·mah
ah·foh·roh·<u>loh</u>·yee·tohn

E

each κάθε ένα kah·theh eh·nah
ear αυτί ahf·tee
earache πόνος στο αυτί poh·nohs stoh ahf·tee
early νωρίς noh·rees
east ανατολικά ah·nah·toh·lee·kah
easy *adj* **εύκολος** ehf·koh·lohs
eat τρώω troh·oh
economical οικονομικός
ee·koh·noh·mee·kohs
economy class τουριστική θέση
too·rees·stee·kee theh·see
elastic ελαστικός eh·lahs·tee·kohs
electrical outlet πρίζα pree·zah
e-mail ηλεκτρονικό ταχυδρομείο
(e-mail) ee·lehk·troh·nee·koh
tah·hee·dro·mee·oh (ee·meh·eel)
embassy πρεσβεία prehz·vee·ah
emerald σμαράγδι zmah·rahgh·THee
emergency έκτακτη ανάγκη
ehk·tahk·tee ah·nah·gee
emergency exit έξοδος κινδύνου
eh·ksoh·THohs keen·THee·noo
empty *adj* **άδειος** ahTH·yohs
end *n* **τέλος** teh·lohs; *v* **τελειώνω**
teh·lee·oh·noh
engine μηχανή mee·khah·nee
England Αγγλία ahng·lee·ah
English *adj* **αγγλικός** ahng·lee·kohs;
(nationality) **Άγγλος** ahng·lohs;
(language) **αγγλικά** ahng·lee·kah
enjoy ευχαριστιέμαι
ehf·khah·rees·tieh·meh
enough αρκετά ahr·keh·tah
entertainment guide οδηγός
ψυχαγωγίας oh·THee·ghohs
psee·khah·ghoh·yee·ahs

entrance fee τιμή εισόδου tee·mee
ee·soh·THoo
epileptic επιληπτικός
eh·pee·leep·tee·kohs
error λάθος lah·thohs
escalator κυλιόμενες σκάλες
kee·lee·oh·meh·nehs skah·lehs
essential απαραίτητος
ah·pah·reh·tee·tohs
e-ticket ηλεκτρονικό εισιτήριο
ee·leh·ktroh·nee·koh ee·see·tee·ree·oh
European Union Ευρωπαϊκή Ένωση
ehv·roh·pah·ee·kee eh·noh·see
euro ευρώ ehv·roh
evening βράδυ vrah·THee
examination (medical) **ιατρική εξέταση**
ee·ah·tree·kee eh·kseh·tah·see
example παράδειγμα
pah·rah·THeegh·mah
excess baggage υπέρβαρο
ee·pehr·vah·roh
exchange *v* (money) **αλλάζω** ah·lah·zoh
exchange rate τιμή συναλλάγματος
tee·mee see·nah·lahgh·mah·tohs
excursion εκδρομή ehk·THroh·mee
exhibition έκθεση ehk·theh·see
exit *n* **έξοδος** eh·ksoh·THohs
expensive ακριβός ahk·ree·vohs
expiration date ημερομηνία λήξεως
ee·meh·roh·mee·nee·ah lee·kseh·ohs
exposure (photos) **στάση** stah·see
express (mail) **εξπρές** ehk·sprehs
extension (number) **εσωτερική**
γραμμή eh·soh·teh·ree·kee
ghrah·mee
extra (additional) **άλλο ένα** ah·loh
eh·nah
eye *n* **μάτι** mah·tee

F

fabric ύφασμα ee·fahs·mah

face n **πρόσωπο** proh·soh·poh

facial καθαρισμός προσώπου
kah·thah·reez·mohs proh·soh·poo

facility εξυπηρέτηση
eh·ksee·pee·reh·tee·see

faint λιποθυμώ lee·poh·thee·moh

fall v **πέφτω** pehf·toh

family οικογένεια ee·koh·yeh·nee·ah

famous διάσημος THee·ah·see·mohs

fan n (air) **ανεμιστήρας**
ah·neh·mees·tee·rahs

far adv **μακριά** mahk·ree·ah

fare εισιτήριο ee·see·tee·ree·oh

farm n **φάρμα** fahr·mah

fast adv **γρήγορα** ghree·ghoh·rah

fat adj (person) **παχύς** pah·khees

faucet βρύση vree·see

fault λάθος lah·thohs

favorite αγαπημένος
ah·ghah·pee·meh·nohs

fax facility υπηρεσία φαξ
ee·pee·reh·see·ah fahks

feed v **ταΐζω** tah·ee·zoh

female θηλυκός thee·lee·kohs

fence n **φράχτης** frahkh·tees

ferry φέρυ-μπωτ feh·ree·boht

festival φεστιβάλ fehs·tee·vahl

fever πυρετός pee·reh·tohs

fiancé αρραβωνιαστικός
ah·rah·voh·niahs·tee·kohs

fiancée αρραβωνιαστικιά
ah·rah·voh·niahs·tee·kiah

filling (dental) **σφράγισμα**
sfrah·yeez·mah

film n (camera) **φιλμ** feelm

filter n **φίλτρο** feel·troh

fine adv **καλά** kah·lah; n **πρόστιμο**
prohs·tee·moh

finger n **δάχτυλο** THakh·tee·loh

fire n **φωτιά** foh·tiah

fire brigade [BE] πυροσβεστική
pee·rohz·vehs·tee·kee

fire escape έξοδος κινδύνου
eh·ksoh·THohs keen·THee·noo

fire extinguisher πυροσβεστήρας
pee·rohz·vehs·tee·rahs

first class πρώτη θέση
proh·tee theh·see

first-aid kit κουτί πρώτων βοηθειών
koo·tee proh·tohn voh·ee·thee·ohn

fishing ψάρεμα psah·reh·mah

flag n **σημαία** see·meh·ah

flashlight φακός fah·kohs

flat adj **επίπεδος** eh·pee·peh·Thohs; n
διαμέρισμα THee·ah·mehr·ees·mah

flea ψύλλος psee·lohs

flight πτήση ptee·see

flight number αριθμός πτήσεως
ah·reeth·mohs ptee·seh·ohs

flip-flops σαγιονάρες sah·yoh·nah·rehs

flood n **πλημμύρα** plee·mee·rah

florist ανθοπωλείο ahn·thoh·poh·lee·oh

flower n **λουλούδι** loo·loo·THee

flu γρίπη ghree·pee

flush τραβώ το καζανάκι trah·voh toh
kah·zah·nah·kee

fly n **μύγα** mee·ghah; v **πετάω** peh·tah·oh

follow v **ακολουθώ** ah·koh·loo·thoh

foot πόδι poh·THee

football [BE] ποδόσφαιρο
poh·THohs·feh·roh

footpath μονοπάτι moh·noh·pah·tee

forecast n **πρόβλεψη** prohv·leh·psee

foreign ξένος kseh·nohs

foreign currency **ξένο συνάλλαγμα**
kseh·noh see·<u>nah</u>·lahgh·mah

forest n **δάσος** <u>THah</u>·sohs

forget **ξεχνώ** ksehkh·<u>noh</u>

form n **έντυπο** <u>ehn</u>·dee·poh

fortunately **ευτυχώς** ehf·tee·<u>khohs</u>

forward **προωθώ** proh·oh·<u>thoh</u>

fountain **συντριβάνι** seen·dree·<u>vah</u>·nee

free adj (available) **ελεύθερος**
eh·<u>lehf</u>·theh·rohs

freezer **κατάψυξη** kah·<u>tah</u>·psee·ksee

frequent adj **συχνός** seekh·<u>nohs</u>

fresh adj **φρέσκος** <u>frehs</u>·kohs

friend n **φίλος** <u>fee</u>·lohs

frightened **φοβισμένος**
foh·veez·<u>meh</u>·nohs

from **από** ah·<u>poh</u>

front n **προκυμαία** proh·kee·<u>meh</u>·ah

full adj **γεμάτος** yeh·<u>mah</u>·tohs

furniture **έπιπλα** <u>eh</u>·peep·lah

fuse n **ασφάλεια** ahs·<u>fah</u>·lee·ah

G

gambling **τζόγος** <u>joh</u>·ghohs

game (toy) **παιχνίδι** pehkh·<u>nee</u>·THee

garage **γκαράζ** gah·<u>rahz</u>

garden n **κήπος** <u>kee</u>·pohs

gas **βενζίνη** vehn·<u>zee</u>·nee

gas station **βενζινάδικο**
vehn·zee·<u>nah</u>·THee·koh

gastritis **γαστρίτιδα** ghahs·<u>tree</u>·tee·THah

gate (airport) **έξοδος** <u>eh</u>·ksoh·THohs

genuine **αυθεντικός** ahf·thehn·dee·<u>kohs</u>

get off (transport) **κατεβαίνω**
kah·teh·<u>veh</u>·noh

get out (of vehicle) **βγαίνω** <u>vyeh</u>·noh

gift **δώρο** <u>THoh</u>·roh

gift store **κατάστημα με είδη δώρων**
kah·<u>tahs</u>·tee·mah meh ee·THee <u>THoh</u>·rohn

girl **κορίτσι** koh·<u>ree</u>·tsee

girlfriend **φίλη** <u>fee</u>·lee

give **δίνω** <u>THee</u>·noh

glass (container) **ποτήρι** poh·<u>tee</u>·ree

glasses (optical) **γυαλιά** yah·<u>liah</u>

glove n **γάντι** <u>ghahn</u>·dee

go **πηγαίνω** pee·<u>yeh</u>·noh

gold n **χρυσός** khree·<u>sohs</u>

golf **γκόλφ** gohlf

golf course **γήπεδο γκολφ** <u>yee</u>·peh·THoh
gohlf

good **καλός** kah·<u>lohs</u>

grass **γρασίδι** ghrah·<u>see</u>·THee

gratuity **φιλοδώρημα**
fee·loh·<u>THoh</u>·ree·mah

greasy (hair, skin) **λιπαρός** lee·pah·<u>rohs</u>

Greece **Ελλάδα** eh·<u>lah</u>·THah

Greek adj **ελληνικός** eh·lee·nee·<u>kohs</u>;
(nationality) **Έλληνας** <u>eh</u>·lee·nahs

greengrocer [BE] **οπωροπωλείο**
oh·poh·roh·poh·<u>lee</u>·oh

ground (earth) **έδαφος** <u>eh</u>·THah·fohs

group n **γκρουπ** groop

guarantee n **εγγύηση** eh·<u>gee</u>·ee·see; v
εγγυώμαι eh·gee·<u>oh</u>·meh

guide book **τουριστικός οδηγός**
too·ree·stee·<u>kohs</u> oh·THee·<u>ghohs</u>

guided tour **ξενάγηση** kseh·<u>nah</u>·yee·see

guitar **κιθάρα** kee·<u>thah</u>·rah

gynecologist **γυναικολόγος**
yee·neh·koh·<u>loh</u>·ghohs

H

hair **μαλλιά** mah·<u>liah</u>

hairbrush **βούρτσα** <u>voor</u>·tsah

hair dresser κομμωτήριο
koh·moh·<u>tee</u>·ree·oh

hair dryer σεσουάρ seh·soo·<u>ahr</u>

half μισός mee·<u>sohs</u>

hammer σφυρί sfee·<u>ree</u>

hand *n* **χέρι** kheh·ree

hand luggage αποσκευές χειρός
ah·pohs·keh·<u>vehs</u> khee·<u>rohs</u>

handbag τσάντα <u>tsahn</u>·dah

handicraft λαϊκή τέχνη lah·ee·<u>kee</u>
tehkh·nee

handicapped-accessible toilet
προσβάσιμη τουαλέτα για
ανάπηρους prohs·<u>vah</u>·see·mee
too·ah·<u>leh</u>·tah yah ah·<u>nah</u>·pee·roos

handkerchief χαρτομάντηλο
khah·rtoh·<u>mahn</u>·dee·loh

handle *n* **πόμολο** poh·moh·loh

hanger κρεμάστρα kreh·<u>mahs</u>·trah

harbor *n* **λιμάνι** lee·<u>mah</u>·nee

hat καπέλο kah·<u>peh</u>·loh

have (possession) **έχω** <u>eh</u>·khoh

have to (obligation) **οφείλω**
oh·<u>fee</u>·loh

head *n* **κεφάλι** keh·<u>fah</u>·lee

headache πονοκέφαλος
poh·noh·<u>keh</u>·fah·lohs

health food store κατάστημα με
υγιεινές τροφές kah·<u>tahs</u>·tee·mah meh
ee·yee·ee·<u>nehs</u> troh·<u>fehs</u>

health insurance ασφάλεια υγείας
ahs·<u>fah</u>·lee·ah ee·<u>yee</u>·ahs

hearing aid ακουστικό βαρυκοΐας
ah·koo·stee·<u>koh</u> vah·ree·koh·<u>ee</u>·ahs

heart *v* **καρδιά** kahr·THee·<u>ah</u>

heart attack καρδιακό έμφραγμα
kahr·THee·ah·<u>koh</u> ehm·frahgh·mah

heat wave καύσωνας <u>kahf</u>·soh·nahs

heater (water) **θερμοσίφωνας**
thehr·moh·<u>see</u>·foh·nahs

heating θέρμανση <u>thehr</u>·mahn·see

heavy βαρύς vah·<u>rees</u>

height ύψος <u>ee</u>·psohs

helicopter ελικόπτερο
eh·lee·<u>kohp</u>·teh·roh

help *n* **βοήθεια** voh·<u>ee</u>·thee·ah; *v* **βοηθώ**
voh·ee·<u>thoh</u>

here εδώ eh·<u>THoh</u>

highway εθνική οδός ehth·nee·<u>kee</u>
oh·<u>THohs</u>

hike *v* **κάνω πεζοπορία** <u>kah</u>·noh
peh·zoh·poh·<u>ree</u>·ah

hill λόφος loh·fohs

hire [BE] *v* **νοικιάζω** nee·<u>kiah</u>·zoh

history ιστορία ee·stoh·<u>ree</u>·ah

hitchhiking οτοστόπ oh·toh·<u>stohp</u>

hobby (pastime) **χόμπι** <u>khoh</u>·bee

hold on περιμένω peh·ree·<u>meh</u>·noh

hole (in clothes) **τρύπα** <u>tree</u>·pah

holiday [BE] **διακοπές** THee·ah·koh·<u>pehs</u>

honeymoon μήνας του μέλιτος
<u>mee</u>·nahs too <u>meh</u>·lee·tohs

horse track ιπποδρόμιο
ee·poh·<u>THroh</u>·mee·oh

hospital νοσοκομείο
noh·soh·koh·<u>mee</u>·oh

hot (weather) **ζεστός** zehs·<u>tohs</u>

hot spring θερμή πηγή thehr·<u>mee</u>
pee·<u>yee</u>

hotel ξενοδοχείο kseh·noh·<u>THoh·khee</u>·oh

household articles **είδη οικιακής χρήσεως**
<u>ee</u>·THee ee·kee·ah·<u>kees</u> khree·seh·ohs

husband σύζυγος <u>see</u>·zee·ghohs

I

ice *n* **πάγος** pah·ghohs

identification **ταυτότητα**
tahf·<u>toh</u>·tee·tah

illegal **παράνομος** pah·<u>rah</u>·noh·mohs

illness **αρρώστεια** ahr·<u>ohs</u>·tee·ah

imitation **απομίμηση**
ah·poh·<u>mee</u>·mee·see

immediately **αμέσως** ah·<u>meh</u>·sohs

impressive **εντυπωσιακός**
ehn·dee·poh·see·ah·<u>kohs</u>

included **συμπεριλαμβάνεται**
seem·beh·ree·lahm·<u>vah</u>·neh·teh

indigestion **δυσπεψία**
THehs·peh·<u>psee</u>·ah

indoor **εσωτερικός** eh·soh·teh·ree·<u>kohs</u>

indoor pool **εσωτερική πισίνα**
eh·soh·teh·ree·<u>kee</u> pee·<u>see</u>·nah

inexpensive **φτηνός** ftee·<u>nohs</u>

infected **μολυσμένος**
moh·leez·<u>meh</u>·nohs

inflammation **φλεγμονή**
flegh·moh·<u>nee</u>

information **πληροφορίες**
plee·roh·foh·<u>ree</u>·ehs

information office **γραφείο**
πληροφοριών ghrah·<u>fee</u>·oh
plee·roh·foh·ree·<u>ohn</u>

injection **ένεση** <u>eh</u>·neh·see

injured **τραυματισμένος**
trahv·mah·teez·<u>meh</u>·nohs

innocent **αθώος** ah·<u>thoh</u>·ohs

insect bite **τσίμπημα από έντομο**
<u>tseem</u>·bee·mah ah·<u>poh</u> ehn·doh·moh

insect repellent **εντομοαπωθητικό**
ehn·doh·moh·ah·poh·thee·tee·<u>koh</u>

inside **μέσα** <u>meh</u>·sah

insist **επιμένω** eh·pee·<u>meh</u>·noh

insomnia **αϋπνία** ah·eep·<u>nee</u>·ah

instruction **οδηγία** oh·THee·<u>yee</u>·ah

insulin **ινσουλίνη** een·soo·<u>lee</u>·nee

insurance **ασφάλεια** ahs·<u>fah</u>·lee·ah

insurance certificate **πιστοποιητικό**
ασφάλειας pees·toh·pee·ee·tee·<u>koh</u>
ahs·<u>fah</u>·lee·ahs

insurance claim **ασφάλεια**
αποζημίωσης ahs·<u>fah</u>·lee·ah
ah·poh·zee·<u>mee</u>·oh·sees

insurance company **ασφαλιστική**
εταιρία ahs·fah·lees·tee·<u>kee</u>
eh·teh·<u>ree</u>·ah

interest rate **επιτόκιο**
eh·pee·<u>toh</u>·kee·oh

interesting **ενδιαφέρων**
ehn·THee·ah·<u>feh</u>·rohn

international **διεθνής** THee·eth·<u>nees</u>

International Student Card **διεθνής**
φοιτητική κάρτα THee·ehth·<u>nees</u>
fee·tee·tee·<u>kee</u> kahr·tah

internet **ίντερνετ** <u>ee</u>·nteh·rnet

internet cafe **ίντερνετ καφέ**
<u>ee</u>·nteh·rnet kah·<u>feh</u>

interpreter **διερμηνέας**
THee·ehr·mee·<u>neh</u>·ahs

interval **διάλειμμα** THee·<u>ah</u>·lee·mah

introduce **συστήνω** see·<u>stee</u>·noh

introductions **συστάσεις** see·<u>stah</u>·sees

invitation **πρόσκληση** <u>prohs</u>·klee·see

invite *v* **προσκαλώ** prohs·kah·<u>loh</u>

iodine **ιώδειο** ee·<u>oh</u>·THee·oh

iron *n* **σίδερο** <u>see</u>·THeh·roh; *v* **σιδερώνω**
see·THeh·<u>roh</u>·noh

itemized bill **αναλυτικός**
λογαριασμός ah·nah·lee·tee·<u>kohs</u>
loh·ghahr·yahz·<u>mohs</u>

J

jacket σακάκι sah·<u>kah</u>·kee
jammed σφηνωμένος sfee·noh·<u>meh</u>·nohs
jar n βάζο <u>vah</u>·zoh
jaw σαγόνι sah·<u>ghoh</u>·nee
jeans μπλου-τζην bloo·jeen
jellyfish μέδουσα <u>meh</u>·THoo·sah
jet-ski τζετ-σκι jeht·skee
jeweler κοσμηματοπωλείο
   kohz·mee·mah·toh·poh·<u>lee</u>·oh
job δουλειά THoo·liah
jogging τζόγκιγκ joh·geeng
joke n ανέκδοτο ah·<u>nehk</u>·THoh·toh
journey ταξίδι tah·<u>ksee</u>·THee
junction (intersection) κόμβος <u>kohm</u>·vohs

K

keep v κρατώ krah·<u>toh</u>
key n κλειδί klee·<u>THee</u>
key card κάρτα-κλειδί <u>kahr</u>·tah·klee·<u>dee</u>
key ring μπρελόκ breh·<u>lohk</u>
kidney νεφρό nehf·<u>roh</u>
kind είδος ee·THohs
king βασιλιάς vah·see·<u>liahs</u>
kiosk περίπτερο peh·<u>ree</u>·pteh·roh
kiss n φιλί fee·<u>lee</u>; v φιλώ fee·<u>loh</u>
kitchen χαρτί κουζίνας khah·<u>rtee</u>
   koo·<u>zee</u>·nahs
knapsack σάκκος <u>sah</u>·kohs
knee γόνατο <u>ghoh</u>·nah·toh
knife μαχαίρι mah·<u>kheh</u>·ree
know γνωρίζω ghnoh·<u>ree</u>·zoh

L

label n ετικέτα eh·tee·<u>keh</u>·tah
ladder σκάλα <u>skah</u>·lah

lake λίμνη <u>leem</u>·nee
lamp λάμπα <u>lahm</u>·bah
land n γη ghee; v προσγειώνομαι
   prohz·yee·<u>oh</u>·noh·meh
language course μάθημα ξένης
   γλώσσας <u>mah</u>·thee·mah <u>kseh</u>·nees
   ghloh·sahs
large adj μεγάλος meh·<u>ghah</u>·lohs
last τελευταίος teh·lehf·<u>teh</u>·ohs
late adv αργά ahr·<u>ghah</u>
laugh v γελώ yeh·<u>loh</u>
laundry facility πλυντήριο
   pleen·<u>dee</u>·ree·oh
lavatory μπάνιο <u>bah</u>·nioh
lawyer δικηγόρος THee·kee·<u>ghoh</u>·rohs
laxative καθαρτικό kah·thahr·tee·<u>koh</u>
learn μαθαίνω mah·<u>theh</u>·noh
leave v (depart) φεύγω <u>fehv</u>·ghoh; (let
   go) αφήνω ah·<u>fee</u>·noh
left adj αριστερός ah·rees·teh·<u>rohs</u>; adv
   αριστερά ah·rees·teh·<u>rah</u>
leg πόδι poh·THee
legal νόμιμος <u>noh</u>·mee·mohs
lend δανείζω THah·<u>nee</u>·zoh
length μήκος <u>mee</u>·kohs
lens φακός fah·<u>kohs</u>
lens cap κάλυμμα φακού <u>kah</u>·lee·mah
   fah·<u>koo</u>
less λιγότερο lee·<u>ghoh</u>·teh·roh
letter γράμμα <u>ghrah</u>·mah
level (even) επίπεδο eh·<u>pee</u>·peh·THoh
library βιβλιοθήκη veev·lee·oh·<u>thee</u>·kee
lie down ξαπλώνω ksah·<u>ploh</u>·noh
life boat ναυαγοσωστική λέμβος
   nah·vah·ghoh·sohs·tee·<u>kee</u> <u>lehm</u>·vohs
lifeguard ναυαγοσώστης
   nah·vah·ghoh·<u>sohs</u>·tees
life jacket σωσίβιο soh·<u>see</u>·vee·oh

lift [BE] *n* (elevator) **ασανσέρ**
ah-sahn-<u>sehr</u>

lift pass άδεια σκι ah-<u>THee</u>-ah skee

light *adj* (color) **ανοιχτός** ah-neekh-<u>tohs</u>;
n (electric) **φως** fohs

light bulb λάμπα <u>lahm</u>-bah

lighter *adj* **ανοιχτότερος**
ah-neekh-<u>toh</u>-teh-rohs; *n* **αναπτήρας**
ah-nahp-<u>tee</u>-rahs

lighthouse φάρος <u>fah</u>-rohs

lights (car) **φώτα** <u>foh</u>-tah

line *n* (subway) **γραμμή** ghrah-<u>mee</u>

lips χείλη <u>khee</u>-lee

lipstick κραγιόν krah-<u>yohn</u>

liter λίτρο <u>lee</u>-troh

little μικρός meek-<u>rohs</u>

liver συκώτι see-<u>koh</u>-tee

living room σαλόνι sah-<u>loh</u>-nee

local τοπικός toh-pee-<u>kohs</u>

location (space) **θέση** <u>theh</u>-see

lock *n* (door) **κλειδαριά** klee-THahr-<u>yah</u>;
(river, canal) **φράγμα** <u>frahgh</u>-mah; *v*
κλειδώνω klee-<u>THoh</u>-noh

long *adj* **μακρύς** mak-<u>rees</u>

**long-distance bus υπεραστικό
λεωφορείο** ee-peh-rahs-tee-<u>koh</u>
leh-oh-foh-<u>ree</u>-oh

**long-distance call υπεραστικό
τηλεφώνημα** ee-pehr-ahs-tee-<u>koh</u>
tee-leh-<u>foh</u>-nee-mah

long-sighted [BE] πρεσβύωπας
prehz-<u>vee</u>-oh-pahs

look *v* **κοιτάω** kee-<u>tah</u>-oh

look for ψάχνω <u>psahkh</u>-noh

loose (fitting) **φαρδύς** fahr-<u>THees</u>

loss *n* **απώλεια** ah-<u>poh</u>-lee-ah

lotion λοσιόν loh-<u>siohn</u>

loud *adj* **δυνατός** THee-nah-<u>tohs</u>

love *v* **αγαπώ** ah-ghah-<u>poh</u>

lower *adj* (berth) **κάτω** <u>kah</u>-toh

lubricant λιπαντικό lee-pahn-dee-<u>koh</u>

luck τύχη <u>tee</u>-khee

luggage αποσκευές ah-pohs-keh-<u>vehs</u>

luggage cart καροτσάκι αποσκευών
kah-roh-<u>tsah</u>-kee ah-pohs-keh-<u>vohn</u>

luggage locker θυρίδα thee-<u>ree</u>-THah

lukewarm χλιαρός khlee-ah-<u>rohs</u>

lump *n* **σβώλος** <u>svoh</u>-lohs; (medical)
εξόγκωμα eh-<u>ksoh</u>-goh-mah

lunch *n* **μεσημεριανό**
meh-see-mehr-yah-<u>noh</u>

lung πνεύμονας <u>pnehv</u>-moh-nahs

luxury πολυτέλεια poh-lee-<u>teh</u>-lee-ah

M

magazine περιοδικό
peh-ree-oh-<u>THee</u>-<u>koh</u>

magnificent μεγαλοπρεπής
meh-ghah-lohp-reh-<u>pees</u>

mailbox ταχυδρομικό κουτί
tah-kheeTH-roh-mee-<u>koh</u> koo-<u>tee</u>

mail *n* **αλληλογραφία**
ah-lee-lohgh-rah-<u>fee</u>-ah

main κύριος <u>kee</u>-ree-ohs

make-up μακιγιάζ mah-kee-<u>yahz</u>

man (male) **άνδρας** <u>ahn</u>-THrahs

manager διευθυντής
THee-ehf-theen-<u>dees</u>

manicure μανικιούρ mah-nee-<u>kioor</u>

manual (car) **χειροκίνητος**
khee-roh-<u>kee</u>-nee-tohs

map *n* **χάρτης** <u>khahr</u>-tees

market *n* **αγορά** ah-ghoh-<u>rah</u>

married παντρεμένος
pahn-dreh-<u>meh</u>-nohs

mask n (diving) **μάσκα** <u>mahs</u>·kah

mass n (church) **λειτουργία**
lee·toor·<u>yee</u>·ah

massage n **μασάζ** mah·<u>sahz</u>

match n (sport) **αγώνας** ah·<u>ghoh</u>·nahs;
(fire starter) **σπίρτο** <u>speer</u>·toh

maybe **ίσως** <u>ee</u>·sohs

meal **γεύμα** <u>yehv</u>·mah

mean v **σημαίνω** see·<u>meh</u>·noh

measure v **μετρώ** meht·<u>roh</u>

measurement **μέτρηση** <u>meh</u>·tree·see

medication **φάρμακα** <u>fahr</u>·mah·kah

meet **συναντώ** see·nahn·<u>doh</u>

memorial **μνημείο** mnee·<u>mee</u>·oh

mend **διορθώνω** THee·ohr·<u>thoh</u>·noh

menstrual cramp **πόνος περιόδου**
<u>poh</u>·nohs peh·ree·<u>oh</u>·THoo

mention **αναφέρω** ah·nah·<u>feh</u>·roh

message n **μήνυμα** <u>mee</u>·nee·mah

metal n **μέταλλο** <u>meh</u>·tah·loh

microwave (oven) **φούρνος**
μικροκυμάτων <u>foor</u>·nohs
mee·kroh·kee·<u>mah</u>·tohn

migraine **ημικρανία** ee·mee·krah·<u>nee</u>·ah

mileage **χιλιόμετρα** khee·<u>lioh</u>·meh·trah

mini-bar **μινι-μπαρ** <u>mee</u>·nee·bahr

minimart **παντοπωλείο**
pahn·doh·poh·<u>lee</u>·oh

minimum **ελάχιστος** eh·<u>lah</u>·khees·tohs

minute n (time) **λεπτό** lehp·<u>toh</u>

mirror n **καθρέφτης** kah·<u>threhf</u>·tees

mistake **λάθος** <u>lah</u>·thohs

misunderstanding **παρεξήγηση**
pah·reh·<u>ksee</u>·yee·see

mobile phone [BE] **κινητό** kee·nee·<u>toh</u>

modern **μοντέρνος** moh·<u>deh</u>·rnohs

moisturizer (cream) **ενυδατική κρέμα**
eh·nee·THah·tee·<u>kee</u> kreh·mah

money **χρήματα** <u>khree</u>·mah·tah

money order **ταχυδρομική επιταγή**
tah·kheeTH·roh·mee·<u>kee</u> eh·pee·tah·<u>yee</u>

money-belt **ζώνη για χρήματα** <u>zoh</u>·nee
yah <u>khree</u>·mah·tah

monument **μνημείο** mnee·<u>mee</u>·oh

moped **μοτοποδίλατο**
moh·toh·poh·<u>THee</u>·lah·toh

more **παραπάνω** pah·rah·<u>pah</u>·noh

morning **πρωί** proh·<u>ee</u>

mosquito **κουνούπι** koo·<u>noo</u>·pee

mosquito bite **τσίμπημα κουνουπιού**
<u>tseem</u>·bee·mah koo·noo·<u>piooh</u>

motorboat **εξωλέμβιο**
eh·ksoh·<u>lehm</u>·vee·oh

motorway [BE] **εθνική οδός**
ehth·nee·<u>kee</u> oh·<u>THohs</u>

mountain **βουνό** voo·<u>noh</u>

moustache **μουστάκι** moos·<u>tah</u>·kee

mouth n **στόμα** <u>stoh</u>·mah

move v (room) **μετακομίζω**
meh·tah·koh·<u>mee</u>·zoh

movie **ταινία** teh·<u>nee</u>·ah

movie theater **κινηματογράφος**
kee·nee·mah·tohgh·<u>rah</u>·fohs

much **πολύ** poh·<u>lee</u>

muscle n **μυς** mees

museum **μουσείο** moo·<u>see</u>·oh

music **μουσική** moo·see·<u>kee</u>

musician **μουσικός** moo·see·<u>kohs</u>

must v **πρέπει** <u>preh</u>·pee

N

nail salon **σαλόνι νυχιών** sah·<u>loh</u>·nee
nee·<u>khiohn</u>

name n **όνομα** <u>oh</u>·noh·mah

napkin **πετσέτα** peh·<u>tseh</u>·tah

nappy [BE] **πάνα μωρού** pah·nah moh·**roo**

narrow **στενός** steh·**nohs**

national **εθνικός** eth·nee·**kohs**

nationality **υπηκοότητα** ee·pee·koh·**oh**·tee·tah

nature **φύση** **fee**·see

nature reserve **εθνικός δρυμός** eth·nee·**kohs** THree·**mohs**

nature trail **μονοπάτι** moh·noh·**pah**·tee

nausea **ναυτία** nahf·**tee**·ah

near adv **κοντά** kohn·**dah**

nearby **εδώ κοντά** eh·**THoh** kohn·**dah**

necessary **απαραίτητος** ah·pah·**reh**·tee·tohs

necklace **κολλιέ** koh·**lieh**

need v **χρειάζομαι** khree·**ah**·zoh·meh

neighbor n **γείτονας** **yee**·toh·nahs

nerve **νεύρο** **nehv**·roh

never **ποτέ** poh·**teh**

new **καινούργιος** keh·**noor**·yohs

newspaper **εφημερίδα** eh·fee·meh·**ree**·THah

newsstand **περίπτερο** peh·**ree**·pteh·roh

next **επόμενος** eh·**poh**·meh·nohs

next to **δίπλα** **THeep**·lah

night **νύχτα** **neekh**·tah

night club **νυχτερινό κέντρο** neekh·teh·ree·**noh** **kehn**·droh

noisy **θορυβώδης** thoh·ree·**voh**·THees

none adj **κανένας** kah·**neh**·nahs

non-smoking **μη καπνίζοντες** mee kap·**nee**·zohn·dehs

north **βόρεια** **voh**·ree·ah

nose n **μύτη** **mee**·tee

nudist beach **παραλία γυμνιστών** pah·rah·**lee**·ah yeem·nees·**tohn**

nurse n **νοσοκόμα** noh·soh·**koh**·mah

O

occupied **κατειλημένος** kah·tee·lee·**meh**·nohs

office **γραφείο** ghrah·**fee**·oh

old adj (thing) **παλιός** pah·**liohs**; (person) **γέρικος** **yeh**·ree·kohs

old town **παλιά πόλη** pah·**liah** **poh**·lee

old-fashioned **ντεμοντέ** deh·mohn·**deh**

once **μια φορά** miah foh·**rah**

one-way ticket **απλό εισιτήριο** ahp·**loh** ee·see·**tee**·ree·oh

open adj **ανοιχτός** ah·neekh·**tohs**; v **ανοίγω** ah·**nee**·ghoh

opening hours **ώρες λειτουργίας** **oh**·rehs lee·toor·**yee**·ahs

opera **όπερα** **oh**·peh·rah

opposite **απέναντι** ah·**peh**·nahn·dee

optician **οφθαλμίατρος** ohf·thahl·**mee**·aht·rohs

orchestra **ορχήστρα** ohr·**khees**·trah

order v **παραγγέλνω** pah·rah·**gehl**·noh

organized **οργανωμένος** ohr·ghah·noh·**meh**·nohs

others **άλλα** **ah**·lah

out adv **έξω** **eh**·ksoh

outdoor **εξωτερικός** eh·ksoh·teh·ree·**kohs**

outside adj **έξω** **eh**·ksoh

oval **οβάλ** oh·**vahl**

oven **φούρνος** **foor**·nohs

over there **εκεί** eh·**kee**

overnight (package) **ένα βράδυ** <u>eh</u>·nah <u>vrah</u>·THee

owe χρωστώ khroh·<u>stoh</u>

owner κάτοχος <u>kah</u>·toh·khohs

P

pacifier πιπίλα pee·<u>pee</u>·lah

pack v (baggage) **φτιάχνω τις βαλίτσες** ftee·<u>ahkh</u>·noh tees vah·<u>lee</u>·tsehs

paddling pool [BE] **ρηχή πισίνα** ree·<u>khee</u> pee·<u>see</u>·nah

padlock λουκέτο loo·<u>keh</u>·toh

pain n **πόνος** <u>poh</u>·nohs

painkiller παυσίπονο pahf·<u>see</u>·poh·noh

paint v **ζωγραφίζω** zohgh·rah·<u>fee</u>·zoh

pair ζευγάρι zehv·<u>ghah</u>·ree

pajamas πυτζάμες pee·<u>jah</u>·mehs

palace ανάκτορα ah·<u>nahk</u>·toh·rah

panorama πανόραμα pah·<u>noh</u>·rah·mah

pants παντελόνι pahn·deh·<u>loh</u>·nee

paper χαρτί khar·<u>tee</u>

paralysis παραλυσία pah·rah·lee·<u>see</u>·ah

parcel πακέτο pah·<u>keh</u>·toh

parents γονείς ghoh·<u>nees</u>

park n **πάρκο** <u>pahr</u>·koh

parking lot χώρος στάθμευσης <u>khoh</u>·rohs <u>stahth</u>·mehf·sees

parking meter παρκόμετρο pahr·<u>koh</u>·meht·roh

party n (social gathering) **πάρτυ** <u>pah</u>·rtee

pass v **περνώ** pehr·<u>noh</u>

passenger επιβάτης eh·pee·<u>vah</u>·tees

passport διαβατήριο THiah·vah·<u>tee</u>·ree·oh

pastry store ζαχαροπλαστείο zah·khah·rohp·lahs·<u>tee</u>·oh

path μονοπάτι moh·noh·<u>pah</u>·tee

pay v **πληρώνω** plee·<u>roh</u>·noh

payment πληρωμή plee·roh·<u>mee</u>

peak n **κορυφή** koh·ree·<u>fee</u>

pearl μαργαριτάρι mahr·ghah·ree·<u>tah</u>·ree

pebbly (beach) **με χαλίκια** meh khah·<u>lee</u>·kiah

pedestrian crossing διάβαση πεζών THee·<u>ah</u>·vah·see peh·<u>zohn</u>

pedestrian zone πεζόδρομος peh·<u>zohTH</u>·roh·mohs

pen n **στυλό** stee·<u>loh</u>

per την teen

perhaps ίσως ee·sohs

period (menstrual) **περίοδος** peh·<u>ree</u>·oh·THohs; (time) **χρονική περίοδος** khroh·nee·<u>kee</u> peh·<u>ree</u>·oh·Thohs

permit n **άδεια** <u>ah</u>·THee·ah

petrol [BE] **βενζίνη** vehn·<u>zee</u>·nee

pewter κασσίτερος kah·<u>see</u>·teh·rohs

phone n **τηλέφωνο** tee·<u>leh</u>·foh·noh

phone call τηλεφώνημα tee·leh·<u>foh</u>·nee·mah

phone card τηλεκάρτα tee·leh·<u>kahr</u>·tah

photo v **φωτογραφία** foh·tohgh·rah·<u>fee</u>·ah

photocopier φωτοτυπικό foh·toh·tee·pee·<u>koh</u>

phrase n **φράση** <u>frah</u>·see

pick up παίρνω <u>pehr</u>·noh

picnic area περιοχή για πικνίκ peh·ree·oh·<u>khee</u> yah peek·neek

piece τεμάχιο teh·<u>mah</u>·khee·oh

pillow μαξιλάρι mah·ksee·<u>lah</u>·ree

pillow case μαξιλαροθήκη mah·ksee·lah·roh·<u>thee</u>·kee pipe (smoking) **πίπα** <u>pee</u>·pah

piste [BE] **μονοπάτι** moh·noh·<u>pah</u>·tee

pizzeria **πιτσαρία** pee·tsah·<u>ree</u>·ah

plan n **σχέδιο** <u>skheh</u>·THee·oh

plane n **αεροπλάνο** ah·eh·rohp·<u>lah</u>·noh

plant n **φυτό** fee·<u>toh</u>

plastic wrap **διαφανή μεμβράνη**
THee·ah·fah·<u>nee</u> mehm·<u>vrah</u>·nee

platform **αποβάθρα** ah·poh·<u>vahth</u>·rah

platinum **πλατίνα** plah·<u>tee</u>·nah

play v (games) **παίζω** <u>peh</u>·zoh; (music)
παίζω <u>peh</u>·zoh

playground **παιδική χαρά** peh·THee·<u>kee</u>
khah·<u>rah</u>

pleasant **ευχάριστος** ehf·<u>khah</u>·rees·tohs

plug n **πρίζα** <u>pree</u>·zah

point n **σημείο** see·<u>mee</u>·oh; v **δείχνω**
<u>THeekh</u>·noh

poison n **δηλητήριο** THee·lee·<u>tee</u>·ree·oh

poisonous **δηλητηριώδης**
THee·lee·tee·ree·<u>oh</u>·THees

police n **αστυνομία** ah·stee·noh·<u>mee</u>·ah

police station **αστυνομικό τμήμα**
ah·stee·noh·mee·<u>koh</u> <u>tmee</u>·mah

pond n **λιμνούλα** leem·<u>noo</u>·lah

popular **δημοφιλής** THee·moh·fee·<u>lees</u>

porter **αχθοφόρος** ahkh·thoh·<u>foh</u>·rohs

portion n **μερίδα** meh·<u>ree</u>·THah

possible **πιθανός** pee·thah·<u>nohs</u>

postbox [BE] **ταχυδρομικό κουτί**
tah·kheeTH·roh·mee·<u>koh</u> koo·<u>tee</u>

post card **καρτποστάλ** kahrt·poh·<u>stahl</u>

post office **ταχυδρομείο**
tah·kheeTH·roh·<u>mee</u>·oh

pottery **αγγειοπλαστική**
ahn·gee·ohp·lahs·tee·<u>kee</u>

pound (sterling) **λίρα** <u>lee</u>·rah

pregnant **έγκυος** <u>eh</u>·gee·ohs

prescribe **συνταγογραφώ**
seen·dah·ghoh·ghrah·<u>foh</u>

prescription **συνταγή γιατρού**
seen·dah·<u>yee</u> yaht·<u>roo</u>

present **δώρο** <u>THoh</u>·roh

press v **σιδερώνω** see·THeh·<u>roh</u>·noh

pretty adj **όμορφος** oh·mohr·fohs

prison n **φυλακή** fee·lah·<u>kee</u>

private bathroom **ιδιωτικό μπάνιο**
ee·THee·oh·tee·<u>koh</u> <u>bah</u>·nioh

problem **πρόβλημα** <u>prohv</u>·lee·mah

program n **πρόγραμμα** <u>prohgh</u>·rah·mah

program of events **πρόγραμμα
θεαμάτων** <u>prohgh</u>·rah·mah
theh·ah·<u>mah</u>·tohn

prohibited **απαγορευμένος**
ah·pah·ghoh·rehv·<u>meh</u>·nohs

pronounce **προφέρω** proh·<u>feh</u>·roh

public **δημόσιος** THee·<u>moh</u>·see·ohs

public holiday **αργία** ahr·<u>yee</u>·ah

pump n **τρόμπα** <u>troh</u>·mbah

purpose **σκοπός** skoh·<u>pohs</u>

put v **βάζω** <u>vah</u>·zoh

Q

quality **ποιότητα** pee·<u>oh</u>·tee·tah

quantity **ποσότητα** poh·<u>soh</u>·tee·tah

quarantine n **καραντίνα**
kah·rahn·<u>dee</u>·nah

quarter (quantity) **ένα τέταρτο** <u>eh</u>·nah
<u>teh</u>·tah·rtoh

quay **αποβάθρα** ah·poh·<u>vath</u>·rah

question n **ερώτηση** eh·<u>roh</u>·tee·see

queue [BE] v **περιμένω στην ουρά**
peh·ree·<u>meh</u>·noh steen oo·<u>rah</u>

quick **γρήγορος** <u>ghree</u>·ghoh·rohs

quiet adj **ήσυχος** <u>ee</u>·see·khohs

R

racket (tennis, squash) **ρακέτα**
rah‧<u>keh</u>‧tah

radio n **ραδιόφωνο** rah‧<u>THee</u>‧oh‧foh‧noh

railway station [BE] **σιδηροδρομικός
σταθμός** see‧THee‧rohTH‧roh‧mee‧<u>kohs</u>
stahth‧<u>mohs</u>

rain n **βροχή** vroh‧<u>khee</u>; v **βρέχει** <u>vreh</u>‧khee

raincoat αδιάβροχο
ah‧THee‧<u>ahv</u>‧roh‧khoh

rapids ρεύμα ποταμού <u>rehv</u>‧mah
poh‧tah‧<u>moo</u>

rare (unusual) **σπάνιος** <u>spah</u>‧nee‧ohs

rash n **εξάνθημα** eh‧<u>ksahn</u>‧thee‧mah

ravine ρεματιά reh‧mah‧<u>tiah</u>

razor ξυραφάκι ksee‧rah‧<u>fah</u>‧kee

razor blade ξυραφάκι ksee‧rah‧<u>fah</u>‧kee

ready adj **έτοιμος** eh‧<u>tee</u>‧mohs

real (genuine) **γνήσιος** <u>ghee</u>‧see‧ohs;
(true) **αληθινός** ah‧lee‧thee‧nohs

receipt απόδειξη ah‧<u>poh</u>‧THee‧ksee

reception (hotel) **ρεσεψιόν**
reh‧seh‧<u>psiohn</u>

recommend συστήνω sees‧<u>tee</u>‧noh

reduction έκπτωση <u>ehk</u>‧ptoh‧see

refund n **επιστροφή χρημάτων**
eh‧pees‧troh‧<u>fee</u> khree‧<u>mah</u>‧tohn

region περιοχή peh‧ree‧oh‧<u>khee</u>

**registration number αριθμός
κυκλοφορίας** ah‧reeth‧<u>mohs</u>
kee‧kloh‧foh‧<u>ree</u>‧ahs

religion θρησκεία three‧<u>skee</u>‧ah

remember θυμάμαι thee‧<u>mah</u>‧meh

rent v **νοικιάζω** nee‧<u>kiah</u>‧zoh

repair n **επισκευή** eh‧pee‧skeh‧<u>vee</u>; v
επισκευάζω eh‧pee‧skeh‧<u>vah</u>‧zoh

repeat v **επαναλαμβάνω**
eh‧pah‧nah‧lahm‧<u>vah</u>‧noh

replacement part ανταλλακτικό
ahn‧dah‧lahk‧tee‧<u>koh</u>

report v **αναφέρω** ah‧nah‧<u>feh</u>‧roh

restaurant εστιατόριο
ehs‧tee‧ah‧<u>toh</u>‧ree‧oh

restroom τουαλέτα too‧ah‧<u>leh</u>‧tah

retired συνταξιούχος
seen‧dah‧ksee‧<u>oo</u>‧khohs

return ticket [BE] **εισιτήριο με
επιστροφή** ee‧see‧<u>tee</u>‧ree‧oh meh
eh‧pee‧stroh‧<u>fee</u>

**reverse the charges με χρέωση του
καλούμενου** meh <u>khreh</u>‧oh‧see too
kah‧<u>loo</u>‧meh‧noo

revolting αηδιαστικός
ah‧ee‧THee‧ah‧stee‧<u>kohs</u>

rib πλευρό plehv‧<u>roh</u>

right adj (correct) **σωστός** soh‧<u>stohs</u>;
(side) **δεξιός** THeh‧ksee‧<u>ohs</u>

river ποταμός poh‧tah‧<u>mohs</u>

road δρόμος THroh‧<u>mohs</u>

road assistance οδική βοήθεια
oh‧THee‧<u>kee</u> voh‧<u>ee</u>‧thee‧ah

road sign πινακίδα pee‧nah‧<u>kee</u>‧Thah

robbery ληστεία lees‧<u>tee</u>‧ah

rock n **βράχος** <u>vrah</u>‧khohs

rock climbing αναρρίχηση
ah‧nah‧<u>ree</u>‧khee‧see

romantic ρομαντικός
roh‧mahn‧dee‧<u>kohs</u>

roof n **στέγη** <u>steh</u>‧yee

room n **δωμάτιο** THoh‧<u>mah</u>‧tee‧oh

room service υπηρεσία δωματίου
ee‧pee‧reh‧<u>see</u>‧ah THoh‧mah‧<u>tee</u>‧oo

rope n **σχοινί** skhee‧<u>nee</u>

round adj **στρογγυλός**
strohn‧gkee‧<u>lohs</u>; n (of golf) **παιχνίδι**
pehkh‧<u>nee</u>‧THee

round-trip ticket **εισιτήριο με επιστροφή** ee·see·<u>tee</u>·ree·oh meh eh·pee·stroh·<u>fee</u>

route n **διαδρομή** THee·ahTH·roh·<u>mee</u>

rowing **κωπηλασία** koh·pee·lah·<u>see</u>·ah

rubbish [BE] **σκουπίδια** skoo·<u>peeTH</u>·yah

rude **αγενής** ah·yeh·<u>nees</u>

rug **χαλί** khah·<u>lee</u>

run v **τρέχω** <u>treh</u>·khoh

rush hour **ώρα αιχμής** <u>oh</u>·rah ehkh·<u>mees</u>

S

safe adj (not dangerous) **ασφαλής** ahs·fah·<u>lees</u>

sailing boat **ιστιοπλοϊκό** ees·tee·oh·ploh·ee·<u>koh</u>

sales tax **ΦΠΑ** fee·pee·<u>ah</u>

same **ίδιος** <u>ee</u>·THee·ohs

sand **άμμος** <u>ah</u>·mohs

sandals **πέδιλα** <u>peh</u>·THee·lah

sandy (beach) **με άμμο** meh <u>ah</u>·moh

sanitary napkin **σερβιέτα** sehr·vee·<u>eh</u>·tah

satin **σατέν** sah·<u>tehn</u>

saucepan **κατσαρόλα** kah·tsah·<u>roh</u>·lah

sauna **σάουνα** <u>sah</u>·oo·nah

scarf **κασκόλ** kahs·<u>kohl</u>

scissors **ψαλίδι** psah·<u>lee</u>·THee

scratch **γρατζουνιά** ghrah·joo·<u>niah</u>

screw n **βίδα** <u>vee</u>·THah

screwdriver **κατσαβίδι** kah·tsah·<u>vee</u>·THee

sea **θάλασσα** <u>thah</u>·lah·sah

seafront **προκυμαία** proh·kee·<u>meh</u>·ah

seat n **θέση** <u>theh</u>·see

second-hand shop **κατάστημα μεταχειρισμένων** kah·<u>tah</u>·stee·mah meh·tah·khee·reez·<u>meh</u>·nohn ee·<u>THohn</u>

sedative **ηρεμιστικό** ee·reh·mee·stee·<u>koh</u>

see **βλέπω** <u>vleh</u>·poh

send **στέλνω** <u>stehl</u>·noh

senior citizen **ηλικιωμένος** ee·lee·kee·oh·<u>meh</u>·nohs

separately **ξεχωριστά** kseh·khoh·ree·<u>stah</u>

service n (business) **υπηρεσία** ee·pee·reh·<u>see</u>·ah; (mass) **λειτουργία** lee·toor·<u>yee</u>·ah

service charge **χρέωση υπηρεσίας** <u>khreh</u>·oh·see ee·pee·reh·<u>see</u>·ahs

sewer **υπόνομος** ee·<u>poh</u>·noh·mohs

shade (color) **απόχρωση** ah·<u>pohkh</u>·r oh·see; (darkness) **σκιά** skee·<u>ah</u>

shampoo n **σαμπουάν** sahm·poo·<u>ahn</u>

shape n **σχήμα** <u>skhee</u>·mah

shaving cream **κρέμα ξυρίσματος** <u>kreh</u>·mah ksee·<u>reez</u>·mah·tohs

shelf n **ράφι** <u>rah</u>·fee

ship n **πλοίο** <u>plee</u>·oh

shirt **πουκάμισο** poo·<u>kah</u>·mee·soh

shock (electric) **ηλεκτροπληξία** ee·leh·ktroh·plee·<u>ksee</u>·ah

shoe **παπούτσι** pah·<u>poo</u>·tsee

shoe polish **βερνίκι παπουτσιών** vehr·<u>nee</u>·kee pah·poo·<u>tsiohn</u>

shoe repair **επισκευή παπουτσιών** eh·pee·skeh·<u>vee</u> pah·poo·<u>tsiohn</u>

shoe store **κατάστημα υποδημάτων** kah·<u>tah</u>·stee·mah ee·poh·THee·<u>mah</u>·tohn

shop (store) **κατάστημα** kah·<u>tah</u>·stee·mah

shopping mall εμπορικό κέντρο
ehm·boh·ree·<u>koh</u> keh·ntroh

shore *n* **ακτή** ak·tee

short *adj* **κοντός** kohn·<u>dohs</u>

shorts *n* **σορτς** sohrts

short-sighted [BE] μύωπας <u>mee</u>·oh·pahs

shoulder *n* (anatomy) **ώμος** <u>oh</u>·mohs

show δείχνω <u>THeekh</u>·noh

shower *n* **ντουζ** dooz

shower gel αφρόλουτρο για ντουζ
ahf·<u>roh</u>·loot·roh yah dooz

shut *adj* **κλειστός** klees·<u>tohs</u>

sick *adj* **άρρωστος** <u>ah</u>·rohs·tohs

side (of road) **μεριά** mehr·<u>yah</u>

sightseeing sight αξιοθέατο
ah·ksee·oh·<u>theh</u>·ah·toh

sightseeing tour ξενάγηση στα
αξιοθέατα kseh·<u>nah</u>·yee·see stah
ah·ksee·oh·<u>theh</u>·ah·tah

sign (road) **σήμα** <u>see</u>·mah

silk μετάξι meh·<u>tah</u>·ksee

silver ασήμι ah·<u>see</u>·mee

simple απλός ahp·<u>lohs</u>

single (not married) **ελεύθερος**
eh·<u>lehf</u>·theh·rohs

single room μονόκλινο δωμάτιο
moh·<u>noh</u>·klee·noh THoh·<u>mah</u>·tee·oh

single ticket [BE] απλό εισιτήριο
ahp·<u>loh</u> ee·see·<u>tee</u>·ree·oh

sink (bathroom) **νιπτήρας** nee·<u>ptee</u>·rahs

sit κάθομαι <u>kah</u>·thoh·meh

size *n* **μέγεθος** <u>meh</u>·yeh·thohs

skates παγοπέδιλα
pah·ghoh·<u>peh</u>·THee·lah

skating rink παγοδρόμιο
pah·ghohTH·<u>roh</u>·mee·oh

ski boots μπότες του σκι <u>boh</u>·tehs too
skee

ski poles μπαστούνια του σκι
bahs·<u>too</u>·niah too skee

ski school σχολή σκι skhoh·<u>lee</u> skee

skiing σκι skee

skin *n* **δέρμα** <u>Thehr</u>·mah

skirt φούστα <u>foo</u>·stah

sleep *v* **κοιμάμαι** kee·<u>mah</u>·meh

sleeping bag υπνόσακκος
ee·<u>pnoh</u>·sah·kohs

sleeping car βαγκόν-λι vah·<u>gohn</u>·lee

sleeping pill υπνωτικό χάπι
eep·noh·tee·<u>koh</u> khah·pee

slippers παντόφλες pahn·<u>dohf</u>·lehs

slope (ski) **πλαγιά** plah·<u>yah</u>

slow *adj* **αργός** ahr·<u>ghohs</u>

small μικρός meek·<u>rohs</u>

smell *v* **μυρίζω** mee·<u>ree</u>·zoh

smoke *v* **καπνίζω** kahp·<u>nee</u>·zoh

smoking area περιοχή για
καπνίζοντες peh·ree·oh·<u>khee</u> yah
kahp·<u>nee</u>·zohn·dehs

snack bar κυλικείο kee·lee·<u>kee</u>·oh

sneakers αθλητικά παπούτσια
ath·lee·tee·<u>kah</u> pah·<u>poo</u>·tsiah

snorkeling equipment εξοπλισμό
για ελεύθερη κατάδυση
eh·ksohp·leez·<u>moh</u> yah eh·<u>lehf</u>·theh·ree
kah·tah·THee·see

snow *v* **χιονίζει** khioh·<u>nee</u>·zee

soap *n* **σαπούνι** sah·<u>poo</u>·nee

soccer ποδόσφαιρο poh·<u>THohs</u>·feh·roh

socket πρίζα <u>pree</u>·zah

socks κάλτσες <u>kahl</u>·tsehs

sofa καναπές kah·nah·<u>pehs</u>

sole (shoes) **σόλα** <u>soh</u>·lah

something κάτι <u>kah</u>·tee

sometimes μερικές φορές meh·ree·<u>kehs</u>
foh·<u>rehs</u>

soon **σύντομα** seen·doh·mah

soother [BE] **πιπίλα** pee·pee·lah

sore throat **πονόλαιμος**
poh·noh·leh·mohs

sort n **είδος** ee·THohs; v **διαλέγω**
THIah·leh·ghoh

south adj **νότιος** noh·tee·ohs

souvenir **σουβενίρ** soo·veh·neer

souvenir store **κατάστημα σουβενίρ**
kah·tahs·tee·mah soo·veh·neer

spa **σπα** spah

space n (area) **χώρος** khoh·rohs

spare (extra) **επιπλέον** eh·peep·leh·ohn

speak **μιλώ** mee·loh

special requirement **ειδική ανάγκη**
ee·THee·kee ah·nahn·gkee

specialist **ειδικός** ee·THee·kohs

specimen **δείγμα** THeegh·mah

speed v **τρέχω** treh·khoh

spend **ξοδεύω** ksoh·THeh·voh

spine **σπονδυλική στήλη**
spohn·THee·lee·kee stee·lee

spoon n **κουτάλι** koo·tah·lee

sport **αθλητισμός** ahth·lee·teez·mohs

sporting goods store **κατάστημα**
αθλητικών ειδών kah·tahs·tee·mah
ath·lee·tee·kohn ee·THohn

sports massage **αθλητικό μασάζ**
ahth·lee·tee·koh mah·sahz

sports stadium **αθλητικό στάδιο**
ahth·lee·tee·koh stah·THee·oh

square **τετράγωνος** teht·rah·ghoh·nohs

stadium **στάδιο** stah·THee·oh

stain n **λεκές** leh·kehs

stairs **σκάλες** skah·lehs

stale **μπαγιάτικος** bah·yah·tee·kohs

stamp n (postage) **γραμματόσημο**
ghrah·mah·toh·see·moh

start v **αρχίζω** ahr·khee·zoh

statement (legal) **δήλωση** THee·loh·see

statue **άγαλμα** ah·ghahl·mah

stay v **μένω** meh·noh

sterilizing solution **αποστειρωτικό**
διάλυμα ah·pohs·tee·roh·tee·koh
THee·ah·lee·mah

sting n (insect) **τσίμπημα** tsee·bee·mah

stolen **κλεμένος** kleh·meh·nohs

stomach n **στομάχι** stoh·mah·khee

stomachache **στομαχόπονος**
stoh·mah·khoh·poh·nohs

stop n (bus) **στάση** stah·see; v **σταματώ**
stah·mah·toh

store guide [BE] **οδηγός καταστήματος**
oh·THee·ghohs kah·tahs·tee·mah·tohs

stove **κουζίνα** koo·zee·nah

straight ahead **ευθεία** ehf·thee·ah

strange **παράξενος** pah·rah·kseh·nohs

straw (drinking) **καλαμάκι**
kah·lah·mah·kee

stream n **ρυάκι** ree·ah·kee

street **δρόμος** THroh·mohs

string n (cord) **σπάγγος** spah·gohs

student **φοιτητής** fee·tee·tees

study v **σπουδάζω** spoo·THah·zoh

style n **στυλ** steel

subtitled **με υπότιτλους** meh
ee·poh·teet·loos

subway **μετρό** meh·troh

subway station **σταθμός μετρό**
stahth·mohs meh·troh

suggest **προτείνω** proh·tee·noh

suit (men's) **κουστούμι** koos·too·mee;
(women's) **ταγιέρ** tah·yehr

suitable **κατάλληλος** kah·tah·lee·lohs

sunburn n **έγκαυμα ηλίου** ehn·gahv·mah
ee·lee·oo

sunglasses **γυαλιά ηλίου** yah·liah ee·lee·oo

sunshade [BE] **ομπρέλλα** ohm·breh·lah

sunstroke **ηλίαση** ee·lee·ah·see

sun tan lotion **λοσιόν μαυρίσματος** loh·siohn mahv·rees·mah·tohs

sunscreen **αντιηλιακό** ahn·dee·ee·lee·ah·koh

superb **έξοχος** eh·ksoh·khohs

supermarket **σουπερμάρκετ** soo·pehr·mahr·keht

supervision **επίβλεψη** eh·peev·leh·psee

surname **επίθετο** eh·pee·theh·toh

sweatshirt **φούτερ** foo·tehr

swelling **πρήξιμο** pree·ksee·moh

swimming **κολύμβηση** koh·leem·vee·see

swimming pool **πισίνα** pee·see·nah

swimming trunks **μαγιό** mah·yoh

swimsuit **μαγιό** mah·yoh

switch n **διακόπτης** THiah·koh·ptees

swollen **πρησμένος** preez·meh·nohs

symptom **σύμπτωμα** seem·ptoh·mah

T

table **τραπέζι** trah·peh·zee

tablecloth **τραπεζομάντηλο** trah·peh·zoh·mahn·dee·loh

tablet **χάπι** khah·pee

take **παίρνω** pehr·noh

take a photograph **βγάζω φωτογραφία** vghah·zoh foh·tohgh·rah·fee·ah

take away [BE] **πακέτο για το σπίτι** pah·keh·toh yah toh spee·tee

tall **ψηλός** psee·lohs

tampon **ταμπόν** tahm·bohn

tax n **φόρος** foh·rohs

taxi **ταξί** tah·ksee

taxi driver **ταξιτζής** tah·ksee·jees

taxi rank [BE] **πιάτσα ταξί** piah·tsah tah·ksee

teaspoon **κουταλάκι** koo·tah·lah·kee

team n **ομάδα** oh·mah·THah

teenager **έφηβος** eh·fee·vohs

telephone n **τηλέφωνο** tee·leh·foh·noh

telephone booth **τηλεφωνικός θάλαμος** tee·leh·foh·nee·kohs thah·lah·mohs

telephone call **κλήση** klee·see

telephone directory **τηλεφωνικός κατάλογος** tee·leh·foh·nee·kohs kah·tah·loh·ghohs

telephone number **αριθμός τηλεφώνου** ah·reeth·mohs tee·leh·foh·noo

tell **λέω** leh·oh

temperature (body) **θερμοκρασία** theh·rmohk·rah·see·ah

temple **ναός** nah·ohs

temporary **προσωρινός** proh·soh·ree·nohs

tennis **τέννις** teh·nees

tennis court **γήπεδο τέννις** yee·peh·THoh teh·nees

tent **σκηνή** skee·nee

terrible **φοβερός** foh·veh·rohs

theater **θέατρο** theh·aht·roh

theft **κλοπή** kloh·pee

there **εκεί** eh·kee

thermal bath **ιαματικό λουτρό** ee·ah·mah·tee·koh loot·roh

thermos flask **θερμός** thehr·mohs

thick **χοντρός** khohn·drohs

thief **κλέφτης** klehf·tees

thin adj **λεπτός** lehp·tohs

think **νομίζω** noh·mee·zoh

thirsty **διψάω** THee·psah·oh

those **εκείνα** eh·kee·nah

throat **λαιμός** leh·mohs

thumb **αντίχειρας** ahn·dee·khee·rahs

ticket **εισιτήριο** ee·see·<u>tee</u>·ree·oh
ticket office **γραφείο εισιτηρίων**
  ghrah·<u>fee</u>·oh ee·see·tee·<u>ree</u>·ohn
tie n **γραβάτα** ghrah·<u>vah</u>·tah
tight adj **στενός** steh·<u>nohs</u>
tights [BE] n **καλσόν** kahl·<u>sohn</u>
timetable [BE] **δρομολόγιο**
  THroh·moh·<u>loh</u>·yee·oh
tire **λάστιχο** <u>lahs</u>·tee·khoh
tired **κουρασμένος** koo·rahz·<u>meh</u>·nohs
tissue **χαρτομάντηλο**
  khahr·toh·<u>mahn</u>·dee·loh
toaster **τοστιέρα** toh·<u>stieh</u>·rah
tobacco **καπνός** kahp·<u>nohs</u>
tobacconist **καπνοπωλείο**
  kahp·noh·poh·<u>lee</u>·oh
toilet [BE] **τουαλέτα** too·ah·<u>leh</u>·tah
toilet paper **χαρτί υγείας** khahr·tee
  ee·<u>yee</u>·ahs
toiletries **καλλυντικά**
  kah·leen·dee·<u>kah</u>
tongue **γλώσσα** <u>ghloh</u>·sah
too (extreme) **πάρα πολύ** pah·rah poh·lee
tooth **δόντι** <u>THohn</u>·dee
toothache **πονόδοντος**
  poh·noh·<u>THohn</u>·dohs
toothbrush **οδοντόβουρτσα**
  oh·THohn·<u>doh</u>·voor·tsah
toothpaste **οδοντόπαστα**
  oh·THohn·<u>doh</u>·pahs·tah
top adj **πάνω** <u>pah</u>·noh
torn **σχισμένος** skheez·<u>meh</u>·nohs
tour guide **ξεναγός** kseh·nah·<u>ghohs</u>
tourist **τουρίστας** too·<u>rees</u>·tahs
towards **προς** prohs
tower **πύργος** <u>peer</u>·ghohs
town **πόλη** <u>poh</u>·lee
town hall **δημαρχείο** THee·mahr·<u>khee</u>·oh

toy store **κατάστημα παιχνιδιών**
  kah·<u>tahs</u>·tee·mah peh·khnee·<u>THiohn</u>
traditional **παραδοσιακός**
  pah·rah·THoh·see·ah·<u>kohs</u>
traffic **κίνηση** <u>kee</u>·nee·see
trail **μονοπάτι** moh·noh·<u>pah</u>·tee
trailer **τροχόσπιτο** troh·<u>khohs</u>·pee·toh
train **τρένο** <u>treh</u>·noh
train station **σταθμός των τρένων**
  stahth·<u>mohs</u> tohn <u>treh</u>·nohn
tram **τραμ** trahm
transfer **μεταφέρω** meh·tah·<u>feh</u>·roh
transit n **μεταφορά** meh·tah·foh·<u>rah</u>
translate **μεταφράζω** meh·tah·<u>frah</u>·zoh
translation **μετάφραση** meh·<u>tah</u>·frah·see
translator **μεταφραστής**
  meh·tah·frah·<u>stees</u>
trash **σκουπίδια** skoo·<u>peeTH</u>·yah
trash can **κάδος απορριμμάτων**
  <u>kah</u>·THohs ah·poh·ree·<u>mah</u>·tohn
travel agency **ταξιδιωτικό γραφείο**
  tah·ksee·THyoh·tee·<u>koh</u> ghrah·<u>fee</u>·oh
travel sickness [BE] **ναυτία** nahf·<u>tee</u>·ah
traveler's check **ταξιδιωτική επιταγή**
  tah·ksee·THee·oh·tee·<u>kee</u> eh·pee·tah·<u>yee</u>
tray **δίσκος** <u>THees</u>·kohs
tree **δέντρο** <u>THehn</u>·droh
trim n **διόρθωμα** THee·<u>ohr</u>·thoh·mah
trolley [BE] (cart) **καροτσάκι**
  kah·roh·<u>tsah</u>·kee
trolley-bus **τρόλλεϋ** <u>troh</u>·leh·ee
trousers [BE] **παντελόνι** pahn·deh·<u>loh</u>·nee
try on **δοκιμάζω** THoh·kee·<u>mah</u>·zoh
T-shirt **μπλουζάκι** bloo·<u>zah</u>·kee
tunnel **τούνελ** <u>too</u>·nehl
turn v **γυρίζω** yee·<u>ree</u>·zoh
turn down v (volume, heat) **χαμηλώνω**
  khah·mee·<u>loh</u>·noh

turn off v **σβήνω** <u>svee</u>-noh

turn on v **ανάβω** ah-<u>nah</u>-voh

turn up v (volume, heat) **ανεβάζω** ah-neh-<u>vah</u>-zoh

TV τηλεόραση tee-leh-<u>oh</u>-rah-see

twin bed διπλό κρεβάτι THeep-<u>loh</u> kreh-<u>vah</u>-tee

typical τυπικός tee-pee-<u>kohs</u>

U

ugly άσχημος <u>ahs</u>-khee-mohs

unconscious αναίσθητος ah-<u>nehs</u>-thee-tohs

underground [BE] **υπόγειος** ee-<u>poh</u>-ghee-ohs

underpants [BE] **κυλοτάκι** kee-loh-<u>tah</u>-kee

understand καταλαβαίνω kah-tah-lah-<u>veh</u>-noh

uneven (ground) **ανώμαλος** ah-<u>noh</u>-mah-lohs

unfortunately δυστυχώς THees-tee-<u>khohs</u>

uniform n **στολή** stoh-<u>lee</u>

unique μοναδικός moh-nah-THee-<u>kohs</u>

unit μονάδα moh-<u>nah</u>-THah

United Kingdom Ηνωμένο Βασίλειο ee-noh-<u>meh</u>-noh vah-<u>see</u>-lee-oh

United States Ηνωμένες Πολιτείες ee-noh-<u>meh</u>-nehs poh-lee-<u>tee</u>-ehs

university Πανεπιστήμιο pah-neh-pees-<u>tee</u>-mee-oh

unlimited mileage απεριόριστα χιλιόμετρα ah-peh-ree-<u>ohr</u>-ees-tah khee-<u>lioh</u>-meht-rah

unpleasant δυσάρεστος THee-<u>sah</u>-reh-stohs

upper (berth) **πάνω (κουκέτα)** <u>pah</u>-noh (koo-<u>keh</u>-tah)

upstairs επάνω eh-<u>pah</u>-noh

urgent επείγον eh-<u>pee</u>-ghohn

use v **χρησιμοποιώ** khree-see-moh-pee-<u>oh</u>

useful χρήσιμος <u>khree</u>-see-mohs

V

vacancy ελεύθερο δωμάτιο eh-<u>lehf</u>-theh-roh THoh-<u>mah</u>-tee-oh

vacant ελεύθερος eh-<u>lehf</u>-theh-rohs

vacation διακοπές THee-ah-koh-<u>pehs</u>

vacation resort θέρετρο διακοπών <u>theh</u>-reh-troh THee-ah-koh-<u>pohn</u>

vaccination εμβόλιο ehm-<u>voh</u>-lee-oh

valid ισχύει ee-<u>skhee</u>-ee

valley κοιλάδα kee-<u>lah</u>-THah

valuable πολύτιμος poh-<u>lee</u>-tee-mohs

value n **αξία** ah-<u>ksee</u>-ah

VAT [BE] **ΦΠΑ** fee-pee-<u>ah</u>

vegetarian χορτοφάγος khohr-toh-<u>fah</u>-ghohs

vein φλέβα <u>fleh</u>-vah

velvet βελούδο veh-<u>loo</u>-THoh

very πολύ poh-<u>lee</u>

video βιντεοκασέτα vee-deh-oh-kah-<u>seh</u>-tah

video game παιχνίδι βίντεο pehkh-<u>nee</u>-THee vee-deh-oh

village χωριό khohr-<u>yoh</u>

visa βίζα <u>vee</u>-zah

visit n **επίσκεψη** eh-<u>pees</u>-keh-psee

volleyball βόλεϊ <u>voh</u>-leh-ee

vomit v **κάνω εμετό** <u>kah</u>-noh eh-meh-<u>toh</u>

W

wait v **περιμένω** peh•ree•<u>meh</u>•noh
waiter n **γκαρσόν** gahr•<u>sohn</u>
waitress δεσποινίς THehs•pee•<u>nees</u>
wake v **ξυπνώ** kseep•<u>noh</u>
walk v **περπατώ** pehr•pah•<u>toh</u>
walking route διαδρομή περιήγησης
  THee•ah•THroh•<u>mee</u> peh•ree•<u>ee</u>•yee•sees
wall τοίχος <u>tee</u>•khohs
wallet πορτοφόλι pohr•toh•<u>foh</u>•lee
want θέλω <u>theh</u>•loh
warm ζεστός zehs•<u>tohs</u>
washing machine πλυντήριο
  pleen•<u>deer</u>•ee•oh
watch n **ρολόι** roh•<u>loh</u>•ee
watch strap λουρί ρολογιού loo•<u>ree</u>
  roh•loh•<u>yioo</u>
water n **νερό** neh•<u>roh</u>
waterfall καταρράχτης kah•tah•<u>rahkh</u>•tees
waterproof αδιάβροχος
  ah•THee•<u>ahv</u>•roh•khohs
wave n **κύμα** <u>kee</u>•mah
way δρόμος <u>THroh</u>•mohs
wear v **φορώ** foh•<u>roh</u>
weather καιρός keh•<u>rohs</u>
weather forecast πρόβλεψη καιρού
  <u>prohv</u>•leh•psee keh•<u>roo</u>
wedding γάμος <u>ghah</u>•mohs
west δυτικά THee•tee•<u>kah</u>
wetsuit στολή δύτη stoh•<u>lee</u> THee•tee
wheelchair αναπηρική καρέκλα
  ah•nah•pee•ree•<u>kee</u> kah•<u>rehk</u>•lah
wide φαρδύς fahr•<u>THees</u>
wife σύζυγος <u>see</u>•zee•ghohs
window παράθυρο pah•<u>rah</u>•thee•roh
window seat θέση δίπλα στο παράθυρο
  <u>theh</u>•see THeep•lah stoh pah•<u>rah</u>•thee•roh
winery οινοποιείο ee•noh•pee•<u>ee</u>•oh

wireless internet ασύρματο ίντερνετ
  ah•<u>see</u>•rmah•toh ee•nteh•rnet
with με meh
withdraw κάνω ανάληψη <u>kah</u>•noh
  ah•<u>nah</u>•lee•psee
without χωρίς khoh•<u>rees</u>
witness μάρτυρας <u>mahr</u>•tee•rahs
wood (forest) δάσος THah•sohs; **(material)**
  ξύλο <u>ksee</u>•loh
work δουλεύω THoo•<u>leh</u>•voh
worry ανησυχώ ah•nee•see•<u>khoh</u>
worse χειρότερος khee•<u>roh</u>•teh•rohs
wound (cut) πληγή plee•<u>yee</u>
write (down) γράφω <u>ghrah</u>•foh
wrong λάθος <u>lah</u>•thohs

X

x-ray ακτινογραφία
  ahk•tee•nohgh•rah•<u>fee</u>•ah

Y

yacht γιωτ yoht
yellow κίτρινος <u>keet</u>•ree•nohs
young νέος <u>neh</u>•ohs
youth hostel ξενώνας νεότητας
  kseh•<u>noh</u>•nahs neh•<u>oh</u>•tee•tahs

Z

zoo ζωολογικός κήπος
  zoh•oh•loh•yee•<u>kohs</u> <u>kee</u>•pohs

ENGLISH–GREEK

A

ATM ehee·tee·**ehm ATM**

άγαλμα ah·ghahl·mah **statue**

αγαπημένος ah·ghah·pee·<u>meh</u>·nohs **favorite**

αγαπώ ah·ghah·<u>poh</u> v **love**

αγγειοπλαστική ahn·gee·ohp·lahs·tee·<u>kee</u> **pottery**

Αγγλία ahng·<u>lee</u>·ah **England**

αγγλικά ahng·lee·<u>kah</u> **English language**

αγγλικός ahng·lee·<u>kohs</u> adj **English**

Άγγλος <u>ahng</u>·lohs **English (nationality)**

αγενής ah·yeh·<u>nees</u> **rude**

αγορά ah·ghoh·<u>rah</u> n **market**

αγοράζω ah·ghoh·<u>rah</u>·zoh **buy**

αγόρι ah·<u>ghoh</u>·ree **boy**

αγώνας ah·<u>ghoh</u>·nahs n **match (sport)**

άδεια <u>ah</u>·THee·ah n **permit**

άδεια σκι <u>ah</u>·THee·ah skee **lift pass**

άδειος <u>ahTH</u>·yohs adj **empty**

αδιάβροχο ah·THee·<u>ahv</u>·roh·khoh **raincoat**

αδιάβροχος ah·THee·<u>ahv</u>·roh·khohs **waterproof**

αδύναμος ah·<u>THee</u>·nah·mohs **weak**

αεροδρόμιο ah·eh·roh·<u>THroh</u>·mee·oh **airport**

αεροπλάνο ah·eh·rohp·<u>lah</u>·noh n **plane**

αεροπορική εταιρία ah·eh·roh·poh·ree·<u>kee</u> eh·teh·<u>ree</u>·ah **airline**

αεροπορικώς ah·eh·roh·poh·ree·<u>kohs</u> **airmail**

αηδιαστικός ah·ee·THee·ah·stee·<u>kohs</u> **revolting**

αθλητικά παπούτσια ath·lee·tee·<u>kah</u> pah·<u>poo</u>·tsiah **sneakers**

αθλητικό στάδιο ahth·lee·tee·<u>koh</u> stah·THee·oh **sports stadium**

αθλητικός όμιλος ahth·lee·tee·<u>kohs</u> oh·mee·lohs **sports club**

αθλητισμός ahth·lee·teez·<u>mohs</u> **sport**

αθώος ah·<u>thoh</u>·ohs **innocent**

αιμορραγία eh·moh·rah·<u>yee</u>·ah n **bleed**

αιμορραγώ eh·moh·rah·<u>yoh</u> v **bleed**

αίθουσα συναυλιών <u>eh</u>·thoo·sah see·nahv·lee·<u>ohn</u> **concert hall**

ακολουθώ ah·koh·loo·<u>thoh</u> v **follow**

ακουστικό βαρυκοΐας ah·koo·stee·<u>koh</u> vah·ree·koh·<u>ee</u>·ahs **hearing aid**

ακριβός ahk·ree·<u>vohs</u> **expensive**

ακτή ahk·<u>tee</u> n **shore**

ακτινογραφία ahk·tee·nohgh·rah·<u>fee</u>·ah **x-ray**

ακυρώνω ah·kee·<u>roh</u>·noh v **cancel**

αληθινός ah·lee·thee·<u>nohs</u> **real (genuine)**

αλλά ah·<u>lah</u> conj **but**

άλλα <u>ah</u>·lah **others**

αλλαγή ah·lah·<u>yee</u> n **change**

αλλάζω ah·<u>lah</u>·zoh v **exchange (money)**

αλλεργικός ahl·ehr·yee·<u>kohs</u> **allergic**

αλληλογραφία ah·lee·lohgh·rah·<u>fee</u>·ah n **mail**

άλλο ένα <u>ah</u>·loh eh·nah **extra (additional)**

άλλος *ah·lohs* **another**

αλουμινόχαρτο *ah·loo·mee·noh·khah·rtoh* **aluminum foil**

Αμερικανός *ah·meh·ree·kah·nohs n* **American**

αμέσως *ah·meh·sohs* **immediately**

άμμος *ah·mohs* **sand**

ανάβω *ah·nah·voh v* **turn on**

αναίσθητος *ah·nehs·thee·tohs* **unconscious**

ανάκτορα *ah·nahk·toh·rah* **palace**

αναλυτικός λογαριασμός *ah·nah·lee·tee·kohs loh·ghahr·yahz·mohs* **itemized bill**

αναπηρική καρέκλα *ah·nah·pee·ree·kee kah·rehk·lah* **wheelchair**

αναπνευστήρας *ah·nahp·nehf·stee·rahs* **snorkel**

αναπνέω *ah·nahp·neh·oh* **breathe**

αναπτήρας *ah·nahp·tee·rahs n* **lighter (cigarette)**

αναρρίχηση *ah·nah·ree·khee·see* **rock climbing**

ανατολικά *ah·nah·toh·lee·kah* **east**

αναφέρω *ah·nah·feh·roh* **mention (report)**

αναχώρηση *ah·nah·khoh·ree·see* **departure (travel)**

άνδρας *ahn·THrahs n* **male (man)**

ανεμιστήρας *ah·neh·mees·tee·rahs n* **fan (air)**

ανεβάζω *ah·neh·vah·zoh v* **turn up (volume, heat)**

ανέκδοτο *ah·nehk·THoh·toh n* **joke**

ανησυχώ *ah·nee·see·khoh* **worry**

ανθοπωλείο *ahn·thoh·poh·lee·oh* **florist**

ανοίγω *ah·nee·ghoh v* **open**

ανοιχτήρι *ah·neekh·tee·ree* **can opener**

ανοιχτός *ah·neekh·tohs adj* **light (color), open**

ανοιχτότερος *ah·neekh·toh·teh·rohs adj* **lighter (color)**

ανταλλακτικό *ahn·dah·lahk·tee·koh* **replacement part**

αντιβιοτικό *ahn·dee·vee·oh·tee·koh* **antibiotic**

αντιηλιακό *ahn·dee·ee·lee·ah·koh* **sunscreen**

αντισηπτική κρέμα *ahn·dee·seep·tee·kee kreh·mah* **antiseptic cream**

αντίχειρας *ahn·dee·khee·rahs* **thumb**

ανώμαλος *ah·noh·mah·lohs* **uneven (ground)**

αξεσουάρ *ah·kseh·soo·ahr* **accessory**

αξία *ah·ksee·ah n* **value**

αξιοθέατο *ah·ksee·oh·theh·ah·tah* **sightseeing sight**

απαγορευμένος *ah·pah·ghoh·rehv·meh·nohs* **prohibited**

απαραίτητος *ah·pah·reh·tee·tohs* **essential, necessary**

απασχολημένος *ah·pahs·khoh·lee·meh·nohs adj* **busy (occupied)**

απέναντι *ah·peh·nahn·dee* **opposite**

απεριόριστα χιλιόμετρα *ah·peh·ree·ohr·ees·tah khee·lioh·meht·rah* **unlimited mileage**

απλό εισιτήριο *ahp·loh ee·see·tee·ree·oh* **one-way [single BE] ticket**

απλός *ahp·lohs* **simple**

από *ah·poh* **from**

απομίμηση ah·poh·<u>mee</u>·mee·see **imitation**

αποβάθρα ah·poh·<u>vahth</u>·rah **platform, quay**

απόγευμα ah·<u>poh</u>·yehv·mah **afternoon**

απόδειξη ah·<u>poh</u>·THee·ksee **receipt**

απορρυπαντικό ah·poh·ree·pahn·dee·<u>koh</u> **detergent**

αποσμητικό ah·pohz·mee·tee·<u>koh</u> **deodorant**

αποσκευές ah·pohs·keh·<u>vehs</u> **baggage [BE]**

αποσκευές χειρός ah·pohs·keh·<u>vehs</u> khee·<u>rohs</u> **hand luggage**

αποστειρωτικό διάλυμα ah·pohs·tee·roh·tee·<u>koh</u> THee·<u>ah</u>·lee·mah **sterilizing solution**

απόχρωση ah·<u>pohkh</u>·roh·see **shade (color)**

απώλεια ah·<u>poh</u>·lee·ah n **loss**

αργά ahr·<u>ghah</u> adv **late**

αργία ahr·<u>yee</u>·ah **public holiday**

αργός ahr·<u>ghohs</u> adj **slow**

αριθμός κυκλοφορίας ah·reeth·<u>mohs</u> kee·kloh·foh·<u>ree</u>·ahs **registration number**

αριθμός πτήσεως ah·reeth·<u>mohs</u> ptee·seh·ohs **flight number**

αριθμός τηλεφώνου ah·reeth·<u>mohs</u> tee·leh·<u>foh</u>·noo **telephone number**

αριστερός ah·rees·teh·<u>rohs</u> **left** (adj)

αριστερά ah·rees·teh·<u>rah</u> **left** (adv)

αρκετά ahr·keh·<u>tah</u> **enough**

αρραβωνιαστικιά ah·rah·voh·niahs·tee·<u>kiah</u> **fiancée**

αρραβωνιαστικός ah·rah·voh·niahs·tee·<u>kohs</u> **fiancé**

αρρώστεια ahr·<u>ohs</u>·tee·ah **illness**

άρρωστος <u>ah</u>·rohs·tohs adj **sick**

αρτοποιείο ah·rtoh·pee·<u>ee</u>·oh **bakery**

αρχάριος ahr·<u>khah</u>·ree·ohs **beginner**

αρχίζω v ahr·<u>khee</u>·zoh **start**

ασανσέρ ah·sahn·<u>sehr</u> n **lift (elevator)**

ασήμι ah·<u>see</u>·mee **silver**

ασύρματο ίντερνετ ah·<u>see</u>·rmah·toh ee·nteh·rnet **wireless internet**

ασθενοφόρο ahs·theh·noh·<u>foh</u>·roh **ambulance**

ασθματικός ahsth·mah·tee·<u>kohs</u> **asthmatic**

ασπιρίνη ahs·pee·<u>ree</u>·nee **aspirin**

αστυνομία ah·stee·noh·<u>mee</u>·ah n **police**

αστυνομικό τμήμα ah·stee·noh·mee·<u>koh</u> tmee·mah **police station**

ασφάλεια ahs·<u>fah</u>·lee·ah n **fuse; insurance**

ασφάλεια αποζημίωσης ahs·<u>fah</u>·lee·ah ah·poh·zee·mee·oh·sees **insurance claim**

ασφάλεια υγείας ahs·<u>fah</u>·lee·ah ee·<u>yee</u>·ahs **health insurance**

ασφαλής ahs·fah·<u>lees</u> adj **safe (not dangerous)**

ασφαλιστική εταιρία ahs·fah·lees·tee·<u>kee</u> eh·teh·<u>ree</u>·ah **insurance company**

άσχημος <u>ahs</u>·khee·mohs **ugly**

άτομο με ειδικές ανάγκες <u>ah</u>·toh·moh meh ee·THee·<u>kehs</u> ah·<u>nahn</u>·gehs **disabled**

ατύχημα ah·<u>tee</u>·khee·mah **accident**

αυθεντικός ahf·thehn·dee·<u>kohs</u> **genuine**

αυθεντικότητα ahf·thehn·dee·koh·tee·tah **authenticity**

αϋπνία ah·eep·<u>nee</u>·ah **insomnia**

αυτοκίνητο ahf·toh·<u>kee</u>·nee·toh **car**

αυχένας ahf·<u>kheh</u>·nahs **neck (part of body)**

αφήνω ah·<u>fee</u>·noh v **leave (let go)**

αφορολόγητα είδη ah·foh·roh·<u>loh</u>·yee·tah ee·THee **duty-free goods**

αφρόλουτρο για ντουζ ahf·<u>roh</u>·loot·roh yah dooz **shower gel**

αχθοφόρος ahkh·thoh·<u>foh</u>·rohs **porter**

В
___

βαμβάκι vahm·<u>vah</u>·kee **cotton**

βαγκόν-λι vah·<u>gohn</u>·lee **sleeping car**

βάζο <u>vah</u>·zoh n **jar**

βάζω <u>vah</u>·zoh v **put**

βαλές vah·<u>lehs</u> **jack**

βαρετός vah·reh·<u>tohs</u> **boring**

βάρκα <u>vahr</u>·kah **boat**

βαρύς vah·<u>rees</u> **heavy**

βασιλιάς vah·see·<u>liahs</u> **king**

βγαίνω <u>vyeh</u>·noh **get out (of vehicle)**

βελούδο veh·<u>loo</u>·THoh **velvet**

βενζινάδικο vehn·zee·<u>nah</u>·THee·koh **gas [petrol BE] station**

βενζίνη vehn·<u>zee</u>·nee **gasoline [petrol BE]**

βερνίκι παπουτσιών vehr·<u>nee</u>·kee pah·poo·<u>tsiohn</u> **shoe polish**

βήχας <u>vee</u>·khahs n **cough**

βήχω <u>vee</u>·khoh v **cough**

βιβλίο veev·<u>lee</u>·oh n **book**

βιβλιοθήκη veev·lee·oh·<u>thee</u>·kee **library**

βιβλιοπωλείο veev·lee·oh·poh·<u>lee</u>·oh **bookstore**

βίδα <u>vee</u>·THah n **screw**

βίζα <u>vee</u>·zah **visa**

βιντεοκασέτα vee·deh·oh·kah·<u>seh</u>·tah **video**

βλάβη <u>vlah</u>·vee **breakdown** n **(car)**

βλέπω <u>vleh</u>·poh **see**

βοήθεια voh·<u>ee</u>·thee·ah n **help**

βοηθώ voh·ee·<u>thoh</u> v **help**

βόλεϋ <u>voh</u>·leh·ee **volleyball**

βόρεια <u>voh</u>·ree·ah **north**

βοτανικός κήπος voh·tah·nee·<u>kohs</u> <u>kee</u>·pohs **botanical garden**

βουνό voo·<u>noh</u> **mountain**

βουρτσίζω voor·<u>tsee</u>·zoh v **brush**

βραδινό vrah·THee·<u>noh</u> **dinner**

βράδυ <u>vrah</u>·THee **evening**

βράζω <u>vrah</u>·zoh **boil**

βράχος <u>vrah</u>·khohs n **rock**

βρετανικός vreh·tah·nee·<u>kohs</u> adj **British**

Βρετανός vreh·tah·<u>nohs</u> **British (nationality)**

βρέχει <u>vreh</u>·khee v **rain**

βροχή vroh·<u>khee</u> n **rain**

βρύση <u>vree</u>·see **faucet**

βρώμικος <u>vroh</u>·mee·kohs adj **dirty**

Γ
___

γάμος <u>ghah</u>·mohs **wedding**

γάζα <u>ghah</u>·zah **bandage**

γαλάκτωμα για τα μαλλιά ghah·<u>lah</u>·ktoh·mah yah tah mah·<u>liah</u> **conditioner (hair)**

γάντι <u>ghahn</u>·dee n **glove**

γαστρίτιδα ghahs·<u>tree</u>·tee·THah **gastritis**

γεμάτος yeh·<u>mah</u>·tohs adj **full**

γείτονας <u>yee</u>·toh·nahs n **neighbor**

γελώ yeh·<u>loh</u> v laugh

γεμιστή yeh·mees·<u>tee</u> stuffed olive

γέρικος <u>yeh</u>·ree·kohs old (person)

γεύμα <u>yehv</u>·mah meal

γέφυρα <u>yeh</u>·fee·rah n bridge (over water)

γη ghee n land

γήπεδο γκολφ <u>yee</u>·peh·THoh gohlf golf course

γήπεδο τέννις <u>yee</u>·peh·THoh <u>teh</u>·nees tennis court

γιατρός yah·<u>trohs</u> doctor

γιωτ yoht yacht

γκαράζ gah·<u>rahz</u> garage

γκαρσόν gahr·<u>sohn</u> waiter

γκόλφ gohlf golf

γκρουπ groop n group

γλώσσα <u>ghloh</u>·sah tongue

γνωρίζω ghnoh·<u>ree</u>·zoh know

γόνατο <u>ghoh</u>·nah·toh knee

γονείς ghoh·<u>nees</u> parents

γράμμα <u>ghrah</u>·mah letter

γραμματόσημο ghrah·mah·<u>toh</u>·see·moh n stamp (postage)

γραμμή ghrah·<u>mee</u> n line (subway)

γραβάτα ghrah·<u>vah</u>·tah n tie

γρασίδι ghrah·<u>see</u>·THee grass

γραφείο ghrah·<u>fee</u>·oh office

γραφείο ανταλλαγής συναλλάγματος ghrah·<u>fee</u>·oh ahn·dah·lah·<u>yees</u> see·nah·<u>lahgh</u>·mah·tohs currency exchange office

γραφείο εισιτηρίων ghrah·<u>fee</u>·oh ee·see·tee·<u>ree</u>·ohn ticket office

γραφείο πληροφοριών ghrah·<u>fee</u>·oh plee·roh·foh·ree·<u>ohn</u> information office

γράφω <u>ghrah</u>·foh write (down)

γρήγορα <u>ghree</u>·ghoh·rah adv fast

γρήγορος <u>ghree</u>·ghoh·rohs quick

γρίππη <u>ghree</u>·pee flu

γυαλιά yah·<u>liah</u> glasses (optical)

γυαλιά ηλίου yah·<u>liah</u> ee·<u>lee</u>·oo sun glasses

γυναικολόγος yee·neh·koh·<u>loh</u>·ghohs gynecologist

γυρίζω yee·<u>ree</u>·zoh v turn

γωνία ghoh·<u>nee</u>·ah corner

Δ

δανείζω THah·<u>nee</u>·zoh lend

δάσος <u>THah</u>·sohs n forest (wood)

δάχτυλο <u>THakh</u>·tee·loh n finger

δείγμα <u>THeegh</u>·mah specimen

δείχνω <u>THeekh</u>·noh v point (show)

δέντρο <u>THehn</u>·droh tree

δεξιός THeh·ksee·<u>ohs</u> adj right (not left)

δέρμα <u>THehr</u>·mah n skin

δημαρχείο THee·mahr·<u>khee</u>·oh town hall

δημοφιλής THee·moh·fee·<u>lees</u> popular

δηλητήριο THee·lee·<u>tee</u>·ree·oh n poison

δηλητηριώδης THee·lee·tee·ree·<u>oh</u>·THees poisonous

δηλώνω THee·<u>loh</u>·noh declare

δήλωση <u>THee</u>·loh·see statement (legal)

δημόσιος THee·<u>moh</u>·see·ohs public

διαμάντι THiah·<u>mahn</u>·dee n diamond

διαμέρισμα THee·ah·<u>meh</u>·reez·mah apartment

διάβαση πεζών THee·<u>ah</u>·vah·see peh·<u>zohn</u> pedestrian crossing διαβατήριο THiah·vah·<u>tee</u>·ree·oh **passport**

διαβητικός THee·ah·vee·tee·<u>kohs</u> **diabetic**

διαδρομή THee·ahTH·roh·<u>mee</u> n **route**

διάδρομος THee·<u>ah</u>·THroh·mohs **aisle seat**

διαζευγμένος THee·ah·zehv·<u>ghmeh</u>·nohs **divorced**

διακοπές THee·ah·koh·<u>pehs</u> **vacation [holiday BE]**

διακόπτης THiah·<u>koh</u>·ptees n **switch**

διαμέρισμα THee·ah·mehr·ees·mah n **flat**

διάρροια THee·<u>ah</u>·ree·ah **diarrhea**

διάσημος THee·<u>ah</u>·see·mohs **famous**

διεθνής THee·eth·<u>nees</u> **international**

διεθνής φοιτητική κάρτα THee·ehth·<u>nees</u> fee·tee·tee·<u>kee</u> kahr·tah **International Student Card**

διερμηνέας THee·ehr·mee·<u>neh</u>·ahs **interpreter**

διεύθυνση THee·<u>ehf</u>·theen·see n **address**

διευθυντής THee·ehf·theen·<u>dees</u> **manager**

δικηγόρος THee·kee·<u>ghoh</u>·rohs **lawyer**

δίκλινο δωμάτιο <u>THeek</u>·lee·noh THoh·<u>mah</u>·tee·oh **double room**

δίνω THee·noh **give**

διόρθωμα THee·<u>ohr</u>·thoh·mah n **trim**

δίπλα <u>THeep</u>·lah **next to**

διπλό κρεβάτι THeep·<u>loh</u> kreh·<u>vah</u>·tee **twin bed**

δίσκος <u>THees</u>·kohs **tray**

διψάω THee·<u>psah</u>·oh **thirsty**

δοκιμάζω THoh·kee·<u>mah</u>·zoh **try on**

δολάριο THoh·<u>lah</u>·ree·oh **dollar**

δόντι <u>THohn</u>·dee **tooth**

δοσολογία THoh·soh·loh·<u>yee</u>·ah **dosage**

δουλειά THoo·<u>liah</u> **job**

δουλεύω THoo·<u>leh</u>·voh **work**

δρομολόγιο THroh·moh·<u>loh</u>·yee·oh **time table**

δρόμος <u>THroh</u>·mohs **road, street, way**

δυνατός THee·nah·<u>tohs</u> adj **loud**

δυσάρεστος THee·<u>sah</u>·reh stohs **unpleasant**

δύσκολος <u>THee</u>·skoh·lohs **difficult**

δυσπεψία THes·peh·<u>psee</u>·ah **indigestion**

δυστυχώς THees·tee·<u>khohs</u> **unfortunately**

δυτικά THee·tee·<u>kah</u> **west**

δωμάτιο THoh·<u>mah</u>·tee·oh n **room**

δώρο <u>THoh</u>·roh **gift**

E

ελιά eh·liah **olive**

εμβόλιο ehm·<u>voh</u>·lee·oh **vaccination**

εμπορικό κέντρο ehm·boh·ree·<u>koh</u> keh·ntroh **shopping mall [centre BE]**

εγγύηση eh·<u>gee</u>·ee·see n **guarantee**

εγγυώμαι eh·gee·oh·meh v **guarantee**

έγκαυμα ηλίου <u>ehn</u>·gahv·mah ee·<u>lee</u>·oo n **sun burn**

έγκυος <u>eh</u>·gee·ohs **pregnant**

έδαφος <u>eh</u>·THah·fohs **ground (earth)**

εδώ eh·<u>THoh</u> **here**

εδώ κοντά eh·<u>THoh</u> kohn·<u>dah</u> **nearby**

εθνική οδός ehth·nee·<u>kee</u> oh·<u>THohs</u> **highway, motorway**

εθνικός eth·nee·<u>kohs</u> **national**

εθνικός δρυμός eth·nee·<u>kohs</u> THree·<u>mohs</u> **nature reserve** είμαι <u>ee</u>·meh **be**

είμαι κουφός koo·<u>fohs</u> **deaf**

είδη οικιακής χρήσεως ee·THee ee·kee·ah·<u>kees</u> <u>khree</u>·seh·ohs **household articles**

ειδική ανάγκη ee·THee·<u>kee</u> ah·<u>nahn</u>·gkee **special requirement**

ειδικός ee·THee·<u>kohs</u> **specialist**

είδος <u>ee</u>·THohs **kind (sort)**

εισιτήριο ee·see·<u>tee</u>·ree·oh **fare (ticket)**

εισιτήριο με επιστροφή ee·see·<u>tee</u>·ree·oh meh eh·pee·stroh·<u>fee</u> **roundtrip [return BE] ticket**

εκδρομή ehk·THroh·mee **excursion**

εκεί eh·<u>kee</u> **there, over there**

εκείνα eh·<u>kee</u>·nah **those**

έκθεση <u>ehk</u>·theh·see **exhibition**

έκπτωση <u>ehk</u>·ptoh·see **reduction**

έκτακτη ανάγκη <u>ehk</u>·tahk·tee ah·<u>nah</u>·gee **emergency**

ελάχιστος eh·<u>lah</u>·khees·tohs **minimum**

ελεύθερο δωμάτιο eh·<u>lehf</u>·theh·roh THoh·<u>mah</u>·tee·oh **vacancy**

ελεύθερος eh·<u>lehf</u>·theh·rohs *adj* **free, single, vacant**

ελικόπτερο eh·lee·<u>kohp</u>·teh·roh **helicopter**

Ελλάδα eh·<u>lah</u>·THah **Greece**

Έλληνας <u>eh</u>·lee·nahs **Greek (nationality)**

ελληνικός eh·lee·nee·<u>kohs</u> *adj* **Greek**

ένα βράδυ <u>eh</u>·nah vrah·THee **overnight**

ένα τέταρτο <u>eh</u>·nah teh·tah·rtoh **quarter (quantity)**

ενδιαφέρων en·THee·ah·<u>feh</u>·rohn **interesting**

ένεση <u>eh</u>·neh·see **injection**

ενήλικας eh·<u>nee</u>·lee·kahs **adult**

ενοχλώ eh·noh·<u>khloh</u> **disturb**

έντομο <u>ehn</u>·doh·moh **insect**

εντομοαπωθητικό ehn·doh·moh·ah·poh·thee·tee·<u>koh</u> **insect repellent**

έντυπο <u>ehn</u>·dee·poh *n* **form**

εντυπωσιακός ehn·dee·poh·see·ah·<u>kohs</u> **impressive**

ενυδατική κρέμα eh·nee·THah·tee·<u>kee</u> <u>kreh</u>·mah **moisturizer (cream)**

εξάνθημα eh·<u>ksahn</u>·thee·mah *n* **rash**

εξαργυρώνω eh·ksahr·ghee·<u>roh</u>·noh *v* **cash**

εξόγκωμα eh·<u>ksoh</u>·goh·mah *n* **lump (medical)**

έξοδος <u>eh</u>·ksoh·THohs *n* **gate (airport); exit**

έξοδος κινδύνου <u>eh</u>·ksoh·THohs keen·<u>THee</u>·noo **emergency, fire exit**

εξοχή eh·ksoh·<u>khee</u> **countryside**

έξοχος <u>eh</u>·ksoh·khohs **superb**

εξπρές ehk·<u>sprehs</u> **express (mail)**

εξυπηρέτηση eh·ksee·pee·<u>reh</u>·tee·see **facility**

έξω <u>eh</u>·ksoh *adv* **out**

έξω <u>eh</u>·ksoh *adj* **outside**

εξωλέμβιο eh·ksoh·<u>lehm</u>·vee·oh **motorboat**

εξωτερικός eh·ksoh·teh·ree·<u>kohs</u> **outdoor**

επαναλαμβάνω eh·pah·nah·lahm·<u>vah</u>·noh *v* **repeat**

επάνω eh·<u>pah</u>·noh **upstairs**

επείγον eh·<u>pee</u>·ghohn **urgent**

επιμένω eh·pee·<u>meh</u>·noh **insist**

επιβάτης eh·pee·<u>vah</u>·tees **passenger**
επιβεβαιώνω eh·pee·veh·veh·<u>oh</u>·noh
confirm
επίβλεψη eh·<u>peev</u>·leh·psee **supervision**
επίθεση eh·pee·<u>theh</u>·see n **attack**
επίθετο eh·<u>pee</u>·theh·toh **surname**
επικοινωνώ eh·pee·kee·noh·<u>noh</u> v
contact
επιληπτικός eh·pee·leep·tee·<u>kohs</u>
epileptic
επίπεδο eh·<u>pee</u>·peh·THoh **level (even)**
επίπεδος eh·<u>pee</u>·peh·THohs adj **flat**
έπιπλα <u>eh</u>·peep·lah **furniture**
επιπλέον eh·peep·<u>leh</u>·ohn **spare (extra)**
επισκευάζω eh·pee·skeh·<u>vah</u>·zoh v
repair
επισκευή eh·pee·skeh·<u>vee</u> n **repair**
επισκευή παπουτσιών eh·pee·skeh·<u>vee</u>
pah·poo·<u>tsiohn</u> **shoe repair**
επίσκεψη eh·<u>pees</u>·keh·psee n **visit**
επιστροφή χρημάτων eh·pees·
troh·<u>fee</u> khree·<u>mah</u>·tohn n **refund**
επιταγή eh·pee·tah·<u>yee</u> n **check [cheque
BE] (bank)**
επιτίθεμαι eh·pee·<u>tee</u>·theh·meh v **attack**
επιτόκιο eh·pee·<u>toh</u>·kee·oh **interest rate**
επόμενος eh·<u>poh</u>·meh·nohs **next**
έρχομαι <u>ehr</u>·khoh·meh **come**
ερώτηση eh·<u>roh</u>·tee·see n **question**
εστιατόριο ehs·tee·ah·<u>toh</u>·ree·oh
restaurant
εσωτερική γραμμή eh·soh·theh·
ree·<u>kee</u> ghrah·<u>mee</u> **extension
(number)**
εσωτερική πισίνα eh·soh·teh·ree·
<u>kee</u> pee·<u>see</u>·nah **indoor pool**

εσωτερικός eh·soh·teh·ree·<u>kohs</u> **indoor**
ετικέτα eh·tee·<u>keh</u>·tah n **label**
έτοιμος eh·tee·mohs adj **ready**
ευθεία ehf·<u>thee</u>·ah **straight ahead**
εύκολος <u>ehf</u>·koh·lohs adj **easy**
ευρώ ehv·<u>roh</u> **euro**
Ευρωπαϊκή Ένωση ehv·roh·pah·
ee·<u>kee</u> <u>eh</u>·noh·see **European Union**
ευτυχώς ehf·tee·<u>khohs</u> **fortunately**
ευχαριστιέμαι ehf·khah·rees·
tieh·meh **enjoy**
ευχάριστος ehf·<u>khah</u>·rees·tohs **pleasant**
εφημερίδα eh·fee·meh·<u>ree</u>·THah
newspaper
έφηβος <u>eh</u>·fee·vohs **teenager**
έχω <u>eh</u>·khoh **have (possession)**

Z

ζαχαροπλαστείο zah·khah·rohp·
lahs·<u>tee</u>·oh **pastry store**
ζεστός zes·<u>tohs</u> **hot, warm (weather)**
ζημιά zee·<u>miah</u> n **damage**
ζητώ zee·<u>toh</u> **ask**
ζωγραφίζω zohgh·rah·<u>fee</u>·zoh v **paint**
ζωγράφος zohgh·<u>rah</u>·fohs **painter**
ζώνη <u>zoh</u>·nee **belt**
ζώνη για χρήματα <u>zoh</u>·nee yah
<u>khree</u>·mah·tah **money-belt**

H

ημερομηνία λήξεως
ee·meh·roh·mee·<u>nee</u>·ah <u>lee</u>·kseh·ohs
expiration date
ημερολόγιο ee·meh·roh·<u>loh</u>·yee·oh
calendar
ημικρανία ee·mee·krah·<u>nee</u>·ah **migraine**

ηλεκτρικός ee·lehk·tree·**kohs electric**

ηλεκτρονικό εισιτήριο ee·leh·ktroh·nee·**koh** ee·see·**tee**·ree·oh **e-ticket**

ηλεκτρονικό ταχυδρομείο ee·lehk·troh·nee·**koh** tah·hee·dro·**mee**·oh (ee)·meh·eel) **e-mail**

ηλεκτροπληξία ee·leh·ktroh·plee·**ksee**·ah **shock (electric)**

ηλίαση ee·lee·ah·see **sun stroke**

ηλικιωμένος ee·lee·kee·oh·**meh**·nohs **senior citizen**

Ηνωμένες Πολιτείες ee·noh·**meh**·nehs poh·lee·**tee**·ees **United States**

Ηνωμένο Βασίλειο ee·noh·**meh**·noh vah·**see**·lee·oh **United Kingdom**

ηρεμιστικό ee·reh·mee·stee·**koh sedative**

ήσυχος ee·see·khohs adj **quiet**

Θ

θάλασσα thah·lah·sah **sea**

θέατρο theh·aht·roh **theater**

θέλω theh·loh **want**

θέρμανση thehr·mahn·see **heating**

θερμή πηγή thehr·**mee** pee·**yee hot spring**

θερμόμετρο thehr·**moh**·meht·roh **thermometer**

θερμοκρασία theh·rmohk·rah·**see**·ah **temperature (body)**

θερμός thehr·**mohs thermos flask**

θέρετρο διακοπών theh·reh·troh THee·ah·koh·**pohn vacation resort**

θέση theh·see n **location (space), seat**

θέση δίπλα στο παράθυρο theh·see THeep·lah stoh pah·**rah**·thee·roh **window seat**

θηλυκός thee·lee·**kohs female**

θορυβώδης thoh·ree·**voh**·THees **noisy**

θρησκεία three·**skee**·ah **religion**

θυμάμαι thee·**mah**·meh **remember**

θυρίδα thee·**ree**·THah **luggage locker (lock-up)**

Ι

ιατρική εξέταση ee·ah·tree·**kee** eh·**kseh**·tah·see **examination (medical)**

ίδιος ee·THee·ohs **same**

ιδιωτικό μπάνιο ee·THee·oh·tee·**koh** bah·nioh **private bathroom**

ιερέας ee·eh·**reh**·ahs **priest**

ινσουλίνη een·soo·**lee**·nee **insulin**

ίντερνετ ee·nteh·rnet **internet**

ίντερνετ καφέ ee·nteh·rnet kah·**feh internet cafe**

ιπποδρομία ee·poh·THroh·**mee**·ah **horse racing**

ιστιοπλοϊκό ees·tee·oh·ploh·ee·**koh sailing boat**

ιστορία ee·stoh·**ree**·ah **history**

ισχύει ee·**skhee**·ee **valid**

ίσως ee·sohs **maybe, perhaps**

ιώδειο ee·**oh**·THee·oh **iodine**

Κ

κάδος απορριμμάτων **kah**·THohs ah·poh·ree·**mah**·tohn **trash can**

καθαρισμός προσώπου kah·thah·reez·**mohs** proh·**soh**·poo **facial**

καθαρός kah·thah·**rohs clean**

καθαρτικό kah·thahr·tee·<u>koh</u> **laxative**

καθεδρικός ναός kah·theh·THree·kohs nah·<u>ohs</u> **cathedral**

καθήκον kah·<u>thee</u>·kohn **duty (obligation)**

κάθομαι <u>kah</u>·thoh·meh **sit**

καθρέφτης kah·<u>threhf</u>·tees n **mirror**

καθυστέρηση kah·thee·<u>steh</u>·ree·see n **delay**

καθυστερώ kah·thee·steh·<u>roh</u> v **delay**

καινούργιος keh·<u>noor</u>·yohs **new**

καιρός keh·<u>rohs</u> **weather**

καλά kah·<u>lah</u> adv **fine (well)**

καλαμάκι kah·lah·<u>mah</u>·kee **straw (drinking)**

καλάθι kah·<u>lah</u>·THee **basket**

καλός kah·<u>lohs</u> **good**

καλσόν kahl·<u>sohn</u> n **tights**

κάλτσες <u>kahl</u>·tsehs **socks**

κάλυμμα φακού <u>kah</u>·lee·mah fah·<u>koo</u> **lens cap**

καλώ kah·<u>loh</u> v **call**

κάμπινγκ <u>kah</u>·mpeeng **camping**

καναπές kah·nah·<u>pehs</u> **sofa**

κανένας kah·<u>neh</u>·nahs adj **none**

κάνω ανάληψη <u>kah</u>·noh ah·<u>nah</u>·lee·psee **withdraw**

κάνω εμετό <u>kah</u>·noh eh·meh·<u>toh</u> v **vomit**

κάνω κράτηση <u>kah</u>·noh krah·tee·see v **book**

κάνω πεζοπορία <u>kah</u>·noh peh·zoh·poh·<u>ree</u>·ah v **hike**

καπέλο kah·<u>peh</u>·loh **hat**

καπνίζω kahp·<u>nee</u>·zoh v **smoke**

καπνοπωλείο kahp·noh·poh·<u>lee</u>·oh **tobacconist**

καπνός kahp·<u>nohs</u> **tobacco**

καραντίνα kah·rahn·<u>dee</u>·nah n **quarantine**

καράφα kah·<u>rah</u>·fah **carafe**

καρδιά kahr·<u>THee</u>·ah v **heart**

καρδιακό έμφραγμα kahr·<u>THee</u>·ah·<u>koh</u> ehm·frahgh·mah **heart attack**

καροτσάκι kah·roh·<u>tsah</u>·kee **trolley (cart)**

καροτσάκια αποσκευών kah·roh·<u>tsah</u>·kiah ah·pohs·keh·<u>vohn</u> **baggage [BE] carts [trolleys]**

κάρτα-κλειδί kahr·tah klee·<u>dee</u> **key card**

καρτποστάλ kahrt·poh·<u>stahl</u> **post card**

κασκόλ kahs·<u>kohl</u> **scarf**

κασσίτερος kah·<u>see</u>·teh·rohs **pewter**

κάστρο kahs·troh **castle**

καταδυτικός εξοπλισμός kah·tah·THee·tee·<u>kohs</u> eh·ksoh·pleez·<u>mohs</u> **diving equipment**

καταλαβαίνω kah·tah·lah·<u>veh</u>·noh **understand**

κατάλληλος kah·<u>tah</u>·lee·lohs **suitable**

καταρράχτης kah·tah·<u>rahkh</u>·tees **waterfall**

κατάστημα kah·<u>tah</u>·stee·mah **shop (store)**

κατάστημα με αντίκες kah·<u>tah</u>·stee·mah meh ahn·<u>tee</u>·kehs **antiques store**

κατάστημα με είδη δώρων kah·<u>tahs</u>·tee·mah meh ee·THee <u>THoh</u>·rohn **gift store**

κατάστημα με υγιεινές τροφές kah·<u>tahs</u>·tee·mah meh ee·yee·ee·<u>nehs</u> troh·<u>fehs</u> **health food store**

κατάστημα μεταχειρισμένων
ειδών kah·<u>tah</u>·stee·mah
meh·tah·khee·reez·<u>meh</u>·nohn ee·<u>THohn</u>
second-hand shop

κατάστημα αθλητικών ειδών
kah·<u>tahs</u>·tee·mah ath·lee·tee·<u>kohn</u>
ee·<u>THohn</u> **sporting goods store**

κατάστημα ρούχων kah·<u>tahs</u>·tee·mah
<u>roo</u>·khohn **clothing store**

κατάστημα σουβενίρ kah·<u>tahs</u>·tee·mah
soo·veh·<u>neer</u> **souvenir store**

κατάστημα υποδημάτων
kah·<u>tah</u>·stee·mah
ee·poh·THee·<u>mah</u>·tohn **shoe store**

καταστρέφω kah·tah·<u>streh</u>·foh v
damage

κατάψυξη kah·<u>tah</u>·psee·ksee **freezer**

κατεβαίνω kah·teh·<u>veh</u>·noh **get off
(transport)**

κατειλημμένος kah·tee·lee·<u>meh</u>·nohs
occupied

κάτι <u>kah</u>·tee **something**

κάτοχος <u>kah</u>·toh·khohs **owner**

κατσαβίδι kah·tsah·<u>vee</u>·THee **screwdriver**

κατσαρόλα kah·tsah·<u>roh</u>·lah **saucepan**

κάτω <u>kah</u>·toh adj **lower (berth)**

καύσωνας <u>kahf</u>·soh·nahs **heat wave**

καφετέρια kah·feh·<u>teh</u>·ree·ah **cafe**

κέντρο της πόλης <u>kehn</u>·droh tees
<u>poh</u>·lees **downtown area**

κεφάλι keh·<u>fah</u>·lee n **head**

κήπος <u>kee</u>·pohs n **garden**

κιθάρα kee·<u>thah</u>·rah **guitar**

κινηματογράφος
kee·nee·mah·tohgh·<u>rah</u>·fohs **movie
theater**

κίνηση <u>kee</u>·nee·see **traffic**

κινητό kee·nee·<u>toh</u> **cell phone [mobile
phone BE]**

κίτρινος <u>keet</u>·ree·nohs **yellow**

κλειδαριά klee·<u>THahr·yah</u> n **lock (door)**

κλειδί klee·<u>THee</u> n **key**

κλειδώνω klee·<u>THoh</u>·noh v **lock (door)**

κλειστός klees·<u>tohs</u> adj **shut**

κλεμένος kleh·<u>meh</u>·nos **stolen**

κλέφτης <u>klehf</u>·tees **thief**

κλήση <u>klee</u>·see n **call**

κλιματισμός klee·mah·teez·<u>mohs</u> **air
conditioning**

κλοπή kloh·<u>pee</u> **theft**

κομμωτήριο koh·moh·<u>tee</u>·ree·oh **hair
dresser**

κόμβος <u>kohm</u>·vohs **junction
(intersection)**

κοιμάμαι kee·<u>mah</u>·meh v **sleep**

κοιλάδα kee·<u>lah</u>·THah **valley**

κοιτάω kee·<u>tah</u>·oh v **look**

κολύμβηση koh·<u>leem</u>·vee·see **swimming**

κοντά kohn·<u>dah</u> adv **near**

κοντός kohn·<u>dohs</u> adj **short**

κορίτσι koh·<u>ree</u>·tsee **girl**

κορυφή koh·ree·<u>fee</u> n **peak**

κοσμηματοπωλείο kohz·mee·mah·
toh·poh·<u>lee</u>·oh **jeweler**

κουβέρτα koo·<u>veh</u>·rtah **blanket**

κουζίνα koo·<u>zee</u>·nah **stove**

κουνούπι koo·<u>noo</u>·pee **mosquito**

κουρασμένος koo·rahz·<u>meh</u>·nohs **tired**

κουστούμι koos·<u>too</u>·mee **men's suit**

κουταλάκι koo·tah·<u>lah</u>·kee **teaspoon**

κουτάλι koo·<u>tah</u>·lee n **spoon**

κουτί koo·<u>tee</u> **carton**

κουτί πρώτων βοηθειών koo·tee proh·tohn voh·ee·thee·ohn **first-aid kit**

κράμπα krahm·bah n **cramp**

κραγιόν krah·yohn **lipstick**

κρατώ krah·toh v **keep**

κρέμα ξυρίσματος kreh·mah ksee·reez·mah·tohs **shaving cream**

κρεμάστρα kreh·mahs·trah **hanger**

κρεβάτι kreh·vah·tee **bed**

κρυολόγημα kree·oh·loh·yee·mah n **cold (flu)**

κρύος kree·ohs adj **cold (temperature)**

κρύσταλλο kree·stah·loh n **crystal**

κύμα kee·mah n **wave**

κυλικείο kee·lee·kee·oh **snack bar**

κυλιόμενες σκάλες kee·lee·oh·meh·nehs skah·lehs **escalator**

Κύπρος kee·prohs **Cyprus**

κύριος kee·ree·ohs **main**

κωδικός περιοχής koh·THee·kohs peh·ree·oh·khees **area code**

κωπηλασία koh·pee·lah·see·ah **rowing**

Λ

λάμπα lahm·bah **lamp, light bulb**

λάθος lah·thohs **error, wrong**

λαιμόκοψη leh·moh·koh·psee **neck (shirt)**

λαιμός leh·mohs **throat**

λάστιχο lahs·tee·khoh **tire [tyre BE]**

λειτουργία lee·toor·yee·ah n **mass (church)**

λεκές leh·kehs n **stain**

λεξικό leh·ksee·koh **dictionary**

λεπτό lehp·toh n **minute (time)**

λεπτός lehp·tohs adj **thin**

λέω leh·oh **tell**

λεωφορείο leh·oh·foh·ree·oh **bus**

ληστεία lees·tee·ah **robbery**

λιμάνι lee·mah·nee n **harbor**

λίμνη leem·nee **lake**

λιμνούλα leem·noo·lah n **pond**

λιγότερο lee·ghoh·teh·roh **less**

λιπαντικό lee·pahn·dee·koh **lubricant**

λιπαρός lee·pah·rohs **greasy (hair, skin)**

λιποθυμώ lee·poh·thee·moh **faint**

λίρα lee·rah **pound (sterling)**

λίτρο lee·troh **liter**

λογαριασμός loh·ghahr·yahz·mohs n **check (bill), account**

λοσιόν loh·siohn **lotion**

λοσιόν μαυρίσματος loh·siohn mahv·rees·mah·tohs **sun tan lotion**

λουκέτο loo·keh·toh **padlock**

λουλούδι loo·loo·THee n **flower**

λουρί ρολογιού loo·ree roh·loh·yioo **watch strap**

λόφος loh·fohs **hill**

M

μαγιό mah·yoh **swimming trunks, swimsuit**

μαθαίνω mah·theh·noh **learn**

μάθημα ξένης γλώσσας mah·thee mah kseh·nees ghloh·sahs **language course**

μακιγιάζ mah·kee·yahz **make-up**

μακριά mahk·ree·ah adv **far**

μακρύς mak·rees adj **long**

μαλλιά mah·liah **hair**

μανικιούρ mah·nee·kioor **manicure**

μαξιλαροθήκη mah·ksee·lah·roh·thee·kee **pillow case**

μαργαριτάρι mahr·ghah·ree·**tah**·ree **pearl**

μάρτυρας **mahr**·tee·rahs **witness**

μας mahs **our**

μασάζ mah·**sahz** n **massage**

μάσκα **mahs**·kah n **mask (diving)**

μάτι **mah**·tee n **eye**

μαχαίρι mah·**kheh**·ree **knife**

με meh **with**

με άμμο meh **ah**·moh **sandy (beach)**

με υπότιτλους meh ee·**poh**·teet·loos **subtitled**

με χαλίκια meh khah·**lee**·kiah **pebbly (beach)**

μεγαλοπρεπής meh·ghah·lohp·reh·**pees** **magnificent**

μεγάλος meh·**ghah**·lohs adj **big, large**

μέγεθος **meh**·yeh·thohs n **size**

μέδουσα meh·THoo·sah **jellyfish**

μένω **meh**·noh v **stay**

μεριά mehr·**yah** **side (of road)**

μερίδα meh·**ree**·THah n **portion**

μερικές φορές meh·ree·**kehs** foh·**rehs** **sometimes**

μέσα **meh**·sah **inside**

μεσημεριανό meh·see·mehr·yah·**noh** n **lunch**

μετά meh·**tah** **after**

μετακομίζω meh·tah·koh·**mee**·zoh v **move (room)**

μέταλλο **meh**·tah·loh n **metal**

μετάξι meh·**tah**·ksee **silk**

μεταφέρω meh·tah·**feh**·roh **transfer**

μεταφορά meh·tah·foh·**rah** n **transit**

μεταφράζω meh·tah·**frah**·zoh **translate**

μετάφραση meh·**tah**·frah·see **translation**

μεταφραστής meh·tah·frah·**stees** **translator**

μέτρηση **meh**·tree·see **measurement**

μετρητά meht·ree·**tah** n **cash**

μετρό meh·**troh** **subway**

μετρώ meht·**roh** v **measure**

μη καπνίζοντες mee kap·**nee**·zon·des **non-smoking**

μήκος **mee**·kohs **length**

μήνας του μέλιτος **mee**·nahs too **meh**·lee·tohs **honeymoon**

μήνυμα **mee**·nee·mah n **message**

μηχανή mee·khah·**nee** **engine**

μια φορά miah foh·**rah** **once**

μικρός meek·**rohs** **little, small**

μιλώ mee·**loh** **speak**

μινι-μπαρ **mee**·nee bahr **mini-bar**

μισός mee·**sohs** **half**

μνημείο mnee·**mee**·oh **memorial, monument**

μολυσμένος moh·leez·**meh**·nohs **infected**

μονάδα moh·**nah**·THah **unit**

μοναδικός moh·nah·THee·**kohs** **unique**

μονόκλινο δωμάτιο moh·**noh**·klee·noh THoh·**mah**·tee·oh **single room**

μονοπάτι moh·noh·**pah**·tee **path, trail**

μοντέρνος moh·**deh**·rnohs **modern**

μοτοποδήλατο moh·toh·poh·**THee**·lah·toh **moped**

μουσείο moo·**see**·oh **museum**

μουσική moo·see·**kee** **music**

μουσικός moo·see·**kohs** **musician**

μουστάκι moos·**tah**·kee **moustache**

μπαγιάτικος bah·<u>yah</u>·tee·kohs **stale**
μπάνιο <u>bah</u>·nioh **bathroom, lavatory**
μπαρ bahr **bar**
μπάσκετ <u>bah</u>·skeht **basketball**
μπαστούνια του σκι bahs·<u>too</u>·niah too
  skee **ski poles**
μπαταρία bah·tah·<u>ree</u>·ah **battery**
μπέιμπι σίτερ beh·ee·bee <u>see</u>·tehr
  babysitter
μπικίνι bee·<u>kee</u>·nee **bikini**
μπλούζα <u>bloo</u>·zah **blouse**
μπλουζάκι bloo·<u>zah</u>·kee **T-shirt**
μπλου-τζην bloo·<u>jeen</u> **jeans**
μποξ bohks n **boxing**
μπότα <u>boh</u>·tah **boot**
μπότες πεζοπορίας <u>boh</u>·tehs
  peh·zoh·poh·<u>ree</u>·ahs **walking boots**
μπότες του σκι <u>boh</u>·tehs too skee **ski boots**
μπουκάλι boo·<u>kah</u>·lee **bottle**
μπρελόκ breh·<u>lohk</u> **key ring**
μύγα <u>mee</u>·ghah n **fly (insect)**
μυρίζω mee·<u>ree</u>·zoh v **smell**
μυς mees n **muscle**
μύτη <u>mee</u>·tee n **nose**
μύωπας <u>mee</u>·oh·pahs **short-sighted [BE]**
μωρό moh·<u>roh</u> **baby**

N

ναός nah·<u>ohs</u> **temple**
ναυαγοσώστης nah·vah·ghoh·<u>sohs</u>·tees
  lifeguard
ναυαγοσωστική λέμβος
  nah·vah·ghoh·sohs·tee·<u>kee</u> lehm·vohs
  lifeboat
ναυτία nahf·<u>tee</u>·ah **nausea, travel
  sickness**

νέος <u>neh</u>·ohs **young**
νερό neh·<u>roh</u> n **water**
νεύρο <u>nehv</u>·roh **nerve**
νεφρό nehf·<u>roh</u> **kidney**
νιπτήρας nee·<u>ptee</u>·rahs **sink (bathroom)**
νόμιμος <u>noh</u>·mee·mohs **legal**
νομίζω noh·<u>mee</u>·zoh **think**
νόμισμα <u>noh</u>·meez·mah **currency**
νοικιάζω nee·<u>kiah</u>·zoh v **hire, rent**
νοσοκόμα noh·soh·<u>koh</u>·mah n **nurse**
νοσοκομείο noh·soh·koh·<u>mee</u>·oh
  hospital
νόστιμος <u>nohs</u>·tee·mohs **delicious**
Νοτιοαφρικανός
  noh·tee·oh·ahf·ree·kah·<u>nohs</u> **South
  African (nationality)**
νότιος <u>noh</u>·tee·ohs adj **south**
ντεμοντέ deh·mohn·<u>deh</u> **old-fashioned**
ντήζελ <u>dee</u>·zehl **diesel**
ντουζ dooz n **shower**
ντουζίνα doo·<u>zee</u>·nah **dozen**
νύχι <u>nee</u>·khee n **nail**
νύχτα <u>neekh</u>·tah **night**
νυχτερινό κέντρο neekh·teh·ree·
  <u>noh</u> kehn·droh **night club**
νωρίς noh·<u>rees</u> **early**

Ξ

ξαπλώνω ksah·<u>ploh</u>·noh **lie down**
ξενάγηση kseh·<u>nah</u>·yee·see **guided
  tour**
ξενάγηση στα αξιοθέατα
  kseh·<u>nah</u>·yee·see stah
  ah·ksee·oh·<u>theh</u>·ah·tah **sightseeing
  tour**
ξεναγός kseh·nah·<u>ghohs</u> **tour guide**

ξένο συνάλλαγμα <u>kseh</u>·noh
see·<u>nah</u>·lahgh·mah **foreign currency**

ξενοδοχείο kseh·noh·<u>THoh</u>·khee·oh
hotel

ξένος <u>kseh</u>·nohs **foreign**

ξενώνας νεότητας kseh·<u>noh</u>·nahs
neh·<u>oh</u>·tee·tahs **youth hostel**

ξεχνώ ksehkh·<u>noh</u> **forget**

ξεχωριστά kseh·khoh·ree·<u>stah</u>
separately

ξινός ksee·<u>nohs</u> **sour**

ξοδεύω ksoh·<u>THeh</u>·voh **spend**

ξύλο <u>ksee</u>·loh **wood (material)**

ξυπνώ kseep·<u>noh</u> v **wake**

ξυραφάκι ksee·rah·<u>fah</u>·kee **razor, razor
blade**

Ο

ομάδα oh·<u>mah</u>·THah n **team**

όμορφος <u>oh</u>·mohr·fohs adj **beautiful,
pretty**

ομπρέλλα ohm·<u>breh</u>·lah **sun shade**

οβάλ oh·<u>vahl</u> **oval**

οδηγία oh·THee·<u>yee</u>·ah **instruction**

οδηγός καταστήματος oh·THee·<u>ghohs</u>
kah·tahs·<u>tee</u>·mah·tohs **store guide**

οδηγός ψυχαγωγίας oh·THee·<u>ghohs</u>
psee·khah·ghoh·<u>yee</u>·ahs
entertainment guide

οδηγώ oh·THee·<u>ghoh</u> v **drive**

οδική βοήθεια oh·THee·<u>kee</u>
voh·<u>ee</u>·thee·ah **road assistance**

οδοντίατρος oh·THohn·<u>dee</u>·ah·trohs
dentist

οδοντόβουρτσα oh·THohn·
<u>doh</u>·voor·tsah **tooth brush**

οδοντόπαστα oh·THohn·<u>doh</u>·
pahs·tah **tooth paste**

οικογένεια ee·koh·<u>yeh</u>·nee·ah **family**

οινοποιείο ee·noh·pee·<u>ee</u>·oh **winery**

όνομα <u>oh</u>·noh·mah n **name**

όπερα <u>oh</u>·peh·rah **opera**

οπωροπωλείο oh·poh·roh·poh·<u>lee</u>·oh
greengrocer [BE]

οργανωμένος ohr·ghah·noh·
<u>meh</u>·nohs **organized**

ορχήστρα ohr·<u>khees</u>·trah **orchestra**

οτιδήποτε oh·tee·<u>THee</u>·poh·teh
anything

οτοστόπ oh·toh·<u>stohp</u> **hitchhiking**

οφείλω oh·<u>fee</u>·loh **have to (obligation)**

οφθαλμίατρος ohf·thahl·<u>mee</u>·aht·rohs
optician

Π

παγοπέδιλα pah·ghoh·<u>peh</u>·THee·lah
skates

πάγος <u>pah</u>·ghohs n **ice**

παιδική χαρά peh·THee·<u>kee</u> khah·<u>rah</u>
playground

παιδικό κρεβάτι peh·THee·<u>koh</u>
kreh·<u>vah</u>·tee **crib [cot BE]**

παίζω <u>peh</u>·zoh v **play (games, music)**

παιχνίδι pehkh·<u>nee</u>·THee n **game (toy),
round**

παιχνίδι βίντεο pehkh·<u>nee</u>·THee
<u>vee</u>·deh·oh **video game**

πακέτο pah·<u>keh</u>·toh **parcel**

πακέτο για το σπίτι pah·<u>keh</u>·toh yah toh
<u>spee</u>·tee **take away**

παλιά πόλη pah·<u>liah</u> <u>poh</u>·lee **old town**

παλιός pah·<u>liohs</u> **old (thing)**

πάνα μωρού pah·nah moh·<u>roo</u> **diaper**

Πανεπιστήμιο pah·neh·pees·<u>tee</u>·mee·oh **university**

πάνες μωρού pah·nehs moh·<u>roo</u> **nappies**

πανόραμα pah·<u>noh</u>·rah·mah **panorama**

παντελόνι pahn·deh·<u>loh</u>·nee **pants [trousers BE]**

παντοπωλείο pahn·doh·poh·<u>lee</u>·oh **minimart**

παντόφλες pahn·<u>dohf</u>·lehs **slippers**

παντρεμένος pahn·dreh·<u>meh</u>·nohs **married**

πάνω pah·noh *adj* **top, upper (berth)**

παπούτσι pah·<u>poo</u>·tsee **shoe**

πάρα πολύ pah·rah poh·<u>lee</u> **too (extreme)**

παραγγέλνω pah·rah·<u>gehl</u>·noh *v* **order**

παράδειγμα pah·<u>rah</u>·THeegh·mah **example**

παραδοσιακός pah·rah·THoh·see·ah·<u>kohs</u> **traditional**

παράθυρο pah·<u>rah</u>·thee·roh **window**

παραλαβή αποσκευών pah·rah·lah·<u>vee</u> ah·poh·skeh·<u>vohn</u> **baggage [BE] claim**

παραλία pah·rah·<u>lee</u>·ah **beach**

παραλία γυμνιστών pah·rah·<u>lee</u>·ah yeem·nees·<u>tohn</u> **nudist beach**

παραλυσία pah·rah·lee·<u>see</u>·ah **paralysis**

παράνομος pah·<u>rah</u>·noh·mohs **illegal**

παράξενος pah·<u>rah</u>·kseh·nohs **strange**

παραπάνω pah·rah·<u>pah</u>·noh **more**

παρεξήγηση pah·reh·<u>ksee</u>·yee·see **misunderstanding**

πάρκο <u>pahr</u>·koh *n* **park**

παρκόμετρο pahr·<u>koh</u>·meht·roh **parking meter**

πάρτυ <u>pah</u>·rtee *n* **party (social gathering)**

παυσίπονο pahf·<u>see</u>·poh·noh **painkiller**

παχύς pah·<u>khees</u> *adj* **fat (person)**

πέδιλα peh·<u>THEE</u>·lah **sandals**

πεζόδρομος peh·<u>zohTH</u>·roh·mohs **pedestrian zone**

περιμένω peh·ree·<u>meh</u>·noh *v* **hold on, wait**

περιμένω στην ουρά peh·ree·<u>meh</u>·noh steen oo·<u>rah</u> *v* **queue [BE]**

περιέχω peh·ree·<u>eh</u>·khoh **contain**

περιοδικό peh·ree·oh·THee·<u>koh</u> **magazine**

περίοδος peh·<u>ree</u>·oh·THohs **period (menstrual)**

περιοχή peh·ree·oh·<u>khee</u> **region**

περιοχή για καπνίζοντες peh·ree·oh·<u>khee</u> yah kahp·<u>nee</u>·zohn·dehs **smoking area**

περιοχή για πικνίκ peh·ree·oh·<u>khee</u> yah peek neek **picnic area**

περίπτερο peh·<u>ree</u>·pteh·roh **newsstand, kiosk**

περνώ pehr·<u>noh</u> *v* **pass**

περπατώ pehr·pah·<u>toh</u> *v* **walk**

περσίδες peh·<u>rsee</u>·THehs **blinds**

πετάω peh·<u>tah</u>·oh *v* **fly**

πετσέτα peh·<u>tseh</u>·tah **napkin**

πέφτω <u>pehf</u>·toh *v* **fall**

πηγαίνω pee·<u>yeh</u>·noh **go**

πιάτσα ταξί <u>piah</u>·tsah tah·<u>ksee</u> **taxi rank [BE]**

πίεση <u>pee</u>·eh·see **blood pressure**

πιθανός pee·thah·<u>nohs</u> **possible**

πινακίδα pee·nah·<u>kee</u>·THah **road sign**

πίνω pee·noh v **drink**

πίπα pee·pah **pipe (smoking)**

πιπίλα pee·pee·lah **pacifier [soother BE]**

πισίνα pee·see·nah **swimming pool**

πιστοποιητικό ασφάλειας
pees·toh·pee·ee·tee·koh ahs·fah·lee·ahs
insurance certificate

πιστωτική κάρτα pees·toh·tee·kee
kahr·tah **credit card**

πιτσαρία pee·tsah·ree·ah **pizzeria**

πλαγιά plah·yah **slope (ski)**

πλαστική σακούλα plahs·tee·kee
sah·koo·lah **plastic bag**

πλατίνα plah·tee·nah **platinum**

πλευρό plehv·roh **rib**

πλημμύρα plee·mee·rah n **flood**

πληγή plee·yee **wound (cut)**

πληροφορίες plee·roh·foh·ree·ehs
information

πληρωμή plee·roh·mee **payment**

πληρώνω plee·roh·noh v **pay**

πλοίο plee·oh n **ship**

πλυντήριο pleen·deer·ee·oh **washing
machine**

πνεύμονας pnehv·moh·nahs **lung**

πόμολο poh·moh·loh n **handle**

ποδήλατο poh·THee·lah·toh **bicycle**

πόδι poh·THee **foot, leg**

ποδόσφαιρο poh·THohs·feh·roh **soccer
[football BE]**

ποιότητα pee·oh·tee·tah **quality**

πόλη poh·lee **town**

πολυκατάστημα
poh·lee·kah·tahs·tee·mah **department
store**

πολυτέλεια poh·lee·teh·lee·ah **luxury**

πολύτιμος poh·lee·tee·mohs **valuable**

πονόδοντος poh·noh·THohn·dohs
toothache

πονοκέφαλος poh·noh·keh·fah·lohs
headache

πονόλαιμος poh·noh·leh·mohs **sore
throat**

πόνος poh·nohs n **pain**

πόνος στο αυτί poh·nohs stoh ahf·tee
earache

πόρτα pohr·tah **door**

πορτοφόλι pohr·toh·foh·lee **wallet**

ποσό poh·soh n **amount**

ποσότητα poh·soh·tee·tah **quantity**

ποταμός poh·tah·mohs **river**

ποτέ poh·teh **never**

ποτήρι poh·tee·ree **glass (container)**

ποτό poh·toh n **drink**

πουκάμισο poo·kah·mee·soh **shirt**

πράσινος prah·see·nohs **green**

πρέπει preh·pee v **must**

πρεσβεία prehz·vee·ah **embassy**

πρεσβύωπας prehz·vee·oh·pahs **long-
sighted [BE]**

πρήξιμο pree·ksee·moh **swelling**

πρησμένος preez·meh·nohs **swollen**

πρίζα pree·zah n **plug, socket**

πριν preen **before**

πρόβλεψη prohv·leh·psee n **forecast**

πρόβλεψη καιρού prohv·leh·psee keh·roo
weather forecast

πρόβλημα prohv·lee·mah **problem**

πρόγραμμα prohgh·rah·mah n **program**

πρόγραμμα θεαμάτων proh·ghrah·
mah theh·ah·mah·tohn **program of
events**

προς prohs **towards**

προσαρμοστής proh-sahr-moh-<u>stees</u> **adaptor**

πρόσβαση <u>prohz</u>-vah-see n **access**

προσγειώνομαι prohz-yee-<u>oh</u>-noh-meh v **land**

προσκαλώ prohs-kah-<u>loh</u> v **invite**

πρόσκληση <u>prohs</u>-klee-see **invitation**

πρόστιμο <u>prohs</u>-tee-moh n **fine (penalty)**

πρόσωπο <u>proh</u>-soh-poh n **face**

προσωρινός proh-soh-ree-<u>nohs</u> **temporary**

προτείνω proh-<u>tee</u>-noh **suggest**

προφέρω proh-<u>feh</u>-roh **pronounce**

προφυλακτικό proh-fee-lah-ktee-<u>koh</u> **condom**

προωθώ proh-oh-<u>thoh</u> **forward**

πρωί proh-<u>ee</u> **morning**

πρωινό proh-ee-<u>noh</u> **breakfast**

πρώτη θέση <u>proh</u>-tee theh-see **first class**

πτήση <u>ptee</u>-see **flight**

πυρετός pee-reh-<u>tohs</u> **fever**

πυροσβεστήρας pee-rohz-vehs-<u>tee</u>-rahs **fire extinguisher**

πυροσβεστική pee-rohz-vehs-tee-<u>kee</u> **fire brigade [BE]**

πυτζάμες pee-<u>jah</u>-mehs **pajamas**

Ρ

ραδιόφωνο rah-THee-<u>oh</u>-foh-noh n **radio**

ρακέτα rah-<u>keh</u>-tah **racket (tennis, squash)**

ραντεβού rahn-deh-<u>voo</u> **appointment**

ράφι <u>rah</u>-fee n **shelf**

ρεματιά reh-mah-<u>tiah</u> **ravine**

ρεσεψιόν reh-seh-<u>psiohn</u> **reception (hotel)**

ρεύμα ποταμού <u>rehv</u>-mah poh-tah-<u>moo</u> **rapids**

ρηχή πισίνα ree-<u>khee</u> pee-<u>see</u>-nah **paddling pool**

ρομαντικός roh-mahn-dee-<u>kohs</u> **romantic**

ρολόι roh-<u>loh</u>-ee n **watch**

ρυάκι ree-<u>ah</u>-kee n **stream**

Σ

σμαράγδι zmah-<u>rahgh</u>-THee **emerald**

σαμπουάν sahm-poo-<u>ahn</u> n **shampoo**

σαγιονάρες sah-yoh-<u>nah</u>-rehs **flip-flops**

σαγόνι sah-<u>ghoh</u>-nee **jaw**

σάκκος <u>sah</u>-kohs **knapsack**

σαλόνι sah-<u>loh</u>-nee **living room**

σάουνα <u>sah</u>-oo-nah **sauna**

σαπούνι sah-<u>poo</u>-nee n **soap**

σατέν sah-<u>tehn</u> **satin**

σβήνω <u>svee</u>-noh v **turn off**

σβώλος <u>svoh</u>-lohs n **lump**

σεζ-λονγκ sehz <u>lohng</u> **deck chair**

σενιάν seh-<u>niahn</u> **rare (steak)**

σερβιέτες sehr-vee-<u>eh</u>-tehs **sanitary towels**

σεσουάρ seh-soo-<u>ahr</u> **hair dryer**

σήμα <u>see</u>-mah **sign (road)**

σημαία see-<u>meh</u>-ah n **flag**

σημαίνω see-<u>meh</u>-noh v **mean**

σημείο see-<u>mee</u>-oh n **point**

σίδερο <u>see</u>-THeh-roh n **iron**

σιδερώνω see-THeh-<u>roh</u>-noh v **iron, press**

σιδηροδρομικός σταθμός see-THee-rohTH-roh-mee-<u>kohs</u> stahth-<u>mohs</u> **rail station**

σκάλα <u>skah</u>-lah **ladder**

σκάλες <u>skah</u>·lehs **stairs**

σκηνή skee·<u>nee</u> **tent**

σκι skee **skiing**

σκιά skee·<u>ah</u> **shade (darkness)**

σκοπός skoh·<u>pohs</u> **purpose**

σκούπα <u>skoo</u>·pah n **broom**

σκουπίδια skoo·<u>peeTH</u>·yah **trash [rubbish BE]**

σκούρος <u>skoo</u>·rohs adj **dark (color)**

σλιπ sleep **briefs**

σόλα <u>soh</u>·lah **sole (shoes)**

σορτς sohrts n **shorts**

σουβενίρ soo·veh·<u>neer</u> **souvenir**

σουπερμάρκετ soo·pehr·<u>mahr</u>·keht **supermarket**

σουτιέν soo·<u>tiehn</u> **bra**

σπα spah **spa**

σπάγγος <u>spah</u>·gohs n **string (cord)**

σπάνιος <u>spah</u>·nee·ohs **rare (unusual)**

σπασμένος spahz·<u>meh</u>·nohs **broken**

σπάω <u>spah</u>·oh v **break**

σπήλαιο <u>spee</u>·leh·oh n **cave**

σπίρτο <u>speer</u>·toh n **match (to start fire)**

σπονδυλική στήλη spohn·THEE·lee·<u>kee stee</u>·lee **spine**

σπουδάζω spoo·<u>THah</u>·zoh v **study**

σταματώ stah·mah·<u>toh</u> v **stop**

στάδιο <u>stah</u>·THee·oh **stadium**

σταθμός μετρό stahth·<u>mohs</u> meh·<u>troh</u> **subway [underground BE] station**

σταθμός λεωφορείων stahTH·<u>mohs</u> leh·oh·foh·<u>ree</u>·ohn **bus station**

στάση <u>stah</u>·see **exposure (photos), stop (bus)**

στάση λεωφορείου <u>stah</u>·see leh·oh·foh·<u>ree</u>·oo **bus stop**

στέγη <u>steh</u>·yee n **roof**

στέλνω <u>stehl</u>·noh **send**

στενός steh·<u>nohs</u> adj **narrow, tight**

στήθος <u>stee</u>·THohs **breast**

στόμα <u>stoh</u>·mah n **mouth**

στομάχι stoh·<u>mah</u>·khee n **stomach**

στομαχόπονος stoh·mah·<u>khoh</u>·poh·nohs **stomach ache**

στολή stoh·<u>lee</u> n **uniform**

στολή δύτη stoh·<u>lee</u> THEE·tee **wetsuit**

στρογγυλός strohn·gkee·<u>lohs</u> adj **round**

στυλ steel n **style**

στυλό stee·<u>loh</u> n **pen**

συμπεριλαμβάνεται seem·beh·ree·lahm·<u>vah</u>·neh·teh **included**

σύζυγος <u>see</u>·zee·ghohs **husband, wife**

συκώτι see·<u>koh</u>·tee **liver**

σύμπτωμα <u>seem</u>·ptoh·mah **symptom**

συναγερμός πυρκαγιάς see·nah·yehr·<u>mohs</u> peer·kah·<u>yahs</u> **fire alarm**

συναντώ see·nahn·<u>doh</u> **meet**

συνέδριο see·<u>neh</u>·THree·oh **conference**

συνταγή γιατρού seen·dah·<u>yee</u> yaht·<u>roo</u> **prescription**

συνταγογραφώ seen·dah·ghoh·ghrah·<u>foh</u> **prescribe**

συνταξιούχος seen·dah·ksee·<u>oo</u>·khohs **retired**

σύντομα <u>seen</u>·doh·mah **soon**

συντριβάνι seen·dree·<u>vah</u>·nee **fountain**

συστάσεις see·<u>stah</u>·sees **introductions**

συστήνω see·<u>stee</u>·noh **introduce, recommend**

συχνός seekh·<u>nohs</u> adj **frequent**

σφηνωμένος sfee·noh·<u>meh</u>·nohs **jammed**

σφράγισμα <u>sfrah</u>·yeez·mah **filling (dental)**

σφυρί sfee·<u>ree</u> **hammer**

σχέδιο <u>skheh</u>·THee·oh *n* **plan**

σχήμα <u>skhee</u>·mah *n* **shape**

σχισμένος skheez·<u>meh</u>·nohs **torn**

σχοινί skhee·<u>nee</u> *n* **rope**

σχολή σκι skhoh·<u>lee</u> skee **ski school**

σωσίβιο soh·<u>see</u>·vee·oh **lifejacket**

σωστός sohs·<u>stohs</u> *adj* **right (correct)**

T

ταμπόν tahm·<u>bohn</u> **tampon**

τάβλι <u>tah</u>·vlee **backgammon**

ταγιέρ tah·<u>yehr</u> **women's suit**

ταΐζω tah·<u>ee</u>·zoh *v* **feed**

ταινία teh·<u>nee</u>·ah **movie**

ταξί tah·<u>ksee</u> **taxi**

ταξίδι tah·<u>ksee</u>·THee **journey**

ταξίδι με πλοίο tah·<u>ksee</u>·THee meh <u>plee</u>·oh **boat trip**

ταξιδιωτική επιταγή tah·ksee·THee·oh·tee·<u>kee</u> eh·pee·tah·<u>yee</u> **traveler's check [traveller's cheque** BE**]**

ταξιδιωτικό γραφείο tah·ksee·THyoh·tee·<u>koh</u> ghrah·<u>fee</u>·oh **travel agency**

ταξιτζής tah·ksee·<u>jees</u> **taxi driver**

ταυτότητα tahf·<u>toh</u>·tee·tah **identification**

ταχυδρομείο tah·kheeTH·roh·<u>mee</u>·oh **post office**

ταχυδρομική επιταγή tah·kheeTH·roh·mee·<u>kee</u> eh·pee·tah·<u>yee</u> **money order**

ταχυδρομικό κουτί tah·kheeTH·roh·mee·<u>koh</u> koo·<u>tee</u> **mailbox [postbox** BE**]**

τεμάχιο teh·<u>mah</u>·khee·oh **piece**

τελειώνω teh·lee·<u>oh</u>·noh *v* **end**

τελευταί ος teh·lehf·<u>teh</u>·ohs **last**

τελεφερίκ teh·leh·feh·<u>reek</u> **cablecar**

τέλος <u>teh</u>·lohs *n* **end**

τελωνειακή δήλωση teh·loh·nee·ah·<u>kee</u> <u>THee</u>·loh·see **customs declaration (tolls)**

τελωνείο teh·loh·<u>nee</u>·oh **customs (tolls)**

τέννις <u>teh</u>·nees **tennis**

τετράγωνος teht·<u>rah</u>·ghoh·nohs **square**

τζετ-σκι jeht skee **jet-ski**

τζόγκιγκ joh·geeng **jogging**

τζόγος <u>joh</u>·ghohs **gambling**

τηλεκάρτα tee·leh·<u>kahr</u>·tah **phone card**

τηλεόραση tee·leh·<u>oh</u>·rah·see **TV**

τηλεφώνημα tee·leh·<u>foh</u>·nee·mah **phone call**

τηλεφωνικός θάλαμος tee·leh·foh·nee·<u>kohs</u> <u>thah</u>·lah·mohs **telephone booth**

τηλεφωνικός κατάλογος tee·leh·foh·nee·<u>kohs</u> kah·<u>tah</u>·loh·ghohs **telephone directory**

τηλέφωνο tee·<u>leh</u>·foh·noh *n* **phone**

την teen **per**

τιμή συναλλάγματος tee·<u>mee</u> see·nah·<u>lahgh</u>·mah·tohs **exchange rate**

τιμή εισόδου tee·<u>mee</u> ee·<u>soh</u>·THoo **entrance fee**

τιρμπουσόν teer·boo·<u>sohn</u> **corkscrew**

τοίχος <u>tee</u>·khohs **wall**

τοπικός toh·pee·<u>kohs</u> **local**

τοστιέρα toh·<u>stieh</u>·rah **toaster**

τουαλέτα too·ah·<u>leh</u>·tah **restroom [toilet BE]**

τούνελ <u>too</u>·nehl **tunnel**

τουρίστας too·<u>rees</u>·tahs **tourist**

τουριστική θέση too·ree·stee·<u>kee</u> <u>theh</u>·see **economy class**

τουριστικός οδηγός too·ree·stee·<u>kohs</u> oh·THee·<u>ghohs</u> **guide book**

τραβώ το καζανάκι trah·<u>voh</u> toh kah·zah·<u>nah</u>·kee **flush**

τραμ trahm **tram**

τράπεζα <u>trah</u>·peh·zah **bank**

τραπέζι trah·<u>peh</u>·zee **table**

τραπεζομάντηλο trah·peh·zoh·<u>mahn</u>·dee·loh **tablecloth**

τραυματισμένος trahv·mah·teez·<u>meh</u>·nohs **injured**

τρένο <u>treh</u>·noh **train**

τρέχω <u>treh</u>·khoh v **run, speed**

τρόμπα <u>troh</u>·mbah n **pump**

τρόλλεϋ <u>troh</u>·leh·ee **trolley-bus**

τρύπα <u>tree</u>·pah **hole (in clothes)**

τρώω <u>troh</u>·oh **eat**

τσάντα <u>tsahn</u>·dah **handbag**

τσίμπημα <u>tsee</u>·bee·mah n **bite, sting (insect)**

τσίμπημα κουνουπιού <u>tseem</u>·bee·mah koo·noo·<u>piooh</u> **mosquito bite**

τυπικός tee·pee·<u>kohs</u> **typical**

τύχη <u>tee</u>·khee **luck**

Υ

υγρό πιάτων eegh·<u>roh</u> piah·tohn **dishwashing detergent**

υπεραστικό λεωφορείο ee·peh·rahs·tee·<u>koh</u> leh·oh·foh·<u>ree</u>·oh **long-distance bus**

υπεραστικό τηλεφώνημα ee·pehr·ahs·tee·<u>koh</u> tee·leh·<u>foh</u>·nee·mah **long-distance call**

υπέρβαρο ee·<u>pehr</u>·vah·roh **excess baggage [BE]**

υπηκοότητα ee·pee·koh·<u>oh</u>·tee·tah **nationality**

υπηρεσία ee·pee·reh·<u>see</u>·ah n **service (administration, business)**

υπηρεσία δωματίου ee·pee·reh·<u>see</u>·ah THoh·mah·<u>tee</u>·oo **room service**

υπηρεσία πλυντηρίου ee·pee·reh·<u>see</u>·ah pleen·dee·<u>ree</u>·oo **laundry service**

υπνόσακκος ee·<u>pnoh</u>·sah·kohs **sleeping bag**

υπνωτικό χάπι eep·noh·tee·<u>koh</u> <u>khah</u>·pee **sleeping pill**

υπόγειος ee·<u>poh</u>·ghee·ohs **underground [BE]**

υπολογιστής ee·poh·loh·yee·<u>stees</u> **computer**

υπόνομος ee·<u>poh</u>·noh·mohs **sewer**

ύφασμα <u>ee</u>·fahs·mah **fabric (cloth)**

ύψος <u>ee</u>·psohs **height**

Φ

φακός fah·<u>kohs</u> **flashlight, lens**

φακός επαφής fah·<u>kohs</u> eh·pah·<u>fees</u> **contact lens**

υπηρεσία φαξ ee·pee·reh·<u>see</u>·ah fahks **fax facility**

φάρμα <u>fahr</u>·mah n **farm**

φάρμακα <u>fahr</u>·mah·kah **medication**

φαρδύς fahr·<u>THees</u> **loose (fitting), wide**

φάρος <u>fah</u>·rohs **lighthouse**

φέρνω <u>fehr</u>·noh **bring**

φέρυ-μπωτ <u>feh</u>·ree boht **ferry**

φεστιβάλ fehs·tee·<u>vahl</u> **festival**

φεύγω <u>fehv</u>·ghoh v **leave (depart)**

φιλμ feelm n **film (camera)**

φίλη <u>fee</u>·lee **girlfriend**

φιλί fee·<u>lee</u> n **kiss**

φιλοδώρημα fee·loh·<u>THoh</u>·ree·mah **gratuity**

φίλος <u>fee</u>·lohs **friend, boyfriend**

φίλτρο <u>feel</u>·troh n **filter**

φιλώ fee·<u>loh</u> v **kiss**

φλέβα <u>fleh</u>·vah **vein**

φλεγμονή flegh·moh·<u>nee</u> **inflammation**

φλυτζάνι flee·<u>jah</u>·nee **cup**

φοβερός foh·veh·<u>rohs</u> **terrible**

φοβισμένος foh·veez·<u>meh</u>·nohs **frightened**

φοιτητής fee·tee·<u>tees</u> **student**

φόρεμα <u>foh</u>·reh·mah n **dress**

φόρος <u>foh</u>·rohs **duty (customs), tax**

φορώ foh·<u>roh</u> v **wear**

φούρνος <u>foor</u>·nohs **oven**

φούρνος μικροκυμάτων <u>foor</u>·nohs mee·kroh·kee·<u>mah</u>·tohn **microwave (oven)**

φούστα <u>foo</u>·stah **skirt**

φούτερ <u>foo</u>·tehr **sweatshirt**

ΦΠΑ fee·pee·<u>ah</u> **sales tax**

φράγμα <u>frahgh</u>·mah n **lock (river, canal)**

φράση <u>frah</u>·see n **phrase**

φράχτης <u>frahkh</u>·tees n **fence**

φρέσκος <u>frehs</u>·kohs adj **fresh**

φτάνω <u>ftah</u>·noh **arrive**

φτηνός ftee·<u>nohs</u> **cheap, inexpensive**

φτιάχνω τις βαλίτσες ftee·<u>ahkh</u>·noh tees vah·<u>lee</u>·tsehs v **pack (baggage)**

φυλακή fee·lah·<u>kee</u> n **prison**

φύση <u>fee</u>·see **nature**

φυτό fee·<u>toh</u> n **plant**

φως fohs n **light (electric)**

φώτα <u>foh</u>·tah **lights (car)**

φωτογραφία foh·tohgh·rah·<u>fee</u>·ah v **photo**

φωτογραφική μηχανή foh·tohgh·rah·fee·<u>kee</u> mee·khah·<u>nee</u> **camera**

φωτοτυπικό foh·toh·tee·pee·<u>koh</u> **photocopier**

Χ

χαμηλώνω khah·mee·<u>loh</u>·noh v **turn down (volume, heat)**

χαλί khah·<u>lee</u> **rug**

χαλκός khahl·<u>kohs</u> **copper**

χάπι <u>khah</u>·pee **tablet**

χάρτης <u>khahr</u>·tees n **map**

χαρτί khar·<u>tee</u> **paper**

χαρτί κουζίνας khah·<u>rtee</u> koo·<u>zee</u>·nahs **kitchen**

χαρτί υγείας khahr·<u>tee</u> ee·<u>yee</u>·ahs **toilet paper**

χαρτομάντηλο khahr·toh·<u>mahn</u>·dee·loh **tissue**

χαρτομάντηλο khah·rtoh·<u>mahn</u>·dee·loh **handkerchief**

χείλη <u>khee</u>·lee **lips**

χειροκίνητος khee·roh·<u>kee</u>·nee·tohs **manual (car)**

χειρότερος khee·roh·teh·rohs **worse**

χιλιόμετρα khee·<u>lioh</u>·meh·trah **mileage**

χιονίζει khioh·<u>nee</u>·zee v **snow**

χλιαρός khlee·ah·<u>rohs</u> **lukewarm**

χόμπυ <u>khoh</u>·bee **hobby (pastime)**

χοντρός khohn·<u>drohs</u> **thick**

χορεύω khoh·<u>reh</u>·voh v **dance**

χορτοφάγος khohr·toh·<u>fah</u>·ghohs **vegetarian**

χρειάζομαι khree·<u>ah</u>·zoh·meh v **need**

χρέωση υπηρεσίας <u>khreh</u>·oh·see ee·pee·reh·<u>see</u>·ahs **service charge**

χρήματα <u>khree</u>·mah·tah **money**

χρησιμοποιώ khree·see·moh·pee·<u>oh</u> v **use**

χρήσιμος <u>khree</u>·see·mohs **useful**

χρονική περίοδος khroh·nee·<u>kee</u> peh·<u>ree</u>·oh·THohs **period (time)**

χρυσός khree·<u>sohs</u> n **gold**

χρώμα <u>khroh</u>·mah n **color**

χρωστώ khroh·<u>stoh</u> **owe**

χτένα <u>khteh</u>·nah n **comb**

χτενίζω khteh·<u>nee</u>·zoh v **comb**

χτες khtehs **yesterday**

χώρα <u>khoh</u>·rah **country (nation)**

χωριό khohr·<u>yoh</u> **village**

χωρίς khoh·<u>rees</u> **without**

χώρος <u>khoh</u>·rohs n **space (area)**

χώρος κάμπινγκ <u>kah</u>·mpeeng <u>khoh</u>·rohs **campsite**

χώρος στάθμευσης <u>khoh</u>·rohs <u>stahth</u>·mehf·sees **car park [BE]**

χώρος στάθμευσης <u>khoh</u>·rohs <u>stahth</u>·mehf·sees **parking lot**

Ψ

ψαλίδι psah·<u>lee</u>·THee **scissors**

ψάρεμα <u>psah</u>·reh·mah **fishing**

ψάχνω <u>psahkh</u>·noh **look for**

ψηλός psee·<u>lohs</u> **tall**

ψύλλος <u>psee</u>·lohs **flea**

Ω

ώμος <u>oh</u>·mohs n **shoulder (anatomy)**

ώρα αιχμής <u>oh</u>·rah ehk·<u>mees</u> **rush hour**

ώρες λειτουργίας <u>oh</u>·rehs lee·toor·<u>yee</u>·ahs **opening hours**